The Strange Sad War Revolving

Studies in English and American Literature,
Linguistics, and Culture

Edited
by
Benjamin Franklin V *(South Carolina)*

The Strange Sad War Revolving

Luke Mancuso

The Strange Sad War Revolving

Walt Whitman, Reconstruction, and the Emergence of Black Citizenship, 1865–1876

CAMDEN HOUSE

Published by Camden House, Inc.
Drawer 2025
Columbia, SC 29202 USA

Printed on acid-free paper.
Binding materials are chosen for strength and
durability.

Printed in the United States of America

Chapter 2, "'Reconstruction is still in abeyance': Walt Whitman's Democratic Vistas
and the Federalizing of National Identity," was originally published in *ATQ*, Volume 8,
No. 3, September 1994. Reprinted by permission of the University of Rhode Island.

Frontispiece photograph of Walt Whitman by Matthew Brady courtesy
of Library of Congress.

ISBN 1–57113–125–6

Library of Congress Cataloging-in-Publication Data

Mancuso, Luke, 1956–
 The strange sad war revolving: Walt Whitman, Reconstruction, and
the emergence of Black citizenship, 1865–1876 / Luke Mancuso
  p. cm. – (Studies in English and American literature,
linguistics and culture)
 Includes bibliographical references and index.
 ISBN 1–57113–125–6 (alk. paper)
 1. Whitman, Walt, 1819–1892 – Political and social views.
2. United States – History – Civil War, 1861–1865 – Literature and the
war. 3. Literature and society – United States – History – 19th century.
4. Afro-Americans – United States – History – 19th century.
5. Citizenship – United States – History – 19th century. 6. War
poetry, American – History and criticism. 7. Whitman, Walt,
1819–1892. Leaves of Grass. 8. Afro-Americans in literature.
9. Reconstruction. I. Title. II. Series: Studies in English and
American literature, linguistics, and culture (Unnumbered)
PS3242.S58M36 1997
811' .3—dc21   97–3940
                                                        CIP

To
Jerome Theisen,
Ed Folsom,
and Kathleen Diffley,
without whose insight
these leaves would not now be existing.

"Individuals may be converted on the instant and change their whole course of life. Nations never. Time and events are required for the conversion of nations."

— Frederick Douglass, 1883

Contents

Acknowledgments

I FIRST NOTICED THE VIGOROUS possibilities in Walt Whitman's work in the now-legendary "Walt Whitman" seminar taught at the University of Iowa by Professor Ed Folsom, editor of the *Walt Whitman Quarterly Review*, in the Spring of 1990. In our prerequisite entrance interview, the previous fall, I ingenuously told Ed that my favorite Whitman poem was "I Saw in Louisiana a Live-Oak Growing," having been always moved by the refusal of the poet to settle for less than comradeship with his readers. I remember saying that I would tenaciously seek a way to locate the source of Whitman's "comradeship" model of social relations in political/public discourse, for the politics of communal identity form the warp and woof of my deepest commitments. In the course of the seminar, I discovered that I had entered a crowded interpretive landscape, for the body of Whitman scholarship is, to use understatement, formidable. Being an extraordinary teacher, however, Ed gave me unflagging encouragement, and has only provided sturdier regard for my Whitman investigations since that time. I am grateful for the hours that Ed managed to scoop out of his dizzying list of duties as Chair, editor, writer, and teacher, in order to generate the most trenchant responses to my chapters that I received through the hectic months of composition.

Also, Professor Kathleen Diffley knows indebtedness comes naturally to me, for Kathleen has helped me to finesse these chapters with far more precision than I thought possible. In her tough but generous responses, I found that I had an audience who took my work seriously, and the benefits are littered across the pages of this project. Above all other books which I have mined, Kathleen's pioneering work, *Where My Heart Is Turning Ever: Civil War Stories and Constitutional Reform, 1861–1876* (Athens: U of Georgia P, 1992), argued compellingly for the yoking of literary and legislative discourse, and did so with a grace and wit that inspired my recovery of Whitman's Reconstruction project. Her book was the departure point for whatever methodological pathway that these pages have scouted.

I also welcomed the responses of Professors Adelaide Morris, Tom Lutz, and Leslie Schwalm to the rougher drafts of these chapters, for they have donated insight, advice, and positive regard in many ports on the map of my progress in the parturition of this project. I know that their schedules are more than filled, and I thank them for helping me polish this manuscript.

Finally, I want to articulate the kind of thanks that virtually defies articulation. To Jerome Theisen who welcomed me without reservation to belong to St. John's; to my former colleague Janet McNew, my present colleagues J. P. Earls and Eva Hooker, and David Rothstein, each of whom has validated my desire to teach English at St. John's University; and to the family of St. John's without whose fraternal affection and support I would not have finished this journey; I also owe a debt of gratitude to Bev Radaich and Anna Klein who made up for my computer illiteracy by copy editing this manuscript; to all of these unique contributors I engrave my thanks in the ink of these pages, in return for the favor of being embedded in our collaborative work.

Abbreviations

Lincoln
Collected Works of Abraham Lincoln. 9 vols. Ed.
Roy P. Basler. New Brunswick, N.J.: Rutgers
U P, 1953.

Corr
Correspondence of Walt Whitman. Ed. Edwin
Haviland Miller. 6 vols. New York: New York
U P, 1961–77.

LG Var
*Leaves of Grass: A Textual Variorum of the
Printed Poems.* Eds. Sculley Bradley, Harold W.
Blodgett, Arthur Golden, and William White. 3
vols. New York: New York U P, 1980.

MDW
*Walt Whitman's Memoranda During the War
and Death of Abraham Lincoln.* Ed. Roy P.
Basler. Bloomington: Indiana U P, 1962.

NUPM
Notebooks and Unpublished Prose Manuscripts.
Ed. Edward F. Grier. 6 vols. New York: New
York U P, 1984.

PW
Prose Works 1892. Ed. Floyd Stovall. 2 vols.
New York: New York U P, 1963–1964.

WWC
With Walt Whitman in Camden. Ed. Horace
Traubel. 7 vols. 1906–1992.

WWW
*Walt Whitman's Workshop: A Collection of
Unpublished Manuscripts.* Ed. Clifton J.
Furness. Cambridge: Harvard UP, 1928.

Introduction:

"Forth from the War emerging"
Drum-Taps, Its *Sequel*, and the Rupture
of the Revolutionary Household

ON 1 DECEMBER 1862, in his second annual message to Congress, Abraham Lincoln concluded his sober appeal for qualified emancipation of Southern black Americans with a warning: "Fellow citizens, we cannot escape history. We of this Congress and this administration, will be remembered in spite of ourselves. No personal significance, or insignificance, can spare one or another of us. The fiery trial through which we pass, will light us down, in honor or dishonor, to the latest generation" (*Lincoln* V, 537). Though Appomattox was two and a half years away, Lincoln's rhetoric had started to widen the moral significance of the Civil War from the Union focus on the fate of ex-states to the amalgamated concerns of the fate of ex-states and the fate of ex-slaves. This rhetorical dilation, which wedded the Union cause to race relations, had a long foreground in Lincoln's speeches and would culminate in his endorsement of the Thirteenth Amendment in 1865, which abolished the institution of slavery.

What coerced Lincoln into grappling with slavery was his anxiety over how history would remember him, though when the war began on 12 April 1861, his notions were far narrower: in his first inaugural address, 4 March 1861, Lincoln declared, "I hold that in contemplation of universal law, and of the Constitution, the Union of these States is perpetual." Thus he relegated the slavery question to a secondary (if not negligible) status (*Lincoln* III, 268). The firing on Fort Sumter four weeks later initiated what has been called the Second American Revolution and catalyzed the greatest cultural upheaval in the American "household" since the Revolutionary War. The "national household" was a rhetorical image deployed (by Whitman, Lincoln, and the Congress) in poetic, political, and congressional texts to signify the ambiguities of domestic language when it was transferred from the sanctum of "hearth and home" onto a postwar public landscape.[1] I would argue that such familial images as "household," "home," "father," "mother," "brother," "sister," "son," and "daughter" signified the postwar rupture with the inherited self-representation of Americans, as heirs of the Revolutionary age, through the discrediting of an untroubled Revolutionary "household" in favor of cultural texts filled with disrupted family blood ties, death, and comradeship among strangers.[2] The rescripting of the Constitution that Lincoln cited as his political cornerstone, through the intrusion of the Civil War amendments, went a long way in remodeling the antebellum American homestead that had legally tolerated slavery in its precincts since the birth of its founding charter.

Opening with *Drum-Taps* (1865) and the *Sequel to Drum-Taps* (1865–1866) and continuing through the Centennial edition of *Leaves of Grass* (1876), Whitman's Reconstruction texts registered more emancipationist density than critics have noted in the scant body of criticism on this prolific phase of his work. In May 1865 Whitman represented the Civil War in *Drum-Taps*, and soon thereafter he appended the *Sequel to Drum-Taps* in an attempt to inscribe into the cultural memory the national conflict, Abraham Lincoln's demise, and the dismantling of slavery. Whitman knew that he too had no escape from history or from the way history would eventually represent the "fruits of victory" ripened in the aftermath of Appomattox, for he wrote to his friend William Douglas O'Connor from Brooklyn on 6 January 1865, "But I am perhaps mainly satisfied with *Drum-Taps* because it delivers my ambition of the task that has haunted me, namely, to express in a poem (& in the way I like, which is not at all by directly stating it) the pending action of this Time & Land we swim in" (*Corr* I, 246). Adrift therefore in the cultural upheaval produced by the war, Whitman had inscribed in *Drum-Taps* "the whirl & deafening din, (yet over all, as by invisible hand, a definite purport & idea)— with the unprecedented anguish of wounded & suffering, . . . everything sometimes as if in blood color, & dripping blood" (*Corr* I, 247). The representational "swim" for Whitman was one that prominently displayed his prowess as an athlete for the Union cause, but *Drum-Taps* nowhere explicitly registered his concern for the competing claims of blacks.

However, the political pressures that had earlier coerced Lincoln into weaving the freedmen's social destiny into the national household, also had their signifying effect on Whitman: the most revealing line in the previously cited letter to O'Connor declared that his historical representation of his "Time and Land" came about "not at all by directly stating it." The indirectness of Whitman's rhetoric has less to do with "dripping blood" than with his investment in "a definite purport & idea"; that is, in a coherent democratic future rising out of the failed racial past. In his deployment of disrupted familial images, read as a cultural text, Whitman's poetic investment in the Union cause forged representational connections with the ongoing emancipation debate over the fate of ex-slaves throughout the Reconstruction period.

Whitman's covertness in his compositions is not as far-fetched as it might appear, for Edward Carpenter recorded a conversation he had with Whitman late in his life, in which Whitman revealed, "There is something in my nature furtive like an old hen! . . . That is how I felt in writing 'Leaves of Grass.' I think there are truths which it is necessary to envelop or wrap up."[3] From the "furtive old hen" to the emancipatory "song" of the hermit thrush in "When Lilacs Last in the Dooryard Bloom'd," signifying the unwritten future of an interracial democracy, a representational linkage of "furtiveness" suggested why Whitman chose "indirectness" in his proclamation of emancipation, arguably the dominant cultural issue of the Reconstruction period. In a rhetorical sense, one fowl does not resemble the other, but they both belong to the same species. After the war, Whitman had begun to camouflage his representations of blacks, but I suggest that behind his furtiveness lay the ongoing cultural work of weaving ex-slaves into the national household. In any case, irrespective of Whitman's intentions, the "whirl & deafening din" of the postwar political landscape shaped his work with ideological resonance and embedded his texts in the same rupture with the antebellum notions about black Americans that had allowed Lincoln no transhistorical escape.

By the time that *Drum-Taps* was published in New York, and followed by the *Sequel to Drum-Taps*, the Union had won the War, Lincoln had been assassinated, and the Thirteenth Amendment had been floating in Congressional debates for over a year. The seventy-two page text of *Drum-Taps* contained sixty-three previously unpublished poems, and only twenty-four pages long, the *Sequel* added eighteen poems.[4] So intense were Whitman's democratic expectations in the last days of the war that he wrote to William Douglas O'Connor from Brooklyn on 7 April 1865, "The grand culminations of the past week impress me profoundly of course. I feel more than ever how America has been entirely re-stated by them — and they will shape the destinies of the future of the whole of mankind" (*Corr* I, 257–58). The oxymoronic linkage of the "reinstatement" of the Revolutionary legacy with the Reconstruction promise of the "whole" American household camouflaged the contentious discourse that pervaded the nation regarding the impending Thirteenth Amendment. Though by no means the first or the last debate over emancipation, the congressional speeches leading up to the ratification of the amendment represented how deeply divided the Union was over emancipation as a war goal. As early as 1862, the war had provoked Lincoln to link the fate of slavery with the fate of the Union, but the constitutional amendment to abolish slavery passed the Senate in April 1864, only to be first defeated in the House of Representatives and then finally approved in the House in January 1865.[5] When Whitman published *Drum-Taps*, therefore, the amendment was on the way to its December 1865 ratification by the states; but this widely disputed legislative renovation, the first constitutional amendment in over a half a century, was elided in Whitman's Civil War collection. Not only was the abolition of slavery not mentioned, but also there was no explicit mention of blacks in *Drum-Taps* at all. Indeed, the absence of race relations in *Drum-Taps* remains the most intriguing fact about these representations of the Civil War.

Before the war, when Whitman wanted to speak with the voice of the slave, he did so most notably in section 10 of "Song of Myself"; but after the war he had begun an indeterminate blurring of the representation of emancipated blacks in his poems. Indeterminacy, however, can be an enabling literary device insofar as the unmooring of cultural images from their ideological boundaries opens up representational spaces for the renegotiation of fundamental issues such as race relations in a racist culture. Such a renegotiation suggests Whitman's textual strategy in *Drum-Taps*, for blacks were still absent from full participation in the forum of civil citizenship in a Union household not quite prepared to let them in. Equally striking is the ironic fact that the word "slavery" did not appear in the Constitution until the ratification of the Thirteenth Amendment, which prohibited "slavery" and "involuntary servitude." Neoabolitionist historians have diluted the significance of this absence in the Constitution, for as Paul Finkelman has stated, though "the word 'slavery' was never mentioned in the Constitution, yet its presence was felt everywhere."[6] However, one of the rhetorical interpretations that followed from the explicit renunciation of the signifier "slavery" in our nation's governmental charter was the potential for emancipation to evolve out of the Founders' reticence to grant moral legitimacy to an institution that was found questionable, at best, by several Constitutional Convention delegates.[7] As James Madison stated, it would be incorrect "to admit in the Constitution the idea that there could be property in man."[8]

Undeniably the extension of slavery was promoted through the national charter, but Frederick Douglass and Abraham Lincoln also contested the notion that the Founders' intention included anxiety-free approbation of the "peculiar institution." Douglass argued that the absence of the explicit authorization of slavery in the Constitution countered William Lloyd Garrison's view that the document was a proslavery "covenant with death."[9] Likewise, Lincoln reasoned that the "covert language" regarding slavery by the Convention delegates "marked" slavery "as an evil not to be extended, but to be tolerated" as an instrument to form a coalition between Southern and Northern states (*Lincoln* III, 307, 535; IV, 22). Given these discursive formations that reinforced the latent emancipation evident in the anxiety over the signification of slavery from Madison to Lincoln, Whitman's silence over blacks seemed to follow in *Drum-Taps* as a rhetorical maneuver that supported Lincoln's gradualist approach to abolition. As Whitman stated to Horace Traubel on 8 June 1889, "the idea of slavery — of holding one man by another, in personal subjection — under dictatorial investments — was palpably bad — damnable — not only condemned by civilization, — by development — but condemned in the first breath of our American genius — of the force and faith at the base of American institutions" (*WWC* V, 276).

Thus, although Whitman was personally antiabolitionist, there existed ample textual evidence that he was at the same time morally opposed to the institution of slavery. Late in his life, on 7 April 1890, Whitman confessed to Horace Traubel, "The abolitionists have always exaggerated the importance of that movement: it was not by any means the beginning or end of things. It was a pimple, a boil — yes, a carbuncle — that's it — out of the nation's bad blood: out of a corpus spoiled, maltreated, bruised, poisoned." Adding to the patchwork of antiabolitionist discourse circulating in the 1860s, "The Southerners, by acts of folly — acts like that of beating down [Charles] Sumner — added to the fuel ... . But something besides the abolitionists brought the matter finally to success" (*WWC* VI, 353). But Whitman concluded his musings with an evasive appraisal of the end of slavery: "And although at one time four-fifths of the country was for slavery, yet slavery seemed doomed. A great something, uncaught yet by writers, explainers, expositors of our history, worked out the great end" (*WWC* VI, 353).

Whitman's awareness of slavery's "doomed" status had a long foreground that antedated *Leaves of Grass* by eight years. In an early notebook, the poet had written, in one of the earliest passages to resemble the loose, flowing style of the 1855 *Leaves of Grass*, "I am the poet of the slave, and of the masters of the slave ... / I am the poet of the body / And I am the poet of the soul / I go with the slaves of the earth equally with the masters / And I will stand between the masters and the slaves, / Entering into both, so that both shall understand me alike" (*NUPM* I, 67). The neutralization of hierarchical social relations in this passage suggests that the entire "language experiment" of *Leaves of Grass* was founded on the potential erasure of chattel slavery from American culture. As the poet of the body politic, and of the political soul of a common Union constructed of diverse pasts,[10] Whitman could not avoid representing the legislative transition from antiabolitionism to emancipation within the Union. Such interracial alliances were legislated by Reconstruction constitutional reform, which from 1865 to 1870 mandated inclusion of ex-slaves in the national household, in the ratification of the Thirteenth, Fourteenth, and Fifteenth Amendments which provided respectively for the abolition of slavery, black citizenship, and black male suffrage. In the same period, Whitman's texts upheld such racial alliances, despite his anxiety over what Kathleen Diffley calls "the fate of freedmen."[11] In 1855 or 1856, Whitman wrote of his distaste for supporters of slavery: "Every one that speaks his word for slavery, is himself the worst slave — the spirit of a freeman is not light enough in him to show that all the fatness of the earth were bitter to a bondaged neck" (*NUPM* VI, 2192). Of course, the most famous of Whitman's anti-slavery passages constituted the runaway slave narrative in "Song of Myself" (section 10): "The runaway slave came to my house and stopped outside, . . . / He staid with me a week before he was recuperated and passed north" (*LG Var* I, 12). This transgressive image of a free white citizen harboring a fugitive slave contradicted the legality of the fugitive slave clause of the Constitution (which forbade the harboring of fugitive slaves), sounded strikingly abolitionist, and signaled a principled resistance to the boundaries of law.

Such a Whitmanian litany of prewar textual evidence demonstrates that Whitman's opposition to abolitionists was severely limited, and it provides a stimulating foreground to the cultural work of emancipationist gestures in *Drum-Taps*. Insofar as he disliked the partisan movement, Whitman silenced the abolitionist voice in his Civil War poems, but insofar as he wrote in "the Time and Land we live in," the constitutional rupture with the Founders' inscription of slavery into the national charter suggested emancipation everywhere. Because of the indirectness of Whitman's rhetorical strategies in *Drum-Taps*, the issue of emancipation was represented through images of disrupted blood ties, death, and comradeship among strangers. The derangement of family ties, as an image mobilized to demonstrate the cultural break between the Revolutionary household and the postwar Union family that included ex-slaves, constitutes Whitman's rhetorical strategy throughout the *Drum-Taps* cluster. Ignoring how the disruption of such domestic ties functions as an emancipationist gesture, critics have read *Drum-Taps* as a humanitarian tract, as a Blakean passage from innocence to experience, and as a homoerotic document of male friendship.[12] But the images of disrupted families and of the corpses of soldiers suggest not simply the dissolving of the personal self in death but also, read as cultural texts, the dissolving of the constitutional compact with slavery. As images of a national household, forced to renovate the foundation it had built on slavery, the separations and deaths of blood relatives were deployed as representations of such a breakage with the Revolutionary past so that a more racially diverse republic might be constructed out of the "whirl & deafening din" in the aftermath of the war. Only then, as the poet of a reconstructed national home, would Whitman make the riskier rhetorical move of reaching out to strangers, beyond kinsfolk, in a gesture that became the cultural cornerstone of his constructing a consolidated nation out of diverse ethnic and racial differences.[13]

The dismantling of nearly a century of sanctioned slaveholding had been long under way through abolitionist activists, but the 1864–65 debate over the Thirteenth Amendment in Congress brought the matter to the center of legislative discourse. Highly contested, the amendment did not initiate cultural stability because of the vociferous resistance of white Southerners and Democratic opponents in the Capitol. These antiemancipationist factions sought to ensure that abolition could destroy one social system, but they did not provide any workable alternative to take its place.

In particular, the disruption of the foundational legacy provoked bitter opposition over the invasion of state sovereignty through federal protection of civil rights. As Congressman Fernando Wood of New York declared during the amendment debates, "The local jurisdiction over slavery was one of the subjects peculiarly guarded and guaranteed to the states, and an amendment ratified by any number of states less than the whole . . . would be contrary to the spirit of the instrument, and so in reality an act of gross bad faith."[14] For Wood and his cohorts, the revolutionizing of the Constitution clearly signified that the abolition of a state-sanctioned "domestic" relation (master-slave) sought to superintend private relations in a public manner.

Undaunted by oppositional claims, the Republicans attached a coda to the amendment that mandated federal jurisdiction over the enforcement of emancipation. Such hegemony gave birth to an expanded national forum to supervise civil liberties, which federalized the Union cause in ways that had not been fully anticipated during the war. This centralized intrusion into state jurisdictions sat uneasily on the heads of Congressional opponents, such as Congressman Robert Mallory of Kentucky, who stated that state jurisdiction would suffice in the governance of the ex-slaves: "You do not intend, however, to leave them to the tender mercies of those states. You propose by a most flagrant violation of their rights to hold the control of this large class in these various states in your own hands."[15]

The disruption of the national household had already claimed over six hundred thousand bodies and a vast expenditure of national treasure. The abolitionist defenders of the amendment in Congress were determined to codify a counter-statement to such a cataclysm in overturning the Founders' "agreement with hell" through the federal government as the arbiter of reconstructing racial relations. Veteran abolitionist Senator Henry Wilson of Massachusetts declared that "if this amendment shall be incorporated by the will of the nation into the Constitution of the United States, it will obliterate the last lingering vestiges of the slave system; its chattelizing, degrading and bloody codes; its dark, malignant barbarizing spirit."[16] Then, invoking the establishment of domestic rhetoric in the social relations of blacks, where it had not existed, he proposed that emancipation would restore "the sacred rights of human nature," and that "the hallowed family relations of husband and wife, parent and child, will be protected by the guardian spirit of that law which makes sacred alike the proud homes and lowly cabins of freedom."[17] Such familial images, which resisted popular images of blacks as not capable of white domestic mores, multiplied in the course of the debates on Capitol Hill.

For instance, Senator James Harlan of Iowa asserted that one of the purposes of the proposed amendment was to right "the breach of the conjugal relationship," and E. C. Ingersoll of Illinois agreed that such legislation would give blacks "a right to the endearments and enjoyment of family ties."[18] Such a restructuring of the legislated household required an overhaul in the constitutional legacy, and the Declaration of Independence was repeatedly cited as a textual antecedent to the proposed amendment: Godlove S. Orth of Indiana asserted in the debates that "the effect of such Amendment will be to prohibit slavery in these United States, and be a practical application of that self-evident truth, 'that all men are created equal; that they are endowed by their Creator with certain inalienable rights; that among these are life, liberty, and the pursuit of happiness.'"[19] Though the real enfranchisement of blacks would come about only gradually over the course of the next century, the momentum of the civil rights revolution in America gained strength in amendment legislation in 1865, which ruptured the inherited constitutional legacy of chattels in the national homestead.[20]

This discursive alienation of American culture from the "covenant with death" formed one of the rhetorical keystones in representing a largely untested national identity. Back in 1862, Lincoln's attorney general, Edward Bates, had puzzled over a request to define national citizenship: "I have often been pained by the fruitless search in our law books and the records of our courts for a clear and satisfactory definition of the phrase citizen of the United States."[21] Likewise, social critic Orestes Brownson declared in 1865 that "among nations, no one has more need of full knowledge of itself, than the United States, and no one has hitherto had less. It has hardly had a distinct consciousness of its own national existence."[22] Despite the amorphous discourse available to national self-representation, the Republicans in Congress founded the enforcement of the abolition amendment on an unprecedented assertion of federal authority over against states' rights.

Weighing in on this divisive issue, Walt Whitman had declared his authorization of state sovereignty on many occasions. In the 1858 unpublished manuscript "Slavery — the Slaveholder — The Constitution — the true America and Americans, the laboring persons," Whitman had stated that "under that vital part or lungs of the American system of government, our independent State Sovereignty . . . or powerful sectarian feeling, have at various times, in their own limits, neglected or palpably offended, the letter and spirit of our Supreme and National Law." Eliding the antebellum federal-state divide, Whitman's optimism led him to declare, "For any neglect or offense of this kind, so long as it is confined in State limits, and to their own citizens and does not seriously annoy the operations of the general government, there is no help" (*NUPM* VI, 2185). Although Whitman judged slavery to be an indefensible insult to white labor and "the greatest undemocratic unAmericanism of all," in 1858 he had interdicted the right of Congress to interfere with the fugitive slave clause enforcement lest the federal subjection of states' rights turn the country into "one vast model plantation" (*NUPM* VI, 2186, 2190). But Whitman was simply echoing the dominant opinion of the 1850s insofar as the loose confederacy of varied antebellum states had always been the main arbiter in legislating race relations. It was not until the abolition of the constitutional tolerance of slavery in December 1865, through the Thirteenth Amendment, that the legislative momentum of federal hegemony in the forum of civil liberties took off; and the watershed of the first Civil War Amendment was simply the opening of a decade of Constitutional revision that would reverberate for black activists down to the present day.

Whitman's representations of Reconstruction in *Drum-Taps* were tied to the legislative debates about the place of ex-slaves in a postwar political culture that was divided over such federal superintendence of domestic relations within states' borders. The images that suggested such ties were related to overturning America's antebellum self-understanding in favor of plunging ahead onto "the road unknown." If the inheritance of the national past had been bankrupted through its complicity in keeping slaves, then Whitman was forced to turn to the unwritten future with a mixture of bafflement, resignation, and guarded optimism for the chances for Reconstruction's success. For instance, in "Year that Trembled and Reel'd Beneath Me," the text registers America's failed social compact through self-doubting rhetoric that calls into question Whitman's uncontested pride in the Revolutionary inheritance: "Must I change my triumphant songs? said I to myself; / Must I indeed learn to chant the cold dirges of the baffled? / And sullen hymns of defeat?" (*LG VAR* II, 505). While such a text's cultural work could be read as an attempt to resist interracial revisionism, the political din over emancipation forced virtually every legislature in the Union to admit its bad faith with regard to slavery. Therefore, read as a voice of indeterminacy, Whitman's questions could be representations of self-criticism and of the cultural space scooped out of the constitutional legacy by the rescindment of the peculiar institution.

However, the 1865 ratification of the Thirteenth Amendment had not initiated cultural stability but rather had exacerbated white racism in every part of the nation. The anxiety-prone voice that crops up so repeatedly in *Drum-Taps*, alternating with the jingoisitic voice of Union propaganda, nevertheless marks a textual space wherein Whitman was renegotiating the relationship between a system of racial segregation from the past and the virtual promise of an interracial democracy in the future. One of the poems that points to this kind of abolitionist cultural negotiation is "Quicksand Years that Whirl Me I Know Not Whither," whose title bespeaks the cultural agitation on the racial divide, wherein the hold of the national family's inheritance gives way under the pressure of legislative change: "Your schemes, politics, fail — lines give way — substances mock and elude me" (*LG Var* II, 479). This text resolves the uncertainty of the overhaul of the

Constitution, in the nullification of such "lines" as the "three-fifths" and fugitive slave clauses, through a competing image of unitary coherence, suggesting the kind of federalist model that the Republicans were agitating for in the first place. If the emancipated Union's promise reverberates as the voice of any poem in *Drum-Taps*, then surely it echoes in the following federalizing lines: "One's-self must never give way — that is the final substance — that out of all is sure; / Out of politics, triumphs, battles, death — what at last finally remains? / When shows break up, what but One's-Self is sure" (*LG Var* II, 479).

The Founders' codification of slavery into the nation's charter may have kept the South attached to the North in 1787, but the constitutional show had revealed its rottenness by the time of Appomattox, the event marking the beginning of the end of the Civil War. Enlisting the female personification of the Union to give voice to the repudiation of the antebellum race relations record in "Lo! Victress on the Peaks!," Whitman gave full vent to remorse over what slavery had done to his Union "Mother," whose household was in ruins: "No poem proud I, chanting, bring to thee — nor mastery's rapturous verse; / But a little book, containing night's darkness, and blood-dripping wounds, / And psalms of the dead" (*LG Var* II 555). Hardly literal, the "wounds" inflicted on the progeny of the Union Mother were rather textual wounds sewn up in the "rapturous verse" of the Constitution's articulations about liberty, which actually meant that liberty was restricted to the gentrified classes and to the masters of slaves. If Whitman's Victress was spotted on the peaks for any purpose other than to illustrate the path toward the dismantling of mastery, then she was no victress at all but rather the victim of conspirators against liberty. Of such conspirators, in "Long, Too Long, O Land," Whitman asked a question resonant with federalist overtones: "But now, ah now, to learn from cries of anguish — advancing, grappling with direst fate, and recoiling not; / And now to conceive, and show to the world, what your children en-masse really are; / (For who except myself has yet conceived what your children en-masse really are?)" (*LG Var* II, 495).

Notes

[1] I am indebted to Kathleen Diffley for her compelling application of rhetorical analysis to the constitutional reform debates in Reconstruction America. See Diffley, *Where My Heart is Turning Ever: Civil War Stories and Constitutional Reform, 1863–1876* (Athens: U of Georgia P, 1992), especially the Introduction (1–12) and chapter 1, "Domestic Narrative and National Stability" (13–53). Diffley is concerned with the textual enlistment of domestic images in an attempt to stabilize the memory of the "civil crisis" of the War, particularly in popular magazine fiction, whereas I am arguing that the domestic rhetoric in Whitman's Civil War texts marked the domestic *instability* of a breakage with the Revolutionary past.

[2] In "The Republican Mother," Linda Kerber argues that the domestic image of the "Republican Mother" in Revolutionary discourse enabled the female representation to engage its power in public political representations, but that in the nineteenth-century the domestic and public spheres split off from each other, neutralizing the political value of the female image, in order to confine female representations to the home. However, Walt Whitman's liberal usage of the "Mother" as the rhetorical image of the Union troubles Kerber's paradigm for gender relations, and Whitman's genius lies in his employment of feminine images as representations of public, political agents.

[3] See Edward Carpenter, *Days With Walt Whitman: With Some Notes on His Life and Works* (London: George Allen, 1906); (New York: Macmillan 1906), 43.

[4] "The first issue of *Drum-Taps*, printed in New York by Peter Eckler and bound by Abraham Simpson, was a thin, 12mo., book of 72 pages, printed on poor quality paper and bound in an unattractive brown, pebble-grain cloth. The typography was neat and clear, but the whole book showed the economy of the times and Whitman's limited income forced upon him. Biographers have long said that after a few copies were distributed Whitman called in the issue and stopped the sale in order that he might add his elegy on Lincoln to the collection. (So stated by H. B. Binns, *A Life of Walt Whitman* [London, 1905, 212], and nearly all biographers since)." Gay Wilson Allen, *The Solitary Singer: A Critical Biography of Walt Whitman* (rev. ed., Chicago: U of Chicago P, 1985) 577n. Allen's book also

contains the finest biographical account of Whitman's activities surrounding the publication of *Drum-Taps*, see chapter 8, "Over the
Carnage," 322–77.

5   The Thirteenth Amendment, which was modeled on the Northwest
Ordinance of 1787, prohibiting slavery in the Northwest territories, is
strikingly brief. Its final form contained two simple declarative sections:

Section 1. Neither slavery nor involuntary servitude, except as a punishment
for crime whereof the party shall have been duly convicted, shall exist
within the United States, or any other place subject to their jurisdiction.
Section 2. Congress shall have the power to enforce this article by appropriate legislation.

The forthright legalese of section 1 provoked nowhere near as much
consternation as the rescripting of federal-state authority which was
encoded in section 2. The ominous promise of federal intrusion into
"state sovereignty" rights over domestic relations proved to be one of
the most disruptive legal revisions of the Reconstruction era. The assertion of federal authority over states' rights was further enforced in
both the Fourteenth and Fifteenth Amendments, the Freedmen's Bureau Bills, and the Military Reconstruction Acts. This "revolution in
federalism" was shut down by the Southern Redemption governments, which neutralized much of the Radical Republican fervor for
black emancipation, but such legislative energies were resurrected in
the 1950s and 1960s during the "Second Reconstruction" of the civil
rights era. Some notable studies of the Thirteenth Amendment include the following: Eric Foner, *Reconstruction: America's Unfinished
Revolution, 1863–1877* (New York: Harper and Row, 1988), 60–68;
Harold M. Hyman and William M. Wiecek, *Equal Justice Under
Law: Constitutional Development, 1835–1875* (New York: Harper &
Row, 1982), 386–438; Herman Belz, *A New Birth of Freedom: The
Republican Party and Freedmen's Rights, 1861–1866* (Westport,
Conn.: Greenwood Press, 1976), 113–37; Harold M. Hyman, *A
More Perfect Union: The Impact of the Civil War and Reconstruction
on the Constitution* (New York: Knopf, 1973), 263–306; and Jacobus
tenBroek, *Equal Under Law: The Antislavery Origins of the Four-
teenth Amendment* (New York: Collier, 1965), 157–97.

6   Paul Finkelman, "Slavery and the Constitutional Convention: Making a Covenant with Death," (224), in eds. Richard Beeman et al, *Beyond Confederation: Origins of the Constitution and American
National Identity* (Chapel Hill: U of North Carolina P, 1987), 188–
225. To illustrate his point about the absence of the word "slavery"
despite its pervasive influence in the Constitution, Finkelman refers to
the fugitive slave clause: "Fugitive slaves were called 'persons owing

service and labour,' and the word 'legally' was omitted so as not to offend northern sensibilities. Northern delegates could return home asserting that the Constitution did not recognize the legality of slavery. In the most technical linguistic sense they were perhaps right" (224).

[7] See John Alvis, "The Slavery Provisions of the U.S. Constitution: Means for Emancipation," *Political Science Reviewer*, 17 (1987): 241–65. "The one thing evidently agreed upon between the delegates from slaveholding states and their opponents at Philadelphia was the propriety of excising any direct mention of slavery from the clauses that would regulate the institution . . . . Consequences attach to the Framers' verbal fastidiousness. Disinfecting the document of any direct acknowledgement of slavery imparts to the concessions regarding the census and the return of fugitive slaves a shame-faced character . . . . More substantial for antislavery constitutionalism, the avoidance of any explicit mention of slavery suggests that one cannot look to the supreme law of the land for authorization in owning human beings" (247).

[8] Madison is quoted in Don E. Fehrenbacher, *The Dred Scott Case: Its Significance in American Law and Politics* (New York, 1978), 27. Also, neoabolitionist scholar Paul Finkelman suggests that the absence of the word "legally" to describe persons "held to service of Labor in one state, under the laws thereof" (Art IV, Sec. 2), "in the most technical linguistic sense" points to the fact that "the Constitution did not recognize the legality of slavery." Finkelman, *Beyond* 224.

[9] See Waldo E. Martin, Jr., *The Mind of Frederick Douglass* (Chapel Hill: U of North Carolina P, 1984) 37.

[10] See Werner Sollors, *Beyond Ethnicity: Consent and Descent in American Culture* (New York: Oxford U P, 1986), 5-7.

[11] Diffley, 24.

[12] There is an enduring body of criticism on *Drum-Taps*, which is extensive and stretches back to its initial publication. Among the most recent influential readings of *Drum-Taps* are the following: James E. Miller, *A Critical Guide to Leaves of Grass* (Chicago: U of Chicago P, 1957), 219–25; George M. Fredrickson, *The Inner Civil War: Northern Intellectuals and the Crisis of the Union* (New York: Harper and Row, 1965), 94–95, 148–49; Daniel Aaron, *The Unwritten War: American Writers and the Civil War* (New York: Oxford U P, 1973), 56–74; Joseph Cady, "*Drum-Taps* and Nineteenth-Century Male Homosexual Literature," in ed. Joann P. Krieg, *Walt Whitman Here and Now* (Westport, Conn.: Greenwood Press, 1985), 49–60;

and Timothy Sweet, *Traces of War: Poetry, Photography, and the Crisis of the Union* (Baltimore: Johns Hopkins U P, 1990), 11–77.

[13] Sollors 5–7.

[14] See *Congressional Globe*, 38th Congress, 1st Session (1864), 2941.

[15] See *Congressional Globe*, 38th Congress, 1st Session (1864), 2982–2983. In his influential study *Equal Under Law*, Jacobus tenBroek summarizes the opponents' arguments against the passage of the Thirteenth Amendment: "Thus, the case of those who resisted the passage of the Thirteenth Amendment was built almost entirely on opposition to the expansion and consolidation of the national power. With slavery already dead, that expansion and consolidation would be neither great nor of continuing importance if the amendment effected only 'simple exemption from personal servitude.' The thing that gave the revolution in federalism significance was the sweeping conception of what the amendment did. Beyond toppling over the corpse of slavery, most if not all the elements of the congressional opposition asserted that the amendment would guarantee to the emancipated Negro a basic minimum of rights — equality before the law, protection in life and person, opportunity to live, work, and move about — and that Congress would be empowered to safeguard and protect these rights" (143).

[16] See *Congressional Globe*, 38th Congress, 1st Session (1864), 1319, 1321, and 1324."

[17] *Congressional Globe*, 38th Congress, 1st Session (1864), 1439–40; 2989–90.

[18] *Congressional Globe*, 38th Congress, 2nd Session (1865), 142–3.

[19] *Congressional Globe*, 38th Congress, 2nd Session (1865), 142–3.

[20] Again TenBroek reveals that the "revolution in federalism" which the amendment would initiate widened the emancipationist scope of Congressional rhetoric: "This, then, was the slavery which the Thirteenth Amendment would abolish: the involuntary personal servitude of the bondsman; the denial to blacks, bond and free, of their natural rights through the failure of the government to protect them and to protect them equally; the denial to whites of their natural and constitutional rights through a similar failure of government. Stated affirmatively, and in the alternative phrases and concepts used repeatedly throughout the debates, the Thirteenth Amendment would: first, guarantee the equal protection of the laws to men in their natural rights and to citizens in their constitutional rights; and/or second, safeguard citizens of the United States equally in their constitutional privileges and immunities; and/or, running a bad but nevertheless articulated third, enforce the constitutional guarantee to

all persons against deprivation of life, liberty, or property without due process of law" (150–51).

[21] Bates is cited in Harold M. Hyman and William M. Wiecek, 412.

[22] Orestes Brownson, *The American Republic* (Boston, 1865), 2.

1

"A vast Similitude interlocks all"

The 1867 *Leaves of Grass*
and the Elephant at the Raffle

IN THE SPRING OF 1867, while in Washington, Walt Whitman wrote to his mother, "Washington is filled with *darkies*. The men & women & wenches swarm in all directions — (I am not sure but the North is like the man that won the elephant in a raffle)" (*Corr* I, 323). Ironically, Whitman was invoking the December 1865 ratification of the Thirteenth Amendment (abolishing slavery), which had disrupted the tacit tolerance of the Founders in drafting a Constitution that had inscribed slavery into the "national household," a domestic representation of the Union that was deployed by conservatives to underwrite historical continuity with the Revolutionary legacy and deployed by progressives to undercut such historical linkages with the incubus of slavery. Whitman's unsettling image of blacks in the nation's capitol registered the ongoing white cultural anxiety about the fate of ex-slaves, which was far from settled when the poet wrote these lines to his mother. In fact, despite the guarantee of legislative emancipation, Radical Republican Reconstruction was almost immediately thrown into a political tailspin because of the recalcitrance of Southern states. These ex-Confederate states resisted the legal effect of the erasure of slavery through the establishment of Black Code laws designed to subjugate blacks all over again with vagrancy and indentured servant rules that made them slaves in all but the technical sense.

The preliminary proposal of the Fourteenth Amendment, which ratified the incorporation of black citizenship into the Union, was first outlined when Congress reconvened in December 1865, and would be contested for two full years before it was appended to the text of the Constitution. The reconstructive energies of postwar culture were lurching forward, however unevenly, but tension created by the coercive domination of the Republican North and the resistance of the unreconstructed South pitched the sectional rivalries squarely on the racial divide. The raffled black "elephant" of millions of ex-slaves had been voted out of the slave quarters, but the white national family was hardly ready to invite them into the parlor of public life. In effect, the familiar rhetoric of a national household, which had underwritten many of the 1864–65 political debates prior to the ratification of the Thirteenth Amendment, was to be strained beyond recognition in the coercive language of the debates over the Fourteenth

Amendment.[1] The assertion of federal hegemony in its deployment of federal troops to supervise the "equal protection" of black civil liberties pushed the resistant South to contravene with the "white elephant" of racism and state sovereignty.

Nevertheless, the federal government had already determined that state sovereignty had narrower boundaries than the antebellum Union had known, through the passage of the Freedmen's Bureau Bill (1865), which extended the jurisdiction of this military bureau to supervise the translation from slave to free labor in the South. Also, the Civil Rights Act of 1866 was passed to protect the black population from infringements on its civil liberties and to bolster the legal mettle of the Thirteenth Amendment. This Civil Rights Act defined national citizenship for the first time, extending legal recognition to all natural-born citizens except Native Americans and providing judicial review for discrimination cases in the federal courts, whereas such cases had previously been handled routinely in the state systems.[2] The hegemony of federal authority had begun in earnest, and national politics were enlisted by Radical Republicans as a mandate against state and local foot-dragging on the protection of civil liberties. This representation of an understanding of "national citizenship" was inextricably woven into the post-war foundation of a Union based on legislative emancipation. Therefore, just as slavery was the dominant cultural issue of antebellum politics, emancipation would dominate the public forum throughout the Reconstruction years. Though hotly contested by racist conservative factions in Washington and elsewhere, federal hegemony, for which the Radical Republican were pushing, became a cornerstone for whatever reconstructed Union would emerge from the discredited slavocracy sanctioned by the Revolutionary Founders.

Just as white America was vexed by the reconfiguration of the Union and the potential for the fuller inclusion of blacks, Walt Whitman published the most chaotic edition of *Leaves of Grass* to that date, the fourth edition of 1867, which bore all the marks of white cultural anxiety over the uncertain future of the Union, and was the container of a repository of literal and indeterminate images of the blacks who demanded adoption into the national household. Whitman had stitched together four separate books into the 1867 issue of *Leaves*, a vastly reedited version of *Leaves of Grass*, a reissue of *Drum-Taps* (1865) and the *Sequel to Drum-Taps* (1865–66), and an intriguing coda called *Songs Before Parting*.[3] This curious volume has been called the "workshop" edition, which has unfortunately relegated its critical stature to the level of a second-rate edition that merits little scrutiny.[4] However, as a text that circulated in the midst of a tumultuous cultural workshop that was reconstituting the ruins of a failed social compact, the 1867 *Leaves*, in its disheveled raggedness, is a fertile site for representing this incipient nationalist ideology founded in the disheveled days after emancipation.

Though Whitman had begun a postwar camouflage of his antebellum frankness in representing blacks, primarily in his neglect of black representations in *Drum-Taps* and its *Sequel*, he was consolidating his images of a coherent Union in this fourth edition of *Leaves of Grass*. Inadvertently, perhaps, Whitman deployed the ghostly presence of blacks due to the highly-charged cultural debates on the future of ex-slaves within the Union as well as the explicit images of blacks that survived from the earlier editions of *Leaves*. Given the legislative renovation of the Revolutionary Constitution, which incorporated black Americans as citizens for the first time, readers of *Leaves of Grass* in 1867 could turn to its representations and find a new kind of cultural work circulating in older poems — as the book materially circulated alongside such dominant representations as the newspaper accounts of the heated congressional debates on the Fourteenth Amendment — and such readers could find that Whitman's 1867 *Leaves* bore the same stress marks that the contentious rhetoric on racial difference bore prior to the 1868 ratification of the Fourteenth Amendment, which has become the most significant citation in civil rights struggles for over a century. With the legislative tide turning toward "equal protection" for all citizens on a national scale, Whitman sought at every turn in his cultural poetics to reinforce this insurgent national self-understanding, through several significant 1867 revisions of his older poems, while carefully superintending his older representations of cultural heterogeneity in the Union landscape.

Beginning with the 1867 *Leaves*, in particular with the coda called *Songs Before Parting*, continuing with *Democratic Vistas* (1871), the 1871–72 *Leaves*, and *Memoranda During the War* (1875–76); and culminating in *Two Rivulets*, the companion volume to the 1876 *Leaves*, Whitman's Reconstruction texts furnished their role as representations of what, in his 1872 preface, he called a book of "an aggregated, inseparable, unprecedented, vast, composite, electric *democratic nationality*" (*PW* II, 463). Insisting that a "composite" future could be constructed out of diverse ethnic and racial pasts, Whitman's Reconstruction cultural poetics served as a mediating gesture in the Union's transition from its localized self-understanding as a confederation of sovereign states toward a centralized national understanding of federal hegemony as the monitor of the regulation of civil liberties in these several states. Through his own appropriation of the binding role of a cultural "minister," seeking coherence in diversity, Whitman believed that his reconstructive poetics could be enlisted as the agent of this growing "aggregate" identity as citizens constituted by the *United* States, in its supersession of localized comrades constituted by the United *States*.

Just as the textual genesis of *Drum-Taps* predated the Civil War, the foreground of the 1867 *Leaves of Grass* stretched back to 1864, when Whitman wrote what was intended to become an introduction to American editions of his book. Though never published, the manuscript reveals in its three versions, written between 1855 and 1870, an ongoing effort by the poet to preface his poetic project with a prose counterpart that condensed his political motivations into coherent form.[5] In the introduction, dated 23 December, 1864 ("good — and must be used"), the same month that Lincoln delivered his "divided house" address, Whitman, in his unabashed nationalism, opens the document with an utterance that suggests the motivation for his entire Reconstruction project: "I claim that in literature, I have judged and felt everything from an American point of view which is no local standard, for America to me, includes humanity and is the universal" (*WWW* 127). Whitman's unitary images for the as-yet-uncongealed Union contained such a macrocosmic scope that they seemed to erase any attempt to sectionalize the cultural text of America. In fact, by the end of 1864, the war had wrecked the nation for three and a half years, and though Whitman was residing in Washington, the axis of the Union, he found no cultural coherence in the capitol, as though Washington itself represented the fragmentation of the United States in microcosm ("this Union Capitol without the first bit of cohesion — this collect of proofs of how low and swift a good stock can deteriorate" [*Corr* I, 69]). Therefore, this aforementioned introduction suggested more than a little compensation on Whitman's part in its appeal to the erasure of localized interests in favor of a national identity.

However, the Union images represented by this intended preface to American readers contained not just geographical metaphors but also temporal ones that disrupted the political models of the past in favor of a reconstructed future. The poet's chant had to "extricate itself from the models of the past," and like America, the poet had to "hold up at all hazards, the banner of inalienable rights, and the divine pride of man in himself" (*WWW* 127). Whitman's implication of the significance of the Declaration of Independence ("inalienable rights") in relation to his poetic project also drew in, alongside his virtual dream of an uncontested Union, the competing claims of blacks in their demands for full citizenship. Throughout 1864 the U.S. Congress had been debating the Thirteenth Amendment because, in February of that year, Lincoln had cautioned that the Emancipation Proclamation (January 1863) could be legitimated only in the theater of a nation at war. Congressional debates on the amendment that would abolish slavery addressed the inscription of the Declaration's unfulfilled promise in the impending legislation, for the "inalienable rights" clause had been a cornerstone in abolitionist legal strategy since the 1830s.[6]

Lincoln had shifted the representational significance of the Revolution of 1776 away from the Confederacy by proclaiming that the original Union had been the progeny of the Declaration: "This issue embraces more than the fate of the United States . . . . It presents to the whole family of man, the question, whether a constitutional republic, or a democracy . . . can, or cannot, maintain its territorial integrity" (*Lincoln* IV, 439, 438). The "integrity" of the reintegration of the North and the South also laid the geographical groundwork for any potential reconstruction based on the emancipation of slaves from "involuntary servitude." By breaking up the legacy of slave economics, Lincoln, like Whitman, projected "a vast future" in which the Union represented "a struggle for maintaining in the world that form and substance of government whose leading object is to elevate the condition of men . . . to afford an unfettered start, and a fair chance in the race of life" (*Lincoln* V, 53).

The unpublished introduction to the 1867 *Leaves* articulated Whitman's program for the fourth edition in three central theses: the American democracy founded on the sacredness of the individual; the fusing of this aggregate of individuals through "Love," thus balancing the private and the public demands of civic life; and finally, "Religion," which denoted the purifying effect of destiny's *purpose* as the key to self-development. Whitman's project paralleled the political fallout of the Civil War, which centered on the give and take between the clout of state sovereignty and the ascendancy of the federal mechanisms used to impose a national agenda on the states. Rather than evading this thorny cultural fracas, the 1867 *Leaves* served as a mediating text between these two governmental rivalries by insisting that a communal future could be built out of diverse sectional pasts. The cultural materials for representing such diversity-in-unity were the political events from which the nation wove its narrative self-understanding: "Our highest themes are things at hand. Current, practical times are to be photographed, embracing the war, commerce inventions, Washington, Abraham Lincoln, . . . the settlement of this Western World, the great railroads &c, — embracing indeed the races and locations of the whole world" (*WWW* 128).

But the third plank of Whitman's program for American Reconstruction, namely "Religion," also bound the nation to the war as the revolutionary trauma out of which a national household could be reconstituted. In Whitman's well-thumbed 1847 *Webster's Dictionary*, the etymology of "religion" read as follows: "Lat. *religio*, either from *relegere*, to gather or collect again, to go through or over again in reading, speech, or in thought . . . or from *religare*, to bind anew or back, to bind fast." Given Whitman's predilection for the perusal of etymologies as a composition technique for his poems, this lexicographical citation provides a key to understand the significance of his Reconstruction project: Whitman had not abandoned the Civil War, but he insisted that the conflict had to be bound anew to the national memory in order to gather all the conflicting political claims that had prevented any real resolution of the two purposes for which it had been pursued, Union and emancipation. The revolutions of the wheels of war had cultural significance only if they reinvigorated the Founders' dream of "a more perfect Union" built on the "inalienable rights" of all persons, minus chattel slavery. Put succinctly in "Starting From Paumonok," the cultural work of religion was linked to the destiny of the reconstituted Union: "I say that the real and permanent grandeur of these States must be their religion, / Otherwise there is no real and permanent grandeur" (*LG Var* II, 279).

Whitman's exertion in printing the 1867 *Leaves* was completed in November 1866, when the first of at least four different formats of the text was undoubtedly bound and ready for shipment.[7] Bibliographers have puzzled over the confusing array of editions, but they speculate that "this edition was crude and poorly put together. [The copies] were probably bound up in small lots as sold. This may account for the many variations."[8] The most notable feature of the 1867 *Leaves* consisted not in new texts, for there were only six new poems, but rather in the radical dismemberment of the 1860 *Leaves* arrangement with hundreds of deletions and emendations of recognizable works.[9] Arriving at the moment that the nation was lost in the labyrinth of a legislative "workshop," seeking to coerce a recalcitrant South to incorporate blacks into the national household, Whitman's renovated *Leaves* claimed an increased significance as a nationalist manifesto. For instance, in *The Good Gray Poet* (1865), Whitman's apologist William Douglas O'Connor proclaimed, based on his reading of the 1860 *Leaves of Grass* and 1865 *Drum-Taps*, "The nation is in it! In form a series of chants, in substance it is an epic of America. It is distinctively and utterly American. Without model, without imitation, without reminiscence, it is evolved entirely from our own polity and popular life."[10] Thus, even Whitman's contemporaries recognized *Leaves of Grass* as a rhetorical containment of all the heterogeneous voices of America into a "Union impregnable." O'Connor continued in hyperbolic form, "To understand Greece, study the *Iliad* and *Odyssey*, study *Leaves of Grass* to understand America. Her Democracy is there. Would you have a text-book of Democracy? The writings of Jefferson are good; De Tocqueville is better; but the great poet always contains historian and philosopher."[11]

Understanding America in 1867, however, may have been more bewildering than it had been prior to Appomattox; the country was poised anxiously between the discredited Revolutionary past and the contested (unreconstructed) future: in response, Whitman's book looked back to the war by literally incorporating *Drum-Taps* and its *Sequel* as separate texts within the evolving *Leaves*, and it looked forward to an unrealized Union (founded on the Thirteenth Amendment and federal supervision of the revision of the disabling alliance with slavery) by appending *Songs Before Parting* as an incipient representation of a national polity.

Affirming Whitman's programmatic intentions in the 1864 Introduction, the 1867 *Leaves* opened with "Inscription," one of the new poems that would thereafter introduce the work to subsequent readers. Gay Wilson Allen has suggested that "Inscription" contained in its six verses the "skeleton plan of the final *Leaves of Grass*, a revelation of the emerging purposes and the congealing form."[12] The dominant image of "ONE'S-SELF" as the subject of the chant "for the use of the New World" shifted its signification in that it made the individual self interchangeable with the collective self: after announcing "Man's physiology complete," the speaker quickly continued, "Nor Cease at the theme of One's-Self. I speak the word of the modern, the word En-Masse" (*LG VAR* II, 557). Here in a single line the metaphorical slippage in the movement from the isolated individual to the collective identity underwrites the historical images that follow, thus troubling their conventional depiction as opposites, and opens the rhetorical path toward reading the 1867 *Leaves* as a cultural text: "My days I sing, and the Lands — with interstice I knew of hapless War" (*LG Var* II, 557).

The image of "ONE'S-SELF" has conventionally been read as a capitalized call for the sovereignty of the individual, the irreducible agent of democratic culture. But the egotistical sublime failed to account for the subsumption of the single self into the "modern" term "En-Masse" in that "one" contained fossilized connotations of not only "single," but also of the "unitary" self. In Whitman's copy of the 1847 *Webster's*, the entry for "one" included the definitions "single in number" and "single in kind" but also "referring to a future time" and denoting "union, a united body." So just as the "Inscription" slipped from "One's-Self" to "En-Masse" in a single line, confirmed by the Webster lexicon, the halls of the Congress were formulating the containment of the individual states' identity within the federal coalition of the "united body" through national superintendence over civil liberties for blacks. As an "epic" utterance, Whitman's programmatic opener actually enacted the cultural work emanating from Washington, where harried lawmakers were grappling with the greatest intervention in individual state sovereignty ("a simple, separate person") in American history. The resulting federal interference in monitoring civil liberties within state jurisdictions, already begun in the enforcement clause of the Thirteenth Amendment and in the Civil Rights Act of 1866, would culminate in the 1868 ratification of the Fourteenth Amendment and further the consolidation of the untested idea of national citizenship ("En-Masse") that had been brewing since the firing on Fort Sumter.

In fact, the South had seceded from the Union on the legal *assertion* of "state sovereignty," and the North had not presumed to negate the undoubted rights of states. This viewpoint was held by General Sherman, who prematurely made conciliatory gestures toward Confederate General Johnston on 18 April 1865, after Appomattox; and simultaneously several ex-rebel governors were assembling their legislatures to submit to the Union. Many Southerners aspired to a painless reentry to their representative status in Washington and hoped that "with the end of war, all affairs should revert to their pre-existing condition; individuals might be guilty of treasonable acts against the United States, but the states themselves, as governmental and territorial entities, had by definition all the same rights and duties as before."[13] Lincoln vetoed this "Southern theory" of Reconstruction following a vociferous uproar in the Northern press. At the opposite rhetorical extreme, Radical Republican Thaddeus Stevens had asserted in Congress in 1863 that the unruly insurrection had obliterated the Constitution and that "we have the right to treat them as we would any provinces that we might conquer."[14] In a much discussed speech at Lancaster, Pennsylvania, on 6 September 1865, Stevens went so far as to advocate confiscation of Southern properties and aver that the federal government would have to put the ex-states through a hard novitiate of reconstitution: "In reconstruction, therefore, no reform can be effected in the Southern States if they have never left the Union. But reformation *must* be effected; the foundation of their institutions, both political, municipal, and social, *must* be broken up and *relaid,* or all our blood and treasure have been spent in vain."[15] But this "conquered provinces" theory never garnered widespread support in the North, primarily because of an aversion to seizing the personal property of citizens.

Given these polarizing discourses that were circulating in the land, Whitman's 1867 mediating stance between the "individual" and the "collective" political identities took on added rhetorical urgency. As he had stated in the 1864 Introduction to American editions of *Leaves,* the "sovereignty, license, and sacredness of the individual" and the "idea of Love [which] fuses and combines the whole" required the arbitrating role of a conciliator: "Out of the fusing of these twain, opposite as they are, I seek to make a homogeneous Song" (*WWW* 128). For Whitman, the poet was the mediating agent who moved public rhetoric from "individual" sovereignty to the "fusion" of a composite identity, and his 1867 *Leaves* became an enactment of this "homogeneous Song." President Andrew Johnson had attempted to provide a "homogeneous" turn away from both Sherman's and Stevens' polar oppositions as soon as Congress reconvened in December 1865, when he stated that "sectional animosity is surely and rapidly merging itself into a spirit of nationality." Ignoring the plight of ex-slaves, the president was promoting the "harmonious restoration of the relations of the States to the national Union."[16] Any such "presidential theory" of Reconstruction always implied the ghost of Abraham Lincoln, who in his last public speech, on 11 April 1865, veered away from disputations over the constitutional status of the ex-states: "Finding themselves safely at home, it would be utterly immaterial whether they had ever been abroad" (*Lincoln* VIII, 403).

The national household that this domestic rhetoric invoked, however, had undergone a rupture so severe that such a civic homestead would not be as welcoming as Lincoln and Johnson implied. Although the Thirteenth Amendment had ended the institution of slavery on parchment, the ex-slaves were finding themselves knocking on the door of the cultural home only to find that there was no easy entrance. Pointing to the coming rhetorical battle over the incorporation of freed blacks, more than three years earlier, Radical Republican Senator Charles Sumner had advocated the notion that the seceded states had effectively committed suicide; and in a series of Senate resolutions on 11 February 1862, Sumner argued that Congress had to intervene in these territories in order to "proceed to establish therein republican forms of government under the Constitution." The termination of constituted states had also ended "those peculiar local institutions which, having no origin in the Constitution, or in natural right independent of the Constitution, are upheld by the sole and exclusive authority of the State."[17] Sumner had reduced the status of the peculiar institution to the forum of state sovereignty, like his abolitionist colleagues, but his "state suicide" theory of Reconstruction was widely judged to be too severe to hold clout in the halls of Congress and elsewhere. The popular understanding of secession interdicted any discontinuity in the historical adherence of the states to the Union; whether they had attempted to split the national household (through secession) or not was construed as a moot point.

The constitutional position that won out in the Reconstruction of the South was delivered on the floor of the House of Representatives on 8 January 1866 by Samuel Shellabarger of Ohio. Subsequently called the "forfeited rights" theory, and closely resembling Sumner's, Shellabarger's concept refined the nuances of state sovereignty to include its territorial integrity, unmolested because secession was null, and held that states had no jurisdiction to leave the Union. Also, however, states had a political integrity with governmental powers, which could be disrupted through attempted severance from Washington. Because the "bodies politic" of these states had been disrupted, "such States and their people ceased to have any rights or powers of government as States of this Union."[18] Shellabarger located the reconstructive power of state governments in the hands of the Congress, and thus the federal superintendence over state self-determination was sealed. Bolstered by Sumner's having planted the emancipation issue squarely on the veranda of state sovereignty in order to delegitimate the slave system, Shellabarger's federalism paved the path for Southern resistance to Reconstruction to such a concerted extent that the Reconstruction Acts of 1867 would send Northern troops back south of the Mason-Dixon. In any Republican scenario, the interwoven fates of ex-states and ex-slaves were crucial to the construction of whatever workable Union that might congeal in the wobbly months after Appomattox.

Whitman's cultural poetics sought at every turn to reinforce the representation of this nationalization of civic identity while carefully superintending the heterogeneous voices that made up the Union. Thus, in the second poem of the 1867 *Leaves*, "Starting From Paumanok" Whitman modified the autobiographical references in the 1860 version, and gave the persona a continental identity: "After roaming many lands — lover of populous pavements; / Dweller in Mannahatta, . . . or on southern savannas; / O a soldier camp'd, . . . or a miner in California; / Or rude in my home in Dakota's woods" (*LG Var* II, 273). The effect of the war is manifested in his representational embrace of diverse geographical sites as well as in the implicit recognition of "Lilacs" in the concluding lines of section 1, where the "unrival'd one, the hermit thrush from the swamp-cedars" motivates the "solitary" speaker "singing in the West" to "strike up for a New World" (*LG Var* II, 274). This echo of his Lincoln elegy, which appeared in the *Sequel to Drum-Taps* (1866), projected the song of the "thrush" as the song of "Death" which is the death of historical continuity with the antebellum tolerance of the slavocracy, to project a reconstructed egalitarian future. Above all else, Whitman's contact with eighty thousand to one hundred thousand soldiers in Washington hospitals from every section of the United States had given him imaginary access to the sprawl of the Union.

Whitman felt "bound" to these visitations in that through them, he could experience directly the regional voices of the Union and fuse them through the poetic texts that managed such vocal diversity with the modern sensibility of the "En-masse." This ministerial fervor suggested that the "epic" stirrings of the national identity were to become a political bond, and one that promised a national allegiance that transcended local family ties. Whitman's "religion" was founded on this "gathering or collecting again," and that coalescence was translated in the "binding" of the war to all cultural poetics. As Whitman told Horace Traubel, the hospital commiserations were "a religion with me. Every man has a religion . . . something which absorbs him . . . . That, whatever it is, seized upon me, made me its servant, slave; induced me to set aside other ambitions: a trail of glory in the heavens, which I followed, with a full heart" (*WWC* III, 581).

In addition, the renovated world that Whitman was inaugurating had already marked the advent of postchattel economics with the ratification of the Thirteenth Amendment, and, as mentioned earlier, the song of the "thrush" had signified the disruption of slave economics in the United States. Such emancipatory potential allowed the text to reincorporate the ex-rebel states with the imperative "Take my leaves America! take them South, as well as North! / Make welcome for them everywhere, for they are your own offspring" (*LG Var* II, 276). The rhetorical recognition of the constitutional crisis that had begun in 1861 with the firing on Fort Sumter and continued in the concurrent debates on the Fourteenth Amendment came up in "Paumanok" at section 6: "I will make a song for These States, that no one State may under any circumstances be subjected to another State; / And I will make a song that there shall be comity by day and by night between all The States, and between any two of them" (*LG Var* II, 277). The "comity" clause of the Constitution (Art IV, Sec 2) stated that "The Citizens of each State shall be entitled to all Privileges and Immunities of Citizens in the several States," and had previously been interpreted to apply strictly to interstate travel (if a citizen crossed state borders, that citizen still had all legal privileges); but by the middle 1840s, the abolitionists had widened the rhetorical scope of the comity clause to include free blacks and slaves under these "Privileges and Immunities" protections of citizenship. Indeed, the abolitionists advanced an embryonic notion of "national citizenship" as its "distinctive doctrine," and "in doing so, they had loosely interchanged 'citizens of the United States' with persons having inalienable natural rights, on the one hand, and with persons having the rights guaranteed by the constitutional amendments, on the other."[19]

Though the states' rights advocates would delay the application of the comity clause to apply to blacks through resistance to racial equality, by the time of the Fourteenth Amendment, in 1868, the notion of "national citizenship" regardless of race had been inscribed in the nation's charter. As Jacobus tenBroek has pointed out, "The comity clause did, however, make a significant though an indirect contribution to paramount national citizenship as that doctrine finally evolved. The national government would naturally be the primary guardian of national citizenship."[20] Therefore Whitman's explicit citation of the comity clause in "Starting From Paumanok" at the outset of the 1867 *Leaves* pointed to the contemporary understanding of that constitutional diction as applying to the renovated concept of national citizenship: the federal government presided over the superintendence of states' conduct in the forum of civil liberties, transcendent from local and regional custom, especially in relation to ex-slaves as they laid claim to authentic civil status as descendants of the Constitution.

Undergirding this national rhetoric, Whitman added the following section to the 1867 version of "Paumanok" to reinforce the postbellum understanding of the "individual" (different from the antebellum 1860 version) that ensued from the subsumption of state sovereignty under the codification of federal hegemony: "And a song make I, of the One form'd out of all; / The fang and glittering One whose head is over all; / Resolute, war-like One, including and over all; / However high the head of any else, that head is over all" (*LG Var* II, 277–78). The sectional trauma that had disrupted the Union ("the One form'd out of all") was interdicted through the greater coherence of a national homestead, formed out of federal legislation that attempted to coerce states to fall in line with its universal claims to constitutional protections: "I will not make a poem with reference to parts, / But I will make poems, songs, thoughts, with reference to ensemble" (*LG Var* II, 283). The projection of a remodeled cultural home with its emancipatory promise for all citizens released the "Paumanok" text for the first time to surge into a continental embrace in section 14, which enfranchised the ex-states of the South in its signification: "Hereby applying these leaves to the new [states], from the hour they unite with the old ones; / Coming among the new ones myself, to be their companion and equal — coming personally to you now; / Enjoining to you acts, characters, spectacles, with me" (*LG Var* II, 286).

The epic spectacle of Whitman's 1867 *Leaves* reached its highest point, in the text "Walt Whitman" (later "Song of Myself"), in which the poet as cartographer drew a cultural map of the management of the diverse social and ethnic factions in the United States. As a fulfillment of the 1855 preface, this teeming epic of America sought to incarnate the maxim "The United States themselves are essentially the greatest poem" (*PW* II, 434). In fact, the 1855 Preface opened Whitman's *Leaves* experiment with the image of the "corpse" of the past borne through the door of the national household so that its descendants could supersede the inheritance of dead forms "into the new life of the new forms" (*PW* II, 434). In order to merge all the conflicting discourses afloat in the culture of the United States, the expansive "I" of the text of "Walt Whitman" represents a cosmopolitan performance of binding heterogeneous cultural voices in all American constituencies, and the "I" always points to the excessive energy of a historical future in which the United States will evolve beyond the cultural traumas of the past and present: "The past and present wilt . . . . I have filled them and emptied them, / And proceed to fill my next fold of the future" (*LG Var* I, 81). Apart from his 1867 ironic reference to the black "elephant" in the cultural raffle, Whitman's representations of black Americans are most frequently cited in the contradictory folds of the poem "Song of Myself." The most celebrated race-relations passage in the text narrated the protection of a runaway slave (section 10): "The runaway slave came to my house and stopped out-side . . . ./ He staid with me a week before he was recuperated and pass'd north; / I had him sit next me at table — my fire-lock lead in the corner" (*LG Var* I, 12). This transgressive image contradicted the legality of the fugitive slave clause of the Constitution as well as the Fugitive Slave Act of 1850, and the text resonated with abolitionist fervor in its principled resistance to the boundaries of enforceable law.

However, the Fugitive Slave Act was never widely enforced, even in antebellum culture, with its largely uncontested state sovereignty ideology. With the passage of the 1850 statute, over three thousand fugitive slaves escaped to Canada, prompting Frederick Douglass to complain that "fugitive slaves who had lived for many years safely and securely in western New York and elsewhere. . . were suddenly alarmed and compelled to flee to Canada . . . and take up a dismal march to a new abode, empty-handed, among strangers."[21] But there was widespread white resistance to the enforcement of the statute, and Whitman's slave escape narrative in "Walt Whitman" embedded this text in the same discursive pattern of defeating such a contested constitutional principle. As Paul Finkelman has pointed out, "Even where it was not a dead letter, the 1850 law was never very effective. Between 1850 and 1860, only 298 fugitives were returned, even though more than 1,000 slaves escaped in 1850 alone. Many northerners refused to stand aside quietly when their black neighbors were threatened with enslavement."[22] Such interracial sympathy reached its representational crux in Whitman's text in section 33, wherein the poet actually spoke with the voice of the runaway: "I am the hounded slave, I wince at the bite of the dogs, / Hell and despair are upon me, crack and again crack the marksmen, / I clutch the rails of the fence, my gore dribs, thinn'd with the ooze of my skin; / . . . The riders . . . / Taunt my dizzy ears and beat me violently over the head with whip-stocks" (*LG Var* I, 51–52).

In another racially charged image that Whitman chose to excise after 1871 and the ratification of the Fifteenth Amendment (enfranchising black males), the text "Sleep-Chasings" (later "The Sleepers") enacted the rage of a black "Lucifer," a voice of resistance to white domination, who possessed fully constituted subjectivity when he stated, "I have been wronged — I am oppress'd — I hate him that oppresses me, / I will either destroy him, or he shall release me. / Damn him! how he does defile me!" (*LG Var* I, 116). The personified "I" of black subjectivity protested the disruption of harmonious domestic family ties in his smoldering resentment of the auctioning of his intimates: "How he informs against my brother and sister, and takes pay for their blood! / How he laughs when I look down the bend, after the steamboat that carries away my woman!" (*LG Var* I, 116). The disruption of familial ties in slave economics provided one of the central rhetorical weapons of the abolitionists against the perpetuation of the peculiar institution. Moreover, the transmutation of domestic into public rhetoric suggested that these literal images of broken family ties articulated the "breakage" of the "national family" as well, through the secession of the "sister states" of the Union. The rage represented in this passage from "Sleep-Chasings" could come only from a fully constituted human subject, not a passive, "half-human" piece of property, and the reconstituted slave promised that, as the potential free citizen, he was only one of many millions: "Now the vast bulk that is the whale's bulk, it seems mine // Warily, sportsman! though I lie so sleepy and sluggish, the tap of my flukes is death" (*LG Var* I, 116). Despite the emancipation from slavery in 1865, the renovation of the postbellum "household" still held the "bulk" of the ex-slaves' threat to demand fuller civil incorporation, including legislative citizenship and the franchise.

In this antebellum passage from the "Sleep-Chasings" text, Whitman chose to translate the white voice into the voice of the brutalized slave, thus performing the social function of pointing out that identities were culturally constructed, not the product of natural (biological) forces. Whitman was aligning himself with the black subculture as a sympathetic white male poet and thereby robbing the dominant culture of its racist construction of black Americans. Such an imaginary access (by a white male) to the experience of brutalized blacks did not seek to collapse racial difference, for the threatening "whale's bulk" was (to mix metaphors) no mere undifferentiated "elephant," or else why would the poet have retained the subjective "I" capable of the experience of alienation from family ties? If the nation had chosen in 1865 to emancipate blacks from such degrading scenarios, then the legislative energy required to adopt ex-slaves into the household of civil liberties performed its social function in the ratification of the Fourteenth Amendment in 1868. Though later rebutted by the debut of Jim Crow's strange career, antebellum images of white civil disobedience transfixed the North in press accounts, between 1850 and 1860, of twenty-two slaves being freed from their slave catchers by Republican sympathizers.[23] Even though Eric Foner has persuasively argued that "the Republican stand on race relations went against the prevailing opinion of the 1850s,"[24] these same Radical Republicans did move the public race debate in a more democratic direction, and "these Republicans who were ahead of northern opinion in the 1850s would write the Fourteenth Amendment in the 1860s."[25]

In the 1867 *Leaves*, Whitman also included as one of the six new compositions a poem titled "Tears!," which contained the indeterminate image of "Moist tears from the eyes of a muffled head, . . . On the white shore dripping, suck'd in by the sand" (*LG Var* II, 559). Given the color coding ("white") and the undeniable remorse in this text, "Tears!" may well have resonated with the concurrent debates over the incorporation of blacks into the national household. Therefore, read as a cultural text, it shows that the full stature of earlier images of blacks, resisting white hegemony over their civic fates, had receded into indeterminacy: "O who is that ghost?—that form in the dark, with tears? / What shapeless lump is that, bent, crouch'd there on the sand?" (*LG Var* II, 559). But the sentimental "lump" suddenly took on a threatening persona, though seemingly "so sedate and decorous by day, with calm countenance and regulated pace"; and the suffering "shade" despaired so deeply that the anguish affected the meterological conditions: "O storm, embodied, rising, careering, with swift steps along the beach; / O wild and dismal night storm, with wind! O belching and desperate!" (*LG Var* II, 559). Thus the text constructed an image of blacks whose "muffled" blankness represented the white antipathy toward ex-slaves that pervaded early Reconstruction America. But the whale's "bulk" of blacks, beaten down by social atrocities for two hundred years, erupted in the "wild and dismal night storm" of demands for inclusion in the material culture. The "white shore" could disregard the stature of emancipation assumed by blacks after the Thirteenth Amendment ("embodied, rising, careering"), but the threat to social relations sounded portentous if the cultural exclusion of ex-slaves continued indefinitely.

Whitman's texts of social solidarity, which had been strengthened through his Civil War experience of comradeship among strangers, comprised the longest cluster of poems in the 1867 *Leaves*, "Calamus," which the representative poet shifted closer to the front of the book. "Calamus" and this "Children of Adam" cluster were the least destabilized of any clusters from the 1860 edition. The growing coherence of a political awareness of national citizenship provided Whitman with the material in "Calamus" to represent a movement away from localized and ethnic factional identities in favor of comradeship among strangers from diverse backgrounds. The congressional debates on the Fourteenth Amendment were simultaneously grappling with the creation of a federated identity of unionized states while at the same time meeting the resistance of regional affiliations and local customs, a cultural tension that Werner Sollors has suggested in his political model of "consent" versus "descent" rhetoric in American self-representations. Sollors's generational-cultural dialectic suggests that "[d]escent language emphasizes our positions as heirs, our hereditary qualities, liabilities, and entitlements; consent language stresses our abilities as mature free agents and 'architects of our fates' to choose our spouses, our destinies, and our political systems."[26] According to Sollors, the movement toward cultural consensus in American life arises from the transformation of un-American pasts into a voluntary relation to the American past, rooted in the Revolutionary heritage of the eighteenth century but always on the open road toward the freedom of a revised future.

Whitman's rhetorical images in "Calamus" also invoked the domination of forward-looking "consent" language against the divisive language of inherited "descent." His religious fervor in comforting hospitalized comrades from every corner of the United States during the war had its representational effect on the 1867 "Calamus" cluster. The poet deleted three of the most privatized confessions from the 1860 edition ("Long I Thought that Knowledge Alone Would Suffice" [No. 8], "Hours Continuing Long, Sore, and Heavy-Hearted" [No. 9], and "Who is Now Reading This?" [No. 16]) in favor of a greater sense of public solidarity among citizens. Later, in the 1876 Preface to *Leaves of Grass*, Whitman was to declare his consensual politics of "universal democratic comradeship" to be the "special meaning" and "political significance" of the "Calamus" cluster: "In my opinion, it is by a fervent, accepted development of comradeship . . . latent in all the young fellows, north and south, east and west — it is by this, I say, . . . that the United States of the future, (I cannot too often repeat,) are to be most effectually welded together, intercalated, anneal'd into a living Union" (*PW* II, 471). Rather than the pull of local family ties, then, in "Calamus" Whitman announced his political model for the pull of national solidarity built on affiliations between citizens enlisted in the quest for the purchase of a "living Union."

Whitman's "Calamus" images of social solidarity were enlisted in the representation of a solidified sense of national identity, but the cluster also recognized the fragility of such a coalition: "Here the frailest leaves of me, and yet my strongest — lasting, / Here I shade down and hide my thoughts — I do not expose them, / And yet they expose me more than all my other poems" (*LG Var* II, 407). By the time this text appeared in the 1867 *Leaves*, the governmental battle lines had been drawn between the Republican Congress and President Johnson, who, along with the Democrats and the unreconstructed Southerners, was opposed to any centralizing federal intentions. On 27 March 1866, in his veto of the Civil Rights Bill of 1866, Johnson complained, "In all our history, in all our experience as a people, living under federal and State law, no such system as that contemplated by the details of this bill has ever before been proposed or adopted." Having supported the Thirteenth Amendment a year earlier, and having vetoed the Freedmen's Bureau Bill on 19 February 1866, Johnson now applied the executive brakes on "an absorption and assumption of power by the General Government which . . . must sap and destroy our federative system of limited powers . . . . It is another step, or rather stride, towards centralization, and the concentration of all legislative powers in the national Government."[27]

Andrew Johnson had desired the executive pardoning privilege to constitute the main requirement for reseating Southern delegates to Congress, but the Congressional Joint Committee on Reconstruction had wanted more stringent entrance requirements before legitimate representation. President Johnson resented the resistance of Congress to speedy recognition of restored states, as he declared in his veto message: "The tendency of this [Civil Rights] bill must be to resuscitate the spirit of rebellion and to arrest the progress of those influences which are more closely drawing around the States the bonds of union and peace."[28] Such barbed interchanges transfixed the nation in daily newspapers and resonated with the political rancor that would lead to President Johnson's 1868 impeachment proceedings. The labyrinth of Reconstruction rhetoric also gained poignant resonance in "Calamus," where Whitman wrote, "To the East and to the West; / . . . To the Canadian of the north — to the Southerner I love; / . . . I believe the main purport of These States is to found a superb friendship, exalte, previously unknown, / Because it waits, and has always been waiting, latent in all men" (*LG Var* II, 401).

This intersectional comradeship remained only a cultural possibility in 1867 despite the promising beginning of Reconstruction with the 1865 ratification of the Thirteenth Amendment. For the first (and last) time during congressional Reconstruction, the executive and legislative branches in Washington were in concert over a major renovation in cultural self-definition, the erasure of slave economics that had dominated national politics in antebellum America. The dissolution of the national compact with slavery found its way into the "Calamus" texts in the multiple representations of death as an image of cultural revision, not simply as a personal dissolution of individual bodies. In "O Living Always — Always Dying!," Whitman's cultural voice apostrophized while striding ahead "imperious as ever," "O me, what I was for years, now dead, (I lament not — I am content;) / O to disengage myself from those corpses of me, which I turn and look at where I cast them! / To pass on, (O living! always living!) and leave the corpses behind!" (*LG Var* II, 396). Such consent language places the rhetorical weight of "death" on its capacity to incite liberation from the pull of ethnic rivalries and from the Old World ancestries in favor of the fuller cohesion of the federated states. America should be "willing to disregard burial-places and dispense with them" (*LG Var* II, 387) in order to energize the comradeship with strangers that would "anneal" the Union and that indeed had begun so intensely among the untraveled recruits in the war regiments, tens of thousands of whom Whitman had ministered to in the hospitals.

This legislative dismantling of the deadening effect of slavery opened out onto the potential for a national future of as-yet-unrealized solidarity. Such a shucking off of the failed promises of the past in favor of fellow-feeling among citizens found its most extended treatment in "Scented Herbage of My Breast," where the postbellum voice calls out, "Through me shall the words be said to make death exhilarating; / Give me your tone therefore, O Death, that I may accord with it, / Give me yourself — for I see that you belong to me now above all, and are folded inseparably together — you Love and Death are" (*LG Var* II, 367). The contingencies of disunion emanating from Washington gave America pause over "the terrible doubt of appearances" (*LG Var* II, 377), but the bonding of affection and a voluntary cultural discontent with the past held out the possibility that discontinuity with that past "will perhaps dissipate this entire show of appearance, / That may-be you [death] are what it is all for — but [appearance] does not last very long, / But you will last very long" (*LG Var* II, 367).

The sternness of the legislative demand for cutting off the accumulated racial strife of a century, which led to secession, would have to result in a "long and exhausting" novitiate of reorientation toward the future, for "The whole past theory of your life and all conformity to the lives around you would have to be abandon'd" (*LG Var* II, 368). But Whitman's cultural poetics continually holds up a virtual promise of democratic comradeship in the politics of national identification: "Over the carnage rose prophetic a voice, / Be not disharten'd — Affection shall solve the problems of freedom yet; / Those who love each other shall become invincible — they shall make Columbia victorious" (*LG Var* II, 374). The social compact of the Union would have to overcome the "carnage" of the rhetorical divisions on the racial divide in Congressional debates, and the image of "Columbia victorious" would have to attach to the forward-looking national will to face the "open road" of an interracial future by discrediting the racially divided past and its atrocities. Amid the din of conflicting racial discourses, Whitman's clarion call for national indissolubility, in "A Song" ("For You O Democracy"), began, "Come, I will make the continent indissoluble; / . . . I will plant companionship thick as trees along the rivers of America, and along the shores of the great lakes, and over all the prairies; / . . . By the love of comrades, / By the manly love of comrades" (*LG Var* II, 375). In the 1847 *Webster's*, "comrade" was understood to mean "*literally* one who lodges in the same room," but comrades also formed alliances as associates "in occupation." Thus, while comradeship could denote descent from localized blood ties, Whitman expanded his friendly embrace to include extrafamilial ties, indeed with those who were constructing a community of citizens "occupied" with learning to represent themselves as a nation of companions within an interracial social compact.

Invoking such consent language in its most condensed format, Whitman eliminated several verses of the earlier version of "On the Beach at Night Alone" (in 1867 simply "Leaves of Grass, No. 1"), in which the poet had focused on Union complacency with the cultural status quo: "What can the future bring me more than I have?" However, in the 1867 version, stripped of such complacency, the "old mother" of the Union "sways her [progeny, the States] to and fro singing her savage and husky song" and lulls the poet into a reverie over the nation's "future": "A VAST

SIMILITUDE interlocks all" (*LG Var* I, 241–242). The consensus of such a "SIMILITUDE" represented Whitman's absolutizing of the "Calamus" sentiment of social solidarity, but among the lines that catalogue its manifestation were four that were pertinent to the evolving popular understanding of national citizenship at the moment such self-representation was fought over in the halls of Congress and elsewhere: "All nations, colors, barbarisms, civilizations, languages; / All identities that have ever existed, or may exist on this globe . . . ; / . . . The vast similitude spans them, and always has spann'd, and shall forever span them, and compactly hold them" (*LG Var* I, 242).

In this representation, the pull of the future had overcome the unreconstructed resistance to the nationalization of civil rights in the North as well as the South as a result of the entrenched racism of whites against blacks. Indeed, the legislative "compact" of all "races" was to take much longer to enact the kind of cultural amalgam that Whitman's *Leaves* had here prophesied in the winter of 1866. At this moment, the Southern states, with President Johnson's public encouragement, were rejecting one after another the ratification of the Fourteenth Amendment on the grounds that it violated their right to do as they pleased with their citizens. Federal authority would have to exert a muscular superintendence over the ex-states for another year and a half, including the threat of remaining outside the Union indefinitely, before the July 1868 ratification of the Fourteenth Amendment signaled the greatest extension of civil rights in the Union's history since the adoption of the Bill of Rights.

The necessity for federal supervision of an expanded civil rights struggle, as the Union was judicially pushed to recognize its racist inheritance, was resisted by those who wanted to maintain slave economics as the foundation of market productivity. In this moment of an explosion of discourse on civil rights, Whitman represented in a new poem, "The City Dead-House," his regret over the continued insistence that marginal citizens could be discarded through social exclusion. At the heart of this text, the issue of disposable persons in an unrealized democracy was foregrounded with as much rhetorical force as it was by Radical Republicans in the halls of Congress, only the marginal figure in this text was "a poor dead prostitute" brought to the city morgue gate. The poem's speaker notices that "Her corpse they deposit unclaim'd, it lies on the damp brick pavement; / The divine woman, her body — I see the Body — I look on it alone, / That house once so full of passion and beauty" (*LG Var* II, 562).

The poetic voice ranks the corporeal "house" of this discarded woman, though she is socially outcast, above "all the rows of dwellings ever built!" Presiding over this mournful spectacle was Washington's "white-domed Capitol itself, with majestic figure surmounted—," which had failed to generate social affection for this "tenement of a soul," so that the speaker intervenes to offer this "Dead house of love" a token: "take one breath from my tremulous lips; / Take one tear, dropt aside as I go, for thought of you" (*LG Var* II, 562). Addressing the resistance to legislative inclusion for marginal citizens, Whitman here signals his own intervention as the "minister" who bridged the cultural gap between local "comrades," which the prostitute lacked, and voluntary "citizens," which Whitman represented with the stranger's kiss to a discarded woman. If persons were rotting on the pavement within sight of the Capitol, then this compelling textual intervention enacted a recovery of the rightful place of human solidarity among strangers, the same legislative agenda set by constitutional reform when this poem appeared in the 1867 *Leaves*. Both blacks and prostitutes were disenfranchised citizens, beyond the boundaries of white respectability, but Whitman's poetic reconstruction of them placed them at the heart of the Republican polity.

While such cultural restraints as racism and the degradation of women disabled the realization of Whitman's democratic Union dream, Whitman accented the virtual enactment of such an egalitarian polity in the future. Another of the new 1867 compositions, "The Runner," could be read as an allegorical "poemet," which represented the athletic determination that would be required to bring coherence to a Union weakened by sectionalism and racism: "On a flat road runs the well-train'd runner; / He is lean and sinewy, with muscular legs; / He is thinly clothed — he leans forward as he runs, / With lightly closed fists, and arms partially rais'd" (*LG Var* II, 558–559). Without such athletic vigilance, the ever-present danger to the Union lay in its static attachment to a moribund past, inherited by descendants of a failed social compact that had finally come undone in the firing on Fort Sumter. In "Aboard at a Ship's Helm" (in 1867 simply "Leaves of Grass, No. 3"), another of the new compositions in the fourth edition of *Leaves*, Whitman's allegorical ship, an obvious figure of the "Ship of State," only avoided "its wreck-place" on the shore of history through the "ocean-bell" that gave "good notice indeed" and thus allowed "the beautiful and noble ship, with all her precious wealth," to speed "away gayly and safe" (*LG Var* II, 560). Only by engaging in an egalitarian revision of its social relations, to become more inclusive rather than exclusive, would the Union avoid another cataclysm like the Civil War. The "ocean-bell" that rang in the ears of virtually all the citizens of the Union in 1867 was the carillon of civil rights for ex-slaves. Rather than persist in the resistance to such solidarity, the Union's reconstructive potential lay in mobilizing its social relations toward such a revisionist goal by "voyaging, voyaging, voyaging" (*LG Var* II, 560).

Through Republican agitation, the Fourteenth Amendment was finally declared ratified on 28 July 1868.[29] However, the amendment had been debated in Congress in May and June of 1866, after the convocation of the

Thirty-ninth Congress (December 1865) revealed that the political rhetoric of the House and Senate had shifted away from ex-slaves and sought to construct an acceptable image of the ex-states as restored Union states. In traces of domestic imagery, Congress determined that these "wayward sisters," who had severed their familial ties to the Union, would have to meet stringent prerequisites prior to their return to the "national household."[30] When President Andrew Johnson provoked a verbal brawl with Congress, convinced that the speedy return of the Confederate states to the Union was the only justifiable course of action, these states felt executive support as they rejected the proposed Fourteenth Amendment. Therefore, to guarantee that renovated state constitutions would support impartial voting rights and to ensure the ratification of the Fourteenth Amendment,[31] Congress resorted to the Military Reconstruction Acts of 1867, which redeployed federal troops into a South divided into five military districts.

The congressional debates over the amendment focused rhetorical energies on the extension of the machinery of government as the superintendent of "equal protection" of civil liberties. Thus these debates served as a tool in the further overturning of the constitutional sanction of the inheritance of slavery. Building on abolitionist polemics, which had circulated since the 1830s, the Republican majority fought to extend the jurisdiction of the comity clause (Art IV, 2) of the Revolutionary text of the Constitution to ex-slaves. As noted earlier, the comity clause guaranteed the "privileges and immunities" of all citizens of the United States, such as the natural rights to life, liberty, due process, and property. In opening the House debate, California Republican William Higby asserted that the Fourteenth Amendment would confer "force, effect, and vitality" to the comity clause as a protection for black civil identity, which had "been trampled under foot and rendered nugatory."[32]

Concurrently, Pennsylvania Republican William D. Kelley fought for the amendment because it restored the "dormant" power of the comity clause in the existing Constitution, "by which the general government may defend the rights, liberties, privileges, and immunities of the humblest citizen wherever he may be upon our country's soil."[33] According to Vermont Republican Frederick E. Woodbridge, the ex-slaves were now United States citizens, and the impending amendment was "intended to enable Congress to give to all citizens the inalienable rights of life and liberty, and to every citizen in whatever state he may be that protection to his property which is extended to the other citizens of the state."[34] Recapitulating the abolitionist arguments that undergirded this application of the comity clause to emancipated blacks, Republican Representative John A. Bingham countered Democrats who opposed the amendment because of the federal supervision of states: "Who ever heard that any state had reserved to itself the right . . . to withhold from any citizen of the United States within its limits . . . that provision of the Constitution which declared that the citizens shall be entitled . . . to all the immunities of a citizen of the United States?"[35]

The Democratic opponents to the extension of civil rights in the proposed amendment rose to the occasion to delegitimize federal hegemony in its intrusion on the previously unmolested forum of state sovereignty.[36] The momentum for federal action had already been enacted in the enforcement clause of the Thirteenth Amendment as well as in the passage of the Civil Rights Act of 1866, which rankled states' rights advocates and unreconstructed congressmen who were waiting to be seated in the halls of Congress. But this civil rights bill was subject to political shifts of majority parties, and Ohio Representative John Garfield rose to address the urgency with which the Republican coalition pushed the proposed amendment through Congress: "It is precisely for that reason that we propose to lift that [civil rights bill] above the reach of political strife, beyond the reach of the plots and machinations of any party, and fix it in the serene sky, in the eternal firmament of the Constitution."[37] By defining the parameters of national citizenship, which the Civil Rights Act had done for the first time in American history, the first section of the Fourteenth Amendment proposed, as Garfield argued, "to hold over every American citizen, without regard to color, the protecting shield of law."[38] Pennsylvania Representative George F. Miller underscored the urgency of constitutional revision in this explicit representation of national citizenship in "that no state shall deprive any person of life, liberty, or property without due process of law, nor deny equal protection of the laws, and [therefore] so clearly within the spirit of the Declaration of Independence of the 4th of July, 1776, that no member of this House can seriously object to it."[39]

Therefore, while carefully avoiding the danger of legitimizing secession as a constitutional right, Congress had the last word in deciding what demands to place on the South as a territory of "conquered provinces." The months of debate over this reconstitution program crystallized in the five sections of the text of the Fourteenth Amendment, which the returning states would have to ratify, even at bayonet point, to be seated in the halls of Congress: the Amendment stated unequivocally that the South would have to (1) guarantee equal protection of laws to both whites and blacks; (2) face a reduction in congressional representation if laws (such as the infamous Black Codes) attempted to exclude voters from the polls; (3) forbid Confederate officials to vote in national elections until 1870; (4) erase the enormous rebel debt, and the possibility of reimbursement for the emancipated slaves, the loss of whom had ruined many plantation owners; (5) abide by any future enforcement legislation that Congress might see fit to enact to protect the amendment from cultural resistance to its demands.

This interracial revision of the U. S. Constitution, as embodied in the impending amendment, proved so revolutionary in its egalitarian potential that speeches like that of Michigan Senator Jacob M. Howard went a long way in whipping up the fierce opposition of Southern rhetoric. Underscoring the equal rights clause, Howard argued that for the first time in America, the amendment "prohibits the hanging of a black man for a crime for which a white man is not to be hanged. It protects the black man in his fundamental rights as a citizen with the same shield which it throws over the white man."[40] The fifth section of the ratified Fourteenth Amendment, which in effect gave Congress the power to pass legislation to implement basic rights for blacks, gave Senator Howard the rhetorical image of the democratization of legal protection. In a description worthy of Whitman, he declared that "it establishes equality before the law, and it gives to the humblest, the poorest, the most despised of the race the same rights and the same protection before the law it gives to the most powerful, the most wealthy, or the most haughty."[41] But the pervasive Southern sentiment for state sovereignty did not go gently into the night of cultural obscurity.

Leaves of Grass, too, registered the pull of the past on the South in a poem called "Longing for Home," wherein the cultural work of nostalgia for the antebellum heritage, founded on state autonomy (and slave economics), was apostrophized with affection but also with a sense of anachronistic loss: "O magnet-South! O glistening, perfumed South! My South! / O quick mettle, rich blood, impulse, and love! Good and evil! O all dear to me! / O dear to me my birth-things — All moving things, and the trees where I was born" (*LG Var* II, 408). An 1860 poem, "Longing for Home" served a different prewar function in its signification of pacifying the South on the eve of disunion. But Whitman's postwar title, "O Magnet-South," suggests his belated awareness of the inappropriate rhetoric of "nostalgia" after the war. Nevertheless, whether the "[g]ood and evil" South liked it or not, the Fourteenth Amendment would give a constitutional mandate to the equal protection of law on an impartial basis, and the "despised" ex-slaves had a permanent constitutional valve to call on as a precedent in advancing their fuller inclusion in the national household.

With the legislative tide turning toward "equal protection" for citizens on a national scale, Whitman packaged several poems from previous editions of *Leaves of Grass* into a new book, with separate pagination, at the end of the 1867 edition. Called *Songs Before Parting*, this coda resonated with the same federalizing motifs that were rife in public rhetoric as the Fourteenth Amendment made its rough passage to its textual port in the U.S. Constitution. The title itself indicates that this pastiche of earlier poems was enlisted in a different cultural work than the poems had performed prior to secession. These songs represent Whitman's desire for the prevention of "parting" the newly reconstituted Union, but they also were written before the 1861 parting of the North from the South. In 1867, these songs can be reheard in the postwar context of the parts, becoming united again. Later on, the 1872 preface to "As a Strong Bird on Pinions Free" articulated Whitman's intention to write a book apart from *Leaves of Grass* ("the song of a great composite *democratic individual,* male or female"), which was to represent American national self-understanding: "I suppose I have in my mind to run through the chants of this volume, (if ever completed,) the thread-voice, more or less audible, of an aggregated, inseparable, unprecedented, vast, composite, electric *democratic nationality*" (*PW* II, 463).

Critics have uniformly assumed that Whitman never fulfilled this half-hearted assertion because of ill health and a senescence of his inspired poetic genius. However, the textual traces of his Reconstruction project, with its representational mission to register such "democratic nationality," suggest another narrative that revises such a premature dismissal of this middle period of Whitman's cultural poetics. In 1867 *Songs Before Parting* announced the emancipatory momentum of national citizenship at the moment of federal supervision of civil liberties of all citizens, regardless of race. To reinforce such a representation of national identity, Whitman opens his preparting *Songs* with "As I Sat Alone by Blue Ontario's Shore" (titled in 1856 "Poem of Many in One"), which pieced together dozens of lines from the 1855 Preface to *Leaves* and voiced its program in the maxim "A nation announcing itself" for the future. The renovated national household, supported by the determination of Congress to fulfill the Revolutionary promise of liberty, allowed Whitman the textual space in which to represent the fact that "the Republic is ever constructive, and ever keeps vista" (*LG Var* I, 197). The 1847 *Webster's Dictionary* defined "vista" as "a view or prospect through an avenue, as between rows of trees; hence the trees or other things that form the avenue." The grounded vantage point of this vision defies the flight from material history that a more elevated vista might have suggested.

As a result, the avenue of history forced Whitman to recognize that the aftermath of the war had thrown the cultural workshop into a self-critical assessment of its democratic promise: "A Phantom, gigantic, superb, with stern visage, accost'd me; / *Chant me a poem,* it said, / *And chant of the welcome bards that breathe but my native air* — *invoke those bards; / And chant me, before you go, the Song of the throes of Democracy* (*LG Var* I, 190). The "throes" of American Union, in these lines added to the 1867 version of "By Blue Ontario's Shore," a Union that Whitman unequivocally felt was "ever constructive," also contained the traumas of the millions of its citizens who had been held as property just two years before, as well as more than half a million casualties interred across America. In addition, the civil unrest in the ex-states of the South, which were resisting congressional imperatives to preface their reinstatement in the Union, forced the poet to resort to the poignant insertion of a parenthetical second voice in the 1867 text, which ran alongside its announcement of a coherent nation and sounded portentous warnings concerning the racial strife in the Union: "(Democracy — the destined conqueror — yet treacherous lip-smiles everywhere, / And Death and infidelity at every step.)" (*LG Var* I, 190).

This egalitarian democracy Whitman dreamed of continued to be deferred in the fall and winter of 1866 as the Southern states rejected the ratification of the Fourteenth Amendment. Invoking the domestic images of maternity and sisterhood, which had been subverted through domestic intrusion of federal hegemony over the submissive "sister" states of the South, the text locates the cultural worm in the American apple in the refusal to rebuild an emancipated Union "home" on the foundation of freedmen: "(O mother! O sisters dear! / If we are lost, no victor else has destroy'd us; / It is by ourselves we go down to eternal night)" (*LG Var* I, 191). Attempting to avoid such a secession from the Union, Whitman anticipated the cultural eligibility to civil liberties that had been newly extended to blacks in 1868: "All is eligible to all, / All is for individuals — All is for you, / No condition is prohibited, not God's, or any" (*LG Var* I, 191–92). As noted earlier, the postemancipation understanding of "individual," with its reference to states, had been deeply circumscribed through federal superintendence. The maxim "Produce great Persons, the rest follows" must be read in the cultural context of federal hegemony, for its use of individualism was no value-free signifier. Whitman's text challenged the antifederalist charges of "military despotism" that were deployed to preserve the "individual" state sovereignty arguments: "I am he who walks the States with a barbed tongue, questioning every one I meet; / Who are you, that wanted only to be told what you knew before? / Who are you, that wanted only a book to join you in your nonsense?" (*LG Var* I, 192). Such congressional coercion, which superseded the "nonsense" of active rebellion against the cultural force of Union, required the "barbed" voice of support for the civil rights struggle that would determine the future of the marginal persons kept outside the forum of citizenship by "what you knew before," which amounted to white racism. The erasure of such a racial divide would therefore have the chance to put the revolutions of war's wheels to rest.

Whitman's procongressional emancipatory rhetoric found a textual home throughout the *Songs Before Parting*, and nowhere more directly than in the concluding couplet to section 6 of "Blue Ontario's Shore," a section outlining his lengthy catalogue of the vitality of nativist American culture, in which the representative voice stated, "Slavery — the murderous, treacherous conspiracy to raise it upon the ruins of all the rest; / On and on to the grapple with it — Assassin! then your life or ours be the stake

— and respite no more" (*LG Var* I, 196). This couplet is a major rewriting of the 1856 and 1860 versions of the poem: Whitman's earlier "stern opposition" to slavery transmutes into a concern with the "conspiracy to raise it upon the ruins," a conspiracy under way in the attempt to raise the slave mentality again after the war fought to exterminate it. Thus the text refutes the contemporary resurgence of racism, manifested especially in the passage of the Black Code laws, and the vigilante violence that was filtering through the recalcitrant South, as though the incubus of slavery threatened to assassinate the Union all over again. Therefore the text summoned up an image of liberty that mastered the seceded states with a remorseless intensity that rivaled the harsher "conquered provinces" 1863 program for Reconstruction by Thaddeus Stevens. The "Libertad" represented in the poem wears the "new aureola" of federal hegemony, with "war's flames and lambent lightnings playing," in order to extinguish Southern resistance to the inclusion of blacks in civil society: "And your foot on the neck of the menacing one, the scorner, utterly crush'd beneath you; / The menacing, arrogant one, that strode and advanced with senseless scorn, bearing the murderous knife; / Lo! the wide swelling one, the braggart, that would yesterday do so much!" (*LG Var* I, 197). The humiliation of the South suggests not a *fait accompli* in the text, for the postwar resistance to Reconstruction legislation prolonged the status of the South as "To-day a carrion dead and damn'd, the despised of all the earth! / An offal rank, to the dunghill maggots spurn'd" (*LG Var* I, 197). But since the cultural work of Reconstruction held the promise of Congress's stern determination, the text translated to the vista of the future: "O days of the future, I believe in you! I isolate myself for your sake; / O America, because you build for mankind, I build for you!" (*LG Var* I, 197).

Because the cultural poetics in "Blue Ontario's Shore" pointed to a virtual future, the textual space of the poem houses a renovated interracial democracy outside of the ongoing constitutional fist fight. Because of the contingencies of politics, Union democracy would have to be voiced by the "native and grand" bards who would achieve their agency for democratic change because "by them only can The States be fused into the compact organism of a Nation" (*LG Var* I, 198). As a result of the political filibuster blocking the reconstitution of the ex-states, the poet's federalizing persona had to admit that to "hold men together by paper and seal or by compulsion is no account," because the Southern resistance to amendment legislation was resulting in racial violence. The "paper and seal" were both present in 1856, but the referents for such constitutional images had now shifted from the Constitution itself to include its amendments. Even President Johnson is castigated as an agent in cultural disintegration because of his insistence that the ex-states reject the Fourteenth Amendment ("Their Presidents shall not be their common referee so much as their poets shall").

The political Union Mother remained potentially "prolific" but "barren" because the Reconstruction project was finding its representation on the parchment of the Constitution but not in the "living principle" of unreconstructed human hearts.

Therefore Whitman offered *Songs Before Parting* as the incipient representation of a national polity in which the images of federal affiliation were enlisted to perform the cultural work of enlarging national consciousness and racial sympathy as well as dismantling the sectional malice that sought a return to antebellum black subjugation. The uncontested Reconstruction project of the future would work out its destiny, because in America's promise, "Without extinction is Liberty! without retrograde is Equality!" and "For the great Idea! / That, O my brethren, that is the mission of poets," with the "flag of peace quick-folded" in favor of the "Warlike flag of the great Idea" (*LG Var* I, 199–200). Because the cultural work of the poet of "democratic nationality" could be accomplished only on "obdurate" terms, the prerequisites included a textual examination to test familiarity with the emancipatory renovations of the Constitution in the years following the war: "Have you consider'd the organic compact of the first day of the first year of the independence of The States, sign'd by the Commissioners, ratified by The States . . . ? / Have you possess'd yourself of the Federal Constitution? / Do you see who have left all feudal processes"? (*LG Var* I, 201). When the political foundation of America had remembered the promise of "inalienable rights" and thereby discarded the "feudal processes" of "involuntary servitude," then the advent of a veritable national citizenship based on "equal protection" would be a consensual reality, and not before. Since "the American compact is altogether with individuals," and "its crimes, lies, thefts, defections, slavery, are you and me," the poet admitted that "he only suits These States whose manners favor the audacity and sublime turbulence of The States" (*LG Var* I, 206–7). But the "individual" states were not simply to be left autonomous in their "audacity," for the "turbulence" represented only a temporal aberration to the inexorable march of democratic nationality, a nationality formed out of the "unitary" individuals bonded to the "Idea" of Union: "(Democracy! while weapons were everywhere aim'd at your breast, / I saw you serenely give birth to children — saw in dreams your dilating form; / Saw you with spreading mantle covering the world.)" (*LG Var* I, 208). The maternal figure in the rebuilding of the national household must perform her domestic role as an arbitrator in a dysfunctional family, for in her persistence the poet could foresee that "I know not what these plots and deferments are for; / I know not fruition's success — but I know that through war and peace your work goes on, and must yet go on" (*LG Var* I, 209).

Indeed, the work of national citizenship, set in motion by the ratification of the Thirteenth and Fourteenth Amendments, did go on despite presidential vetoes and Southern resistance to change. The promise of "equal protection" to blacks, though stymied by the ineradicable racism of American culture, had begun to exert its legislative influence through its habitation in the remodeled house of the Constitution. Though the Union Congress enforced such interracial alliances through the imposition of martial law, Whitman's *Songs Before Parting* held out the promise of social solidarity in America's cultural workshop. In "O me, man of slack faith so long!" the speaker situated the nation as "standing aloof" from all the momentary resistance and solidified the Union resolve in its "denying portions so long; / Only aware to-day of compact, all-diffused truth" (*LG Var* II, 329).

Such a social compact based on equality regardless of race, Whitman's poetics suggested, must endure the manifestations of the "falsehoods" of white superiority, but the poet projected a future when such racist misreadings would be an anachronism: "(This is curious, and may not be realized immediately — But it must be realized; / I feel in myself that I represent falsehoods equally with the rest, / And that the universe does.)" (*LG Var* II, 330). The elasticity of this textual and cultural solidarity arose from the multivalent materials that composed America, which invited the consent of its citizens to enact a voluntary nation out of the involuntary past of slavery: "Locations and times — what is it in me that meets them all, whenever and wherever, and makes me at home? / Forms, colors, densities, odors — what is it in me that corresponds with them?" (*LG Var* II, 332). America's absorption of different races (and ethnicities) would continue as long as the push for a national identity called forth the representational energies needed to bring political coherence out of competing ideological positions.

The *Songs Before Parting* cluster handled the issue of Southern resistance to federal hegemony as a temporary aberration that would pass away with the inertia of time: "Of these years I sing, / How they pass through and have pass'd through convuls'd pains, as through parturitions; / How America illustrates birth, gigantic youth, the promise, the sure fulfillment, despite of people — Illustrates evil as well as good; / How many hold despairingly yet to the models departed, caste, myths, obedience, compulsion, and to infidelity" (*LG Var* II, 304–5). By adding the past tense of "pass," Whitman has altered the 1860 lines to cast the "convuls'd pains" in the past. The question of the "elephant at the raffle," or the bulk of the millions of ex-slaves who were clamoring for a place in the public parlor, held out a promise to all Americans: the emancipation of these newly protected citizens was to partake of "what the feuillage of America is the preparation for — and of what all the sights, North, South, East and West, are" (*LG Var* II, 306). Whitman's announcement of a nation, which was the reconstructive purpose of this cluster, was represented in tandem with the Re-

publican program of "equal protection" for ex-slaves, for as the poet unequivocally states in "As I Walk, Solitary, Unattended," America's realities
must extend beyond its commodities to include "Libertad, and the divine
average — *Freedom to every slave on the face of the earth,* / The rapt promises and luminé of seers — the spiritual world — these centuries-lasting
songs, / And our visions, the visions of poets, the most solid announce-
ments of any" (*LG Var* II, 318; emphasis added). These prewar lines
resonated with the abolitionist agitation floating in public discourse since
the 1830s. Indeed, after Appomattox, the impetus of Reconstruction legislation had a visionary cultural force that would resonate long after the
racist resistance to constitutional reform had become largely a cultural arti-
fact.

Fortunately, the legislative workshop of Reconstruction was hardly over
in 1867. As Yankee troops patrolled the five military districts of the South
to intervene in discrimination cases against blacks, the cultural dissonance
forced Whitman to mortgage the national homestead to preserve the
promise of liberty in the face of civil turmoil. The Second Reconstruction
of the 1950s and 1960s was almost a hundred years down the open road of
national experience, but Whitman had laid in his store in advance, and "So
Long!," the farewell poem of *Songs Before Parting,* furnished its part toward the more immediate breakthrough of the Fifteenth Amendment,
which enfranchised black males in 1870: "To conclude — I announce
what comes after me, / I announce mightier offspring, orators, days, then
depart. / I remember I said, before my leaves sprang at all, / I would raise
my voice jocund and strong with reference to consummations" (*LG Var*
II, 448). Whitman was compelled to announce a "Union impregnable" in
which the national citizenship that took shape in the text of the Constitution would become a social fact: "I announce that the identity of These
States is a single identity only, / I announce the Union more and more
compact, / I announce splendors and majesties to make all the previous
politics of the earth insignificant" (*LG Var* II, 450). In 1871 Whitman
would federalize the "compact" Union by adding the freighted word
"indissoluble" to his farewell poem, for the intervening four years had witnessed more racial antagonism than before.

Indeed, such a single identity was still only a "consummation" to be
wished, for the Republican Congress's demand for submission in the summer of 1868 had been hardened by the Southern efforts to bleach the
emancipation elephant white. This federal hegemony held as much determination as it had on 8 February 1867, when moderates joined radicals in
the mandate that "we must remove the rubbish and rebuild from the bottom. Whether they are willing or not, we must compel obedience to the
Union, and demand protection for its humblest citizen wherever the flag
floats."[43] The elephant in the cultural raffle wanted interracial alliances of

mutual tolerance and legislated equality, but white racism donated an ironic resonance in Whitman's letter to his mother in the spring of 1867. However, such a raffled leviathan, millions of free black persons, had not lost its agency for cultural inclusion. Blacks were demanding a place at the American table of equality, and, as Michigan Congressman Howard stated on 23 May 1866, "For weal or woe, the destiny of the colored race in this country is wrapped up with our own; they are to remain in our midst, and here spend their years and here bury their fathers and finally repose themselves."[44]

Notes

[1] See Kathleen Diffley, *Where My Heart Is Turning Ever: Civil War Stories and Constitutional Reform, 1863–1876* (Athens: U of Georgia P, 1992), 64–73, for a first-rate discussion of the shutdown of domestic rhetoric in the congressional debates on the Fourteenth Amendment. Diffley's purpose is to move away from the representational value of historical continuity with the Revolutionary past in the rhetoric of the debates, toward intersectional cooperation between the North and the South as represented in the reconstitution of ex-states to the Union in popular magazine Civil War fiction.

[2] See Jacobus tenBroek, *The Antislavery Origins of the Fourteenth Amendment* (Berkeley: U of California P, 1951) 156–80, for a thorough analysis of the debates over the Freedmen's Bureau Bill and the Civil Rights Act of 1866 as interventions to ensure the civil liberties of ex-slaves.

[3] "The title page read: LEAVES/ OF/ GRASS./ New York./ 1867. Like the first edition, the author's name did not appear, except in the copyright notice on verso. Though printed and copyrighted in 1866, this is known as the 1867 edition (from the date on the title page). And the edition is bibliographically confusing in other ways, because small batches were bound up at different times, often with varying contents and occasionally with slightly different arrangements. Four main issues are distinguished by bibliographers, but more could be counted." Gay Wilson Allen, *The Solitary Singer: A Critical Biography of Walt Whitman*, 580n. Allen's book also contains the finest treatment of the biographical details of Whitman's life in 1867; this appears in chapter 9, "Ships at Sea," 378–413.

[4] "The 1867 *Leaves of Grass* might be called 'The Workshop Edition,' for the revisions indicate great critical activity, although in organization it is the most chaotic of all editions. Exclusive of the annexes . . . this edition contains only six new poems, all short and of minor significance. What makes it important is Whitman's great exertion to rework the book by deletion, emendation, and rearrangement of the poems. The confused state of the published work, therefore, bears testimony to the poet's literary and spiritual life during the War." See Gay Wilson Allen, *The New Walt Whitman Handbook*, 118.

[5] See section 4, "Introductions Intended for American Editions of Leaves of Grass," in *Walt Whitman's Workshop: A Collection of Un-*

published Manuscripts, 115–38. Horace Traubel, Whitman's literary executor, located the manuscripts in a box at the poet's Mickle Street home after Whitman's death in 1892.

6   For an indication of how pervasive the citation of the Declaration of Independence was to antebellum abolitionist reformers, see tenBroek, 62–63.

7   "The book was printed for Whitman (whose name appears only in the copyright date, 1866), by a New York printer, William E. Chapin, and was bound and distributed during the year in at least four different forms: (1) *Leaves of Grass* (338 pp.); (2) *Leaves of Grass* with *Drum-Taps* (72 pp.) and *Sequel to Drum-Taps* (24 pp.); (3) *Leaves of Grass* with *Drum-Taps*, *Sequel to Drum-Taps*, and *Songs Before Parting* (36 pp.)." See Allen, *Whitman Handbook*, 119.

8   See Carolyn Wells and Alfred F. Goldsmith, *A Concise Bibliography of the Works of Walt Whitman* (Boston: Houghton Mifflin and Co., 1922) 14.

9   The six new poems printed for the first time in the 1867 *Leaves* are "Inscription (One's Self I Sing)," "The Runner," "Tears! Tears! Tears!," "Aboard at a Ship's Helm," "When I Read the Book," and "The City Dead-House."

10 William Douglas O'Connor's *The Good Gray Poet* is reprinted in Jerome Loving, *Walt Whitman's Champion: William Douglas O'Connor* (College Station: Texas A & M U P, 1978) 157–203. The citation is from page 184. One of the most lyrical passages, which approaches the same intensity as one of Whitman's catalogues and most clearly indicates the nationalist rhetoric of Whitman's project, is on page 184–85.

11 O'Connor, *Good* 185.

12 See Allen, *Whitman Handbook*, 119.

13 See Eric L. McKitrick, *Andrew Johnson and Reconstruction* (Chicago: U of Chicago P, 1960) 97.

14 See *Congressional Globe*, 37th Congress, 3rd Session, 239–40.

15 Thaddeus Stevens's Lancaster speech, which articulated his "conquered provinces" approach to the constitutional theory of Reconstruction, appeared in the *New York Tribune*, 11 September 1865.

16 See *Congressional Globe*, 39th Congress, 1st Session, 78.

17 Charles Sumner's "state suicide" approach to the constitutional theory of Reconstruction was articulated in his Senate resolutions in the *Congressional Globe*, 37th Congress, 1st Session, 736–37.

18 Samuel Shellabarger's comments on the eventually successful understanding of Congressional Reconstruction legislation can be found in *Congressional Globe*, 39th Congress, 1st Session, 142.

[19] See tenBroek, 85.

[20] See tenBroek, 84.

[21] See Frederick Douglass, *The Life and Times of Frederick Douglass* (1892; rpt. New York, 1962), 279–82.

[22] See Paul Finkelman, "Rehearsal for Reconstruction" 16.

[23] Ibid.

[24] See Eric Foner, *Free Soil, Free Labor, Free Men: The Ideology of the Republican Party Before the Civil War* (New York, 1970) 262. The Constitutional guarantees of the remanding of fugitive slaves back to their owners conflicted with the interdiction of such practices by many Northerners, who chose instead to place due process above racist ideology. Even Eric Foner argues that "almost every Republican believed that it had been the intention of the founding fathers to restrict slavery and divorce it from the federal government" (84).

[25] Finkelman, 18.

[26] See Werner Sollors, *Beyond Ethnicity: Consent and Descent in American Culture* (New York: Oxford U P, 1986) 6. Sollors goes on to define his project: "Focusing on the tensions between consent and descent relations permits us to look at American culture anew, including even its familiar and ambiguous semantic safety valves . . . . Most striking in a great variety of American texts are the persistent attempts to construct a sense of natural family cohesion in the new world, especially with the help of naturalizing codes and concepts such as 'love' and 'generations.' The conflicts between descent and consent in American literature thus can tell us much about the creation of an American culture out of diverse pre-American pasts" (6).

[27] See James D. Richardson, comp., *A Compilation of the Messages and Papers of the Presidents*, 20 vols., (New York, 1897), vol. 8, 3601. The full text is 3601–11. The text of President Andrew Johnson's veto of the Civil Rights Bill of 1866 is reprinted, in part, in Michael Les Benedict, *The Fruits of Victory: Alternatives in Restoring the Union, 1865–1877* (Lanham, MD: U P of America, 1986) 108–110.

[28] See Andrew Johnson's Civil Rights Bill veto in Benedict, 110.

[29] On 13 July 1866, the House passed the Senate revisions of the preliminary drafts of the House version of the Fourteenth Amendment. The present constitutional text, as it was finally ratified by the United States and appended to the document on 28 July 1868, reads as follows:

Section 1. All persons born or naturalized in the United States, and subject to the jurisdiction thereof, are citizens of the United States and of the State wherein they reside. No State shall make or enforce any law which shall abridge the privileges or immunities of citizens of the United States; nor shall any State deprive any person of life, liberty, or property, without due process of law; nor deny to any person within its jurisdiction the equal protection of the laws.

Section 2. Representatives shall be apportioned among the several States according to their respective numbers, counting the whole number of persons in each State, excluding Indians not taxed. But when the right to vote at any election for the choice of electors for President and Vice President of the United States, Representatives in Congress, the Executive and Judicial officers of a State, or the members of the Legislature thereof, is denied to any of the male inhabitants of such State, being twenty-one years of age, and citizens of the United States, or in any way abridged except for participation in rebellion, or other crime, the basis of representation therein shall be reduced in the proportion which the number of such male citizens shall bear to the whole number of male citizens twenty-one years of age in such State.

Section 3. No person shall be a Senator or Representative in Congress, or elector of President or Vice President, or hold any office, civil or military, under the United States, or under any State, who, having previously taken an oath, as a member of Congress, or as an officer of the United States, or as a member of any State legislature, or as an executive or judicial officer of any State, to support the Constitution of the United States shall have engaged in insurrection or rebellion against the same or given aid or comfort to the enemies thereof. But Congress may by a vote of two thirds of each House, remove such disability.

Section 4. The validity of the public debt of the United States authorized by law, including debts incurred for payment of pensions and bounties for services in suppressing insurrection or rebellion, shall not be questioned. But neither the United States nor any State shall assume or pay any debt or obligation incurred in aid of insurrection or rebellion against the United States, or any claim for the loss or emancipation of any slave; but all such debts, obligations and claims shall be held illegal and void.

Section 5. The Congress shall have the power to enforce by appropriate legislation, the provisions of this article.

The following are among the notable studies of the legal impact of the Fourteenth Amendment on the understanding of national citizenship as an identification founded on equal protection of the laws for blacks and whites: Michael Kent Curtis, *No State Shall Abridge: The Fourteenth Amendment and the Bill of Rights* (Durham, NC: Duke U P, 1986), 18–91; Harold M. Hyman and William M. Wiecek, *Equal Justice Under Law: Constitutional Development, 1835–1875* (New York: Harper and Row, 1982) 386–438; and Jacobus tenBroek, 183–224.

[30] Diffley, 64.

[31] See *Congressional Globe*, 40th Congress (1867–68), 2nd Session, 2395, and *Congressional Globe*, 40th Congress (1867–68), 2nd Session, 2633).

[32] *Congressional Globe*, 39th Congress (1865–66), 1st Session, 1054.

[33] Ibid., 1057.

[34] Ibid., 1088.

[35] Ibid.

[36] Among the oppositional voices to the "military despotism" of federal hegemony over against a resistant Southern polity were Samuel J. Randall,(*Congressional Globe*, 39th Congress [1865–66], 1st Session, 2530); Andrew J. Rogers (2538); George S. Shanklin (2500); and Aaron Harding (3147).

[37] *Congressional Globe*, 39th Congress (1865–66), 1st Session, 2462.

[38] Ibid.

[39] Ibid., 2510.

[40] Ibid., 2765.

[41] Ibid.

[42] Ibid., 2nd Session, 1104.

[43] Ibid., 1st Session, 2766. Cited in Diffley, 68.

2

"Reconstruction is still in abeyance"

Walt Whitman's *Democratic Vistas* and the Federalizing of National Identity

O N 17 FEBRUARY 1868, Walt Whitman wrote to abolitionist Moncure Conway from Washington with a cautionary enthusiasm for the impending election of Ulysses S. Grant: "The Republicans have exploited the negro too intensely, & there comes a reaction. But that is going to be provided for. According to present appearances the good, worthy, non-demonstrative, average-representing Grant will be chosen President next fall" (*Corr* II, 15). The previous fall, Republicans had begun to discern that their adherence to a demand for black suffrage would cost their party dearly in the North as well as the South.[1] After all, prejudice against blacks was a national cultural fact, whereas slavery had been largely a sectional issue. Since the end of the Civil War, Congress had been reluctant to tamper with the suffrage issue, historically a custom for state regulation. In that respect, both civil and political rights for ex-slaves since 1865 had been grudgingly affirmed, but despite the grumbling, more and more constitutional rights were affirmed through 1870. Nonetheless, abolitionists continued to lobby an increasingly reluctant Republican Congress for the franchise for blacks. As the Democratic *New York World* declared on 14 October 1867, "Negro suffrage is the hinge of the whole Republican policy; it is what they most value in the Reconstruction laws; it is the vital breath of the party." Grant's election victory in the presidential bid for 1868 had been achieved without the endorsement of national black suffrage, which was muffled at the Republican nominating convention; black suffrage was demanded only of the ex-states of the Confederacy, leaving the Northern states free choice in this controversial matter. But Grant won only 52 percent of the popular vote, and he would not have won at all without the black votes tallied in the South.[2] Clearly, the Republicans wanted to enfranchise blacks in the North in order to consolidate their shaky majority in the halls of Congress.

At the same time, Whitman was also composing notes on the franchise question. These would burgeon into the long prose essay *Democratic Vistas* (1871), wherein he attempted, under the headings "Democracy," "Personalism," and "Orbic Literature," to prescribe an antidote to the racial, sectional, governmental, and gender tensions in Reconstruction

America. In his *Vistas*, Whitman noted that as he composed a particular passage in November 1868, "the din of disputations rages around me. Acrid the temper of the parties, vital the pending questions. Congress convenes; the President sends his message; reconstruction is still in abeyance; the nomination and contest for the twenty-first Presidentiad draws close, with loudest threat and bustle" (*PW* II, 384). Slightly less than a year earlier, amid the incoherent "disputations" over the extension of civil rights to blacks, seemingly always in jeopardy to some extent, *Galaxy* carried Whitman's essay "Democracy" in December 1867; a half-year later, in May 1868, it published "Personalism." Subsequently the journal refused to carry the third installment, "Orbic Literature." Whitman's half-jeremiad, half-prognosis on American cultural ills was written to counteract Thomas Carlyle's critique of democracy in "Shooting Niagara: And After?," which was published by the *New York Tribune* on 16 August 1867, two months before the November presidential elections. In "Shooting Niagara," Carlyle had primarily objected to Benjamin Disraeli's Reform Bill of 1867, which would enfranchise the working classes in Britain, though he also took issue with America's abolitionist legislation.[3] Within weeks, Whitman had written the first installment, called "Democracy," thereby leaping into the "Niagara" of public debate on the franchise himself "in some sort of counterblast or rejoinder to Carlyle's late piece . . . " (Corr. I, 342). When Whitman's three essays had been collected into an eighty-four-page pamphlet, published in 1871, as *Democratic Vistas*,[4] Whitman's treatise followed in the wake of the March 1870 ratification of the Fifteenth Amendment, which provided a constitutional guarantee for the enfranchisement of black males and congressional authority to enact legislation to enforce this landmark mandate.

The bicameral debaters on the Fifteenth Amendment in January and February 1869 constructed their tangled rhetorical energies on four central political battlefields: the right of black male suffrage, the right of women's suffrage, the impartial right to hold office, and the consolidation of federal hegemony over against state sovereignty in franchise regulation. In his *Vistas*, Whitman's prose diction reached an almost tortuous level of circumlocution as he tried to articulate a culture that must have appeared virtually incapable of articulation, though his rhetorical images did shed clear light on these four cultural issues and place *Democratic Vistas* squarely in the public debate over the franchise. Whitman's convoluted prose bore more than a passing resemblance to the rhetorical gears grinding in the machinery of the federal government as legislators sought to constitute black Americans more firmly in the democratic "privileges and immunities" promised them in the ratified Fourteenth Amendment. The language, in which the legislature sought to couch such an unprecedented federal mandate, proved to be just as convoluted in the Congressional debates as it had been in Whitman's apology for democratizing cultures here and abroad.

Because of his own unsettled frame of mind, Whitman too had to seek a language in which to voice the "disputations" that threatened to rend the fragile Union coalition along the racial divide. So soon on the heels of the war, the poet agonized over "the lack of a common skeleton, knitting all close" (*PW* II, 368). Because such a reconstructive task lay in his own representative syntax, Whitman had to compose a syntactical skeleton that would perform the cultural work of binding up the competing factions, all veterans of both sectional and racial disputes. This federalizing transaction had to be caught in language so that the representative poet and the Congressional representatives were both articulating rhetorical strategies for reconstructing a composite identity out of which to build a greater sense of social solidarity. Whitman's strategy constituted a push for "Radical Democracy," perhaps best defined as the voluntary embrace of strangers beyond the boundaries of family and neighborhood. Michael Mosher has configured Whitman's democratic cultural theory as the cultivation of "a capacity to extend oneself sympathetically to include the experiences of relative strangers," after admitting that "one must suffer alienation from one's particular attachments."[5] Radical Reconstruction fought its legislative skirmishes along the same trenches, agitating for the inclusion of blacks in the forum of civil liberties despite their status as strangers and despite the resistance of the white majority which did not "suffer alienation" from its settled white dominance without a fight. Thus both the representative Whitman, in his *Vistas*, and the representative legislators, in the Fifteenth Amendment debates, were knitting a common skeleton of solidarity between races, though such syntactic skeletons needed sympathetic readers to give them flesh.

Democratic Vistas has not been an entirely inert document in Whitman studies, but until recently Whitman's 1871 treatise has remained relatively inert in critical commentaries. In his now classic essay "The Theory of America," Richard Chase argued that *Vistas* was too optimistic in its ameliorative reading of an unstoppable democracy "as having under its surface sense of wildness, indeterminacy, and doubt a too simple, even a complacent, faith in the rational unities of democratic society, which in practice meant a too simple faith in the status quo." Chase concluded his critique by effectively turning Whitman's *Vistas* into a transhistorical pipe dream: "History, in so far as it is present at all, is regarded as maternal and beneficent. It therefore has no hazards and can be counted on to foster democracy."[6] This chapter will contest such a transhistorical reading to inspect Whitman's prose as symptomatic of the larger cultural debates over extension of the franchise and the significance of both discourses in the nationalization of civil rights. When juxtaposed with the resonant speeches in the

House and Senate prior to the passage of the Fifteenth Amendment, Whitman's *Vistas* becomes the representational site of enormous emancipatory significance and resists the exclusion of blacks as full-fledged citizens. Such a black expulsion from the fulfillment of constitutional promises did soon follow the short-lived euphoria over the amendment's passage, giving way to the systematic subjugation of blacks on a scale that rivaled antebellum cultural life only in calibration. But *Democratic Vistas* textualized Whitman's conviction that the "great word Solidarity has arisen. Of all dangers to a nation, as things exist in our day, there can be no greater than having certain portions of the people set off from the rest by a line drawn — they not privileged as others, but degraded, humiliated, made of no account" (*PW* II, 382).

When Congress finally passed the Fifteenth Amendment in February 1869, guaranteeing the franchise to black males, the legislative momentum of nationalizing civil rights was already riddled with compromises.[7] Bowing to moderates, the amendment's more radical congressional backers avoided the interdiction of property and literacy tests for voting as well as a supplement promoting the impartial right to hold public office. Slightly less than a year later, on 30 March 1870, the Fifteenth Amendment was ratified, former Confederates were safely seated in the Capitol, and Radical Reconstruction passed from its political dominance as the legislative voice of ex-slaves, who were now left to the mercy of the residual racism that had never evaporated from the white cultural reservoir of antagonism in both the North and the South. Nevertheless, the political fervor over the ratification manifested itself in interracial parades along Washington's avenues, with banners proclaiming "The Nation's second birth" and "the fifteenth amendment, Uncle Sam's bleaching powder."[8] President Grant told Congress that the Fifteenth Amendment "completes the greatest civil change and constitutes the most important event that has occurred since the nation came into life."[9] Radical Republican leader Charles Sumner declared, along with black leaders, that the Declaration of Independence had at last been legislated to apply to all Americans.[10]

Apparently both Sumner and the black leaders were disregarding the widespread vigilante violence by the newly founded Ku Klux Klan. Klan guerrilla terrorism was already being broadcast across the country on front pages and would motivate the legislative action known as the Ku Klux Klan Act of 1871, which would help to punish thousands of Klan perpetrators and lead to a sharp decline in Klan membership in the 1870s. President Grant and Charles Sumner, obviously suffering from political amnesia, were not alone in laundering the racist stains marring the American cultural cloth with "Uncle Sam's bleaching powder" and ignoring the fact that Southern legislatures were quick to seize upon the lack of a prohibition against poll tests and to use such tests to distance blacks from the right to vote. The notorious Black Codes, which in effect institutionalized the disenfranchisement of blacks all over again, would force the hand of Congress to pass the Enforcement Acts of 1870–71, designed to federalize surveillance over fair elections.

In the wake of the euphoria over constitutional reform, however, antislavery societies across America disbanded and disregarded the caveat of the editorial voice of the *New York Tribune* on 31 March 1870, which ominously stated, "Neither Constitutions nor good-will can permanently secure Freedom to those who neglect to make themselves worthy of it." Suffrage was hardly enough to stem the tide of the indelible racism in the institutional structures of American society, but Americans seemed anxious in 1870 to put the fractious cultural work of reconstruction behind them and turn toward the motto of Grant, "Let us have peace," as though it were a bewitching barbiturate. Indeed, when Grant was elected, the 4 November 1868 issue of the *New York Tribune* eulogized the postwar cultural revolution as a moribund fact: "The last of the great issues — the social and political Reconstruction of the South, [is] . . . determined, and we may now look forward to a long era of peace and prosperity." Whitman's *Democratic Vistas* went a long way to interdict such a facile misrepresentation of the state of the Union, for the open road of the reconstructed future needed his diagnostic essay to register a counter-statement in the midst of a de facto racial war.

In Carlyle's "Shooting Niagara: And After?," the immediate catalyst for Whitman's prose response, Carlyle's primary target was the extension of the franchise to the working classes in Britain. However, he paused early in his essay to aim his rhetorical rifle squarely at the United States for the civil rights legislation enacted after the Civil War on behalf of black Americans. This "descent" of the American nation into what he called "Swarmery" or the rule of the polity through the majority rather than an elite class, led him to accuse America of having perpetrated "by far the notablest case of *Swarmery*, in these times," following "the late American War, with the Settlement of the Nigger Question for result."[11] Carlyle's odious views on the "Nigger Question" motivated him to declare the absurdity of the fruits of the Civil War in a "dismal prediction" that sounded menacingly like some sort of genocide for blacks at the hands of the white majority: "A continent of the earth has been submerged, for certain years, by deluges as from the Pit of Hell; half a million . . . of excellent White Men, full of gifts and faculty, have torn and slashed one another into horrid death, in a temporary humour, which will leave centuries of remembrance fierce enough."[12] The result of such mass slaughter, for Carlyle, amounted to only "three million absurd Blacks, men and brothers (of a sort), [who] are completely 'emancipated'; launched into the career of improvement,— likely to be 'improved off the face of the earth' in a generation or two."[13]

His image of a species of "improvement" that would lead to the extinction of blacks, at the prodding of an unnamed American acquaintance, sounded ominously Darwinian, but it was consonant with the racist terrorism that would sweep through the South, impelled by a racial hatred that produced atrocities far more horrific than any offensive, sarcastic rejoinder from Thomas Carlyle.

Whitman's "counterblast" to Carlyle, in the original *Galaxy* serial, contained one explicit denunciation of his British opponent's overt racism,[14] though Whitman conceded, in a footnote to the 1871 *Democratic Vistas*, that he found himself, with reservations, sharing the same vitriolic judgments toward democratization: "I was at first roused to much anger and abuse by this essay from Mr. Carlyle, so insulting to the theory of America — but happening to think afterwards how I had more than once been in like mood, during which his essay was evidently cast, and seen persons and things in the same light" (*PW* II, 375–76). Since the "Swarmery" passage denigrating emancipation constituted the only citation of the United States in the whole Carlylean jeremiad, it seems safe to conclude that Whitman had occasionally entertained the same racist reservations toward emancipation, despite legislative reform, that most Americans had harbored.[15]

On rereading the "Niagara" essay, however, Whitman made a significant qualification to the consonance of his antiemancipationist views with those of Carlyle. While admiring the "earnest" soulfulness of his uniting, Whitman recontextualized Carlyle's political presuppositions outside of democracy altogether, because of the essay's "highest feudal point of view" (*PW* II, 376). Nothing could have been farther from Whitman's approval than feudalism, the antithesis of his desired demolition of hierarchical social relations, so that *Democratic Vistas* had arrived as an apologia for the democratizing social forces at work in England as well as in America. Echoing the opening image of his 1885 preface, Whitman began his *Vistas* by proclaiming that America absorbed the past, "including feudalism," but only as a prelude to the actualization of democratic promise in the future: "For our New World I consider far less important for what it has done, or what it is, than for results to come" (*PW* II, 362). The pull of the future, superseding the lingering claims of the Old World on the New, would only serve to validate the democratizing process that had so unsettled Carlyle in 1867: "Sole among nationalities, these States have assumed the task to put in forms of lasting practicality . . . the democratic republican principle, and the theory of development and perfection by voluntary standards, and self-reliance" (*PW* II, 362). Through such centripetal cultural forces as voluntary inclusion of "the experiences of relative strangers," America's destiny seemed assured from the opening paragraphs of Whitman's essay, insofar as no other nation had even ventured the risk of governing with the widest consent of the governed: "Who else, indeed, except the United States, in history, so far, have accepted in unwitting faith, and, as we now see, stand, act upon, and go security for, these things?" (*PW* II, 362).

Despite the legislative extension of civil rights to blacks in 1868, for the next two years the American public was caught up in a divisive public debate over the extension of the suffrage to black males. Whitman's sensitivity to the political pulse of the nation was evident in his declaration of his purpose in penning *Democratic Vistas*: "I will not gloss over the appaling [sic] dangers of universal suffrage in the United States. In fact, it is to admit and face these dangers I am writing" (*PW* II, 363). Contrary to Richard Chase's assertion that Whitman was domesticating "hazards" to democracy, the "dangers" posed by the bitterness of racial strife in every section of the Union alarmed Whitman, who countered that "America and Democracy are controvertible terms," an assertion that subverted those who were determined to subjugate blacks in order to preserve their inherited privilege of white dominance. In his rhetorical strategy in the *Vistas*, Whitman sought to bridge such racial divisions while admitting that his audience consisted of the citizens "whose thought rages the battle, advancing, retreating, between democracy's convictions, aspirations, and the people's crudeness, vice, caprices" (*PW* II, 363). Clearly, then, Whitman pitched the fate of the democratic urge, already fomenting in the halls of Congress, on the divide between the radical minority favoring black suffrage and the antiextension majority of the populace grudgingly holding out against such a revisionary action.

Though prospects were initially promising, the Fifteenth Amendment was by no means assured ratification even during the successive votes in the states, for the intervening partisan wrangles in the winter of 1869–70 weakened the Republican coalition through intraparty factions, and the Democrats spared no effort to defeat ratification.[16] However, Republicans managed to remain organized enough to achieve ratification against all odds, mainly through federal strong-arming of unwilling states with the threats that they would not be reconstituted in the Union if they failed to ratify. The constitutional certification of the franchise, despite the foot-dragging, offered a dilation of the democratic "opening of the doors" that Whitman advocated in his *Vistas*, but it did not diminish his concern with the "dangers" diffused throughout the land in social resistance to the issue. Sobered by the continued resistance to wider majority rule, Whitman realized that the "United States are destined either to surmount the gorgeous history of feudalism, or else prove the most tremendous failure of time" (*PW* II, 363).

The ratification of the Fifteenth Amendment went a long way toward overthrowing outmoded "feudal" governmental structures of Whitman's image; it was a manifestation of "the priceless value of our political institutions, general suffrage, . . . (and . . . the latest, widest opening of the doors)." (*PW* II, 364). Nonetheless, Whitman the diagnostician bore testimony to the fact that the majority of Americans in 1870 still favored "feudalism, caste, the ecclesiastic traditions, [which,] though retreating from political institutions, still hold essentially, by their spirit, even in this country, entire possession of the more important fields, indeed the very subsoil, of education, and of social standards and literature" (*PW* II, 364–5). Positioned as a partisan who spoke against the "majority," Whitman called out for radical democratic texts that would articulate the overturning of the hierarchical influences of the European past, ostentatiously represented by the elitist Carlyle as well as by the feudal subjugation of blacks in the South. These reconstructive texts had to be written by "native authors, literatuses, far different, far higher in grade than any yet known, sacerdotal, modern, fit to cope with our occasions, lands, permeating the whole mass of American mentality," precisely to create an American *mass culture* (*PW* II, 365). In "mass culture," Whitman was seeking his analogue to the embrace of "relative strangers," in Michael Mosher's terms, represented in prose and poems that would provoke readers to glimpse their "alienation" from "particular attachments." Whitman ranked the publication of such "literatuses" above even the acts of Congress in that the former would bequeath to the mass culture "a religious and moral character beneath the political and productive and intellectual bases of the States" (*PW* II, 365). In their management of cultural diversity in America, these "divine literatuses" would write the "archetypal poems," representative of all races and sections of the Union, that would perform the cultural work of "a great original literature, (in some respects the sole reliance,) of American democracy" (*PW* II, 366). On so doing, the representative poet assumed a hegemonic position in the legislation of an all-inclusive democracy, which would freely embrace the "relative strangers" in its midst.

But such a cosmopolitan textual production, in both *Democratic Vistas* and the enactment of constitutional legislation to safeguard the inviolability of civil rights, had not found its popular reception untroubled in 1871. With striking candor, Whitman admitted that "the fear of conflicting and irreconcilable interiors, and the lack of a common skeleton, knitting all close, continually haunts me" (*PW* II, 368). However, he believed the historical momentum already under way in his texts and in Congress would solidify the future "fusion of the States," resulting in "the true nationality of the States, the genuine union," through "the fervid and tremendous IDEA, melting everything else with resistless heat, and solving all lesser and definite distinctions in vast, indefinite, spiritual, emotional power" (*PW* II, 368). This virtual "fusion" of a national identity would, as mentioned earlier, be founded on the "religious" and "moral" ground of human assent, undergirding all the material prosperity that engulfed public consciousness after the war. Indeed, such "unprecedented materialistic advancement" had borne only "canker'd, crude, superstitious, and rotten" offspring. Underscoring his moral argument, Whitman capped this lengthy antimaterialistic harangue with words that amounted to a précis of his diagnosis of Reconstruction America: "In any vigor, the element of the moral conscience, the most important, the verteber [*sic*] to State or man, seems to me entirely lacking, or seriously enfeebled or ungrown" (*PW* II, 369).

As noted in chapter 2, *Webster's* 1847 denotation of "religion" signified to Whitman its etymological resonance of "to gather or collect again" and "to bind anew, or back, to bind fast." Synonymously, the dictionary illuminated the mid-nineteenth century understanding of "moral" as follows: "morality; the doctrine or practice of the duties of life (not much used)," and furthermore, "The doctrine inculcated by a fiction; the accommodation of a fable to form the moral. 'The moral is the first business of the poet.' Dryden." These definitions of "moral" constituted the syntactic "skeleton" of Whitman's understanding of the diagnosis he proposed for reinvigorating American democracy. Whitman's "first business," in other words, was to constitute texts that sang songs of social solidarity: "Few are aware how the great literature penetrates all, gives hue to all, shapes aggregates and individuals, and after subtle ways, with irresistible power, constructs, sustains, demolishes at will" (*PW* II, 366).

One of the major rhetorical wrangles of the third session of the Fortieth Congress, in the first two months of 1869, was over the suitability of the character of black males as voters. When framing the rationale for the amendment, Representative George S. Boutwell of Massachusetts, on the floor of the House on 23 January 1869, placed the weight of his argument on the high moral ground of human rights: "Now, in this struggle for the establishment of manhood suffrage in the country are we to decline the services of one hundred and fifty thousand men who are ready to do battle for us at the ballot-box in favor of human rights: not of their own rights merely, but of the rights of all men on this continent?"[17] Boutwell, too, seemed to rely on the signification of "morality," again as defined by the 1847 *Webster's* as "the doctrine or system of moral duties, or the duties of men in their social character," applied specifically, as the definition continued, "to actions which accord with justice and human laws, without reference to the motives from which they proceed."

Though morality implied social responsibilities, as already mentioned, the Republicans were far from altruistic in that their majority of Congressional seats was at stake. Thus, in Radical Republican agitation, there coexisted political interest as well as genuine humanitarian concern in this last push for a Civil War amendment to the Constitution. Boutwell concluded his black suffrage apologia in language loaded with moralistic overtones: "If we fail to act, and if, sir, there be a day of retribution for our omission to do our duty, as there has been a day of retribution for those men who omitted to do their duty upon another great question involving public crime [slavery], there can be no defense for us."[18] Whitman agreed with this denigration of the slaveholding class, at the root of the "Late War," as could be discerned in the "General Notes" section at the back of the *Democratic Vistas* text: "Though it was not certain, hardly probable, that the effort by founding a Slave-Holding power, by breaking up the Union, should be successful, it was urged on by indomitable passion, pride and will" (*PW* II, 756). Whitman continued, "The signal downfall of this effort, the abolition of Slavery, and the extirpation of the Slaveholding Class (cut out and thrown away like a tumor by a surgical operation,) makes incomparably the longest advance for Radical Democracy, utterly removing its only really dangerous impediment, and insuring its progress in the United States" (*PW* II, 756). With the same democratic resonance, Boutwell denounced the racism in the North, because while the majority of blacks in the South had already voted in the 1868 elections (Southerners having allowed black voting as mandated by the Fourteenth Amendment), blacks in the North were still disbarred from voting. As a result, Boutwell argued, the "measures before us are part of the great work of harmonizing the country, of pacifying all classes, of reconciling all interests."[19] Thus both Whitman and Boutwell were linking the fate of "Radical Democracy" to granting civil rights to freedmen, a legislative discourse that dismantled hierarchical race relations and promoted inclusive social solidarity.

Such an advancement toward egalitarianism in voting rights would be long deferred, however, for the pull of "moral" social relations would be handicapped by the property and educational requirements of prospective voters under strictly state surveillance. Arguably the greatest legislative failure of the Reconstruction era was the hotly contested defeat of a specific ban on voting qualifications in favor of constitutional reform merely to prohibit discrimination on the basis of race. Such voting qualifications, argued Senator George F. Edmunds of Vermont on 8 February 1869, "leave with the States, after all, the regulation of suffrage, the conferring or withholding it entirely," thereby elevating "a State government to an aristocracy, as it has been in South Carolina and many of the other States under old influences; and where is the benefit to the African, then?"[20] On 5 February 1869, two weeks after Boutwell's statement of purpose, Senator George Vickers of Maryland took the floor of the Senate to reprimand his radical colleagues fighting for the black man, who, he contended, lacked the moral character needed for the franchise: "The negro as a class, as a race, is unfortunately ignorant and superstitious; with some exceptions, he cannot read nor understand your Constitution, is unacquainted with your laws, institutions, history, and policy."[21]

In fact, Vickers's speech was only the most prominent example of the kind of Negrophobia that would permeate the turbulent road to ratification in the border states and elsewhere. But immediately after Vickers asked, "If you had a house to build would you procure ignorant and unskilled hands to erect it?," Senator Waitman T. Willey of West Virginia countered such derisive language by offering a succinct summary of the two weeks of debate. Willey's primary plank for supporting the extension of the franchise was the "true maxim of the fathers of the Republic, that all just government must rest on the consent of the governed. If, therefore, the colored people of this country are to be recognized as citizens and held subject to our laws, then they ought to have a right to . . . a participation in the administration of the Government."[22]

Interestingly enough, Whitman, who was attending these debates intermittently, enlisted the same inclusive image of "popular consent" in his *Vistas* when he commented that "few probably are the minds, even in these republican States, that fully comprehend the aptness of that phrase, 'THE GOVERNMENT OF THE PEOPLE, BY THE PEOPLE, FOR THE PEOPLE,' which we inherit from the lips of Abraham Lincoln; a formula . . . whose scope includes both the totality and all the minutiae of the lesson" (*PW* II, 376). Indeed, the antiemancipationist sentiments of Senator Vickers failed to address the Lincolnian "lesson" that democracy rested on the consent of the governed, mainly to prevent the possibility of the Carlylean "feudal" model of government, exemplified in the Confederate slavocracy, to win out over the Union. Senator Samuel C. P. Pomeroy of Kansas echoed this demand for democratic rule when he rose to ask, "Who gave any class the right to monopolize the elective franchise? If a majority, however large, can strike down one right not forfeited then they can another, and hence, as I have said, all."[23] Likewise, while admitting the "imperfections" of majority rule, Whitman went on to allege that the potential for any viable democracy must *begin* with the settlement of democratic suffrage: "But to become an enfranchised man, and now, impediments removed, to stand and start without humiliation, and equal with the rest; to commence . . . the grand experiment of development, whose end . . . may be the forming of a full-grown man or woman — that is something" (*PW* II, 380).

Of course, while Whitman grasped the "totality" of the franchise lesson, he missed the "minutiae" of the defeat of a prohibition to franchise prerequisites as well as the defeat of the coda that would have legislated the impartial right to hold office. Such measures would have to be recovered by twentieth-century jurists, who in upholding the Civil Rights Act of 1964 and the Voting Rights Act of 1965, certified the Second Reconstruction on the legislative ground trod by such figures as Representative Boutwell and Senator Willey. Whitman ranked with these Radical Republican reformers in appending a sweeping majoritarian brief in the notes to his *Vistas*, which exceeded even the most optimistic Republican hopes for a democratized electorate: "As to general suffrage, after all, since we have gone so far, the more general it is, the better. I favor the widest opening of the doors. Let the ventilation and area be wide enough, and all is safe."[24] Though this validation of black suffrage was relegated to the endnotes of his *Vistas*, such an emendation, like the Fifteenth Amendment, represents a necessary and clarifying amendment to his *Vistas*. Hence, as a syntactic device, Whitman's "General Notes" suggested that their legislative rhetoric was enlisted in the same "ventilation" of "Radical Democracy" as the *Vistas* themselves. In a sense, Whitman's *Vistas* were themselves an attempt to renovate the Constitution for the Union.

Agitating the minds of many on Capitol Hill, the issue of women's suffrage had long been the agenda of a minority seeking a larger political forum. While the Fifteenth Amendment would not enfranchise women, there was a handful of senators who courageously promoted this "widest opening of the doors" to further the realization of democratic rule. On 28 January 1869, Senator Joseph S. Fowler of Tennessee expressed his intention to move an amendment to the proposal at hand to enfranchise women, for if ethnic boundaries to the franchise were to be lifted, then it was no longer fair to "exclude from a voice my mother or my sister or my wife, an American woman, from the exercise of this inestimable privilege."[25] The next day, Senator Samuel C. Pomeroy of Kansas echoed Fowler but nuanced his argument by removing the gender question from the forum of family relations and instead accorded women the right to vote because they were *citizens* of the Republic, coequal partners with men in their subjection to taxation and representation.

Pomeroy went further, however, in articulating what amounted to a revolutionary proposal for "Radical Democracy," with women as coarchitects with men in the civil rights forum: "Let it come, then, by one comprehensive amendment striking out all inequalities among citizens, and the dream of the fathers of a free and pure Republic shall be realized, and there shall be peace throughout the land and good will."[26] Nonetheless, Congress ultimately restricted the amendment to race on the rhetorical ground of Judeo-Christian male dominance in the household and allowed the misogynistic rhetoric of such figures as Senator George F. Edmunds of Vermont to win out for another fifty years against the representation of women in the Constitution. Edmunds sarcastically declared that the franchise could not extend to women because, "the great difficulty I have on that question — but I am not going into a dissertation on it — is that I am very much afraid when it is extended to them all the bad women will vote and the good women will stay at home."[27]

Walt Whitman did not make such demagogic pronouncements on women in *Democratic Vistas*, but he did interlace the essay with several illuminating statements that pointed to the cultural liberation of women from the domination of males, including the validation of women's stature in the political arena of American life. Whitman wrote that the only means toward a "reconstructed sociology depended, primarily, on a new birth, elevation, expansion, invigoration of woman," for "great, great, indeed, far greater than they know, is the sphere of women" (*PW* II, 372). To achieve such a reconstructed female subject, Whitman's prescription included the ridding of the female preoccupation with cosmetic appearances, which were, he argued, a cultural trap that prevented women, through their subjection as objects, from achieving their own equality. One of the purposes of his reconstructed "literatus" was to write texts that redeemed women from "these incredible holds and webs of silliness, millinery, and every kind of dyspeptic depletion — and thus insuring to the States a strong and sweet Female Race, a race of perfect Mothers" (*PW* II, 372).

"Perfect Mothers" may not have sounded like lever-pulling voters, but Whitman did not simply restrict women to the role of motherhood; though he always revered maternity, the legislative poet created a separate space for the "Female Race." As Betsy Erkkila has argued, Whitman was intervening in the cultural conspiracy to keep women locked exclusively into domestic roles when "he included among his *Vistas* models of women in the traditional roles of wife and mother and also in their new roles as worker and business woman outside the home."[28] Unlike Senator Pomeroy, Whitman wrote that women could be equals with men in "all departments" or had the potential to achieve such gender parity "soon as they realize it, and can bring themselves to give up toys and fictions, and launch forth as men do, amid real, independent, stormy life" (*PW* II, 389). This ventilation of the political self-determination of American women was not to be legislated in his own day, but Whitman proleptically foresaw the triumph of the suffragettes in the ratification of the Nineteenth Amendment in 1920: "The day is coming when the deep questions of woman's entrance amid the arenas of practical life, politics, the suffrage, &c., will not only be argued all around us, but may be put to decision, and real experiment" (*PW* II, 401).

Aside from the vexing suffrage issue, early drafts of the Fifteenth Amendment included statements designed to protect not only the right to vote but also the guarantee to hold office regardless of race. On 17 February 1869, Senator Frederick T. Frelinguysen from New Jersey sought to defeat the codification of the right to hold office because "if you give seven hundred and fifty thousand [black] men the right to the ballot they will look out for their own rights as to office."[29] Senator George F. Edmunds of Vermont retorted that such a casuistic argument would only perpetuate racial antagonism, because blacks inhabited every section of the United States, "and if you do not give them the right to hold office as well as to vote you immediately create a white aristocracy in every one of those States with the negroes divided among them."[30] While blacks had the right to vote in the South through the newly revised state constitutions, they were deprived of officeholding simply on account of their skin color. Senator Adonijah S. Welch of Florida argued that this arbitrary decision was absurd and was harmful to "complete and impartial justice": "I believe that men should vote and hold office because they have the capacity to vote and hold office . . . not because of their forefathers, and not because their forefathers have or have not made inventions."[31] The final draft of the amendment excluded the right to governmental office. This was the result of a somewhat desperate compromise by moderates to keep the amendment from being derailed by partisan extremists of both parties and thus never reaching the states to be ratified at all. The third session of the Fortieth Congress was strictly a lame-duck session, and Radical Republicans foresaw that this was perhaps their only chance to complete their legislative legacy on behalf of ex-slaves.

The Whitmanian diatribe against the quality of governmental officers in *Democratic Vistas* was rivaled only by his earlier unpublished essay *The Eighteenth Presidency* (1850?–55?), a jeremiad against the proslavery Fugitive Slave Law. Whitman's *Vistas* revealed a deep suspicion of the factious infighting of Congress as a conduit for transmission of the Lincolnian "lesson" of majoritarian rule in its widest expression. While not doubting that American democracy "supplies a training-school for making first-class men," Whitman judged that the movement toward democracy had failed as often as it had been successful. Echoing the Republican agitators in Congress, opposing the Democratic resistance to change, Whitman declared, "not for nothing does evil play its part among us. Judging from the main portions of the history of the world, so far, justice is always in jeopardy, . . . and of slavery, misery, meanness, the craft of tyrants and the credulity of the populace, in some of their protean forms, no voice can at any time say, They are not"(*PW* II, 385–86). Articulating a sweeping condemnation of the "scoundrelism" of current officeholders, Whitman's prose rivaled Carlyle's in vitriol: "The official services of America, national, state, and municipal, in all their branches and departments, except the judiciary, are saturated in corruption, bribery, falsehood, maladministration; and the judiciary is tainted" (*PW* II, 370). Given the cultural fractures of Reconstruction, Whitman had no choice but to ask, "what prospect have we? We sail a dangerous sea of seething currents, cross and under-currents, vortices — all so dark, untried — and whither shall we turn?" (*PW* II, 422).

The contingencies of the contested political issues of his day gave Whitman pause both to look back to the Civil War as a bracing lesson in the fragility of "our Nationality," which had "just by a hair escaped destruction," and to look forward to the open road of the future, which would be the battlefield for a continual resolution to achieve "greatness" through "the long postponement, the fossil-like lethargy, the ceaseless need of revolutions, prophets, thunderstorms, deaths, births, new projections and invigorations of ideas and men"(*PW* II, 422–23). Conscious of the entropy engendered through politics, Whitman wrote in the general notes to his *Vistas,* "We elect Presidents, Congressmen, &c., not so much to have them consider and decide for us, but as surest practical means of expressing the will of majorities on mooted questions, measures, &c."[32] The most "mooted question" in 1871 was the suitability of black males to vote, and the Congressional settlement of the Fifteenth Amendment did not still the undercurrents of racism and sectionalism that made interracial democracy seem like only a radicalized dream.

Beneath all the verbal sparring over the passage of the Fifteenth Amendment in the early days of 1869 lay the vexing question of the power relations between federalism and state sovereignty. Indeed, this main gear grinding in the machinery of government in Reconstruction Washington prevented any congressional consensus in the passage of every piece of civil rights legislation since Appomattox. Aside from the predictable argument of racial inferiority, the Democrats exploited federal hegemony as the enemy of democracy more heavily than any other issue in the debates. At every turn, the Democrats resisted federal superintendence of civil rights enforcement with particular vehemence under the pretext that states' rights were being trampled under the federal foot of suppression, when the suppression was aimed at their discriminatory practices.

An exemplary performance of such resistance came from Senator James Dixon of Connecticut, who rose on 29 January 1869 to state that although the extension of the suffrage question was "now agitating the public mind of this country to a very great extent," such agitation was merely symptomatic of the deeper malady brought on by four and a half years of the federal demolition of the self-regulation of the states in their own affairs. While qualifications for voters was a significant issue, "The question is not what shall be the qualifications of the voter, but who shall create, establish, and prescribe those qualifications; not who shall be the voter, but who shall make the voter."[33] Senator Dixon's thesis proceeded from the presupposition that each state was an "independent republic," and even if the states "should now consent that a central power should regulate" the suffrage issue, they would be violating nearly a century of constitutional precedent. Such an abdication would exceed the boundaries of the text of the U.S. Constitution, wherein "there was an entire neglect to interfere in the slightest degree with the question of suffrage in the several states."[34] Thus, voicing the alarm of an increasingly restive Democratic minority (including unreconstructed Southern congressmen), Senator Dixon placed the issue of federal hegemony above the abolition of slavery, the extension of civil liberties to blacks, and even suffrage as the most potentially damaging legacy that Reconstruction would hand on to the future republic. He concluded his remarks with the damaging peroration, which resonated far beyond the Senate chambers, that federalism had to be put down because it "strikes at the very root and foundation of the Government; it removes its corner stone, and changes the entire character of the State governments."[35]

On the other hand, the Republican supporters of the amendment argued with equal vehemence that the notion of state sovereignty had been discredited so thoroughly by secession that Dixon and his cohorts were beating a dead donkey. As noted earlier, the political stakes for Republicans were high, and the consolidation of the federal control over the franchise would have swelled the polls by nearly a million additional black male voters and thus increased the chances of a Republican hold over Congress for the near future. The most resonant defense of this federalist ideology was delivered on 29 January 1869 by Senator Oliver P. Morton of Indiana. Sparring with two ex-Confederate Senators, Morton parried with an ad hominem attack that accused them both of treason through their belief "in the right of secession," which "advocated the same theories, urged the same arguments, and cited the same history upon which the right of secession has been based for the last twenty years."[36] Responding to the senator from Delaware, Morton continued, "The Senator told us today frankly that we were not one people. He said in the Senate of the United States, after the culmination of a war that cost this nation six hundred thousand lives, that we were not a nation. He gave us to understand that we were as many separate nationalities as we have states."[37] Morton had shifted the rhetorical charge away from the suffrage issue, the enactment being debated, in order to resurrect the resentments of most Northerners against the South through a numerical count of the war dead.

Clearly, the revolutions of war's wheels were turning in Morton's performance to move the legislative vehicle away from a highly divisive issue, black male suffrage (contested in the North as well as the South), toward an issue on which most Northerners were in agreement, antagonism toward the ex-states that had provoked the slaughter of their husbands, brothers, and sons. Prolonging his war rhetoric, Morton countered the state-sovereignty partisans with the deduction that if the states had self-determination in voter qualifications, then "there was a right of secession; the South was right and we were wrong." Proleptically, Morton projected the unsteady future of enfranchised freedmen with no defense against voting tests when he summed up, "Sir the heresy of secession is not dead; it lives. It lives after this war, although it ought to have been settled by the war." Morton continued, "The whole fallacy lies in denying our nationality. I assert that we are one people and not thirty-seven different peoples; that we are one nation, and as such we have provided for ourselves a national Constitution, and that Constitution has provided the way by which it may be amended."[38]

The rhetorical denial of "nationality," which was afoot in the Capitol chambers, must have given even the staunchest supporters of the right to vote pause in their optimistic forecast of a "second birth" for the Republic. Of course, Radical Republican agitation on behalf of black civil rights was not over, but these same Republicans could not know that Radical Reconstruction had already reached its zenith, for the Klan was murdering and terrorizing blacks in every Southern state, military reconstruction was underfunded and understaffed, and Southern legislatures seized the absence of a check on their right to establish voter qualifications almost immediately after the passage of the Fifteenth Amendment. Indeed, the ideological battle lines had been drawn along the trench between federal authority and state sovereignty, and neither side seemed willing to retreat from its opposing political convictions.

Whitman was not insensate to this ideological struggle for hegemony in the political landscape, and rather than promote more jurisdictional breakdown in the machinery of government, he backed away from absolute adherence to one or the other of these positions. In the representative role of mediator between factions, the poet cast his reconciliation between federalists and states' rights advocates in the future tense. In his *Vistas*, Whitman carved out a middle ground in which federalism and state sovereignty would enter into a dialectical relation, certainly an untried alliance in the governmental structures of the United States. In such a dialectic, Washington and the states became the interlocking partners in the further advancement of "Radical Democracy." In his discussion of "personalism," Whitman argued in favor of individualism only insofar as it provided the matrix from which to build national consensus: "This idea of perfect individualism it is indeed that deepest tinges and gives character to the idea of the aggregate. For it is mainly or altogether to serve independent separatism that we favor a strong generalization, consolidation" (*PW* II, 374). Whitman continued his dialectical argument by stating that "it is to give the best vitality and freedom to the rights of the States, (every bit as important as the right of nationality, the union,) that we insist on the identity of the Union at all hazards" (*PW* II, 374). In a representational sense, Whitman was coercing Senators Dixon and Morton into a handshake in order to avoid further fracturing the already crippled nation that had emerged from the war's violence.

Always pitching such an ideological harmony between Washington and the states down the open road of the future, Whitman still worried about the oppositions among them: "For how can we remain, divided, contradicting ourselves this way?" (*PW* II, 409). The cultural dissonance over the extension of the franchise, as a necessary text in the nationalization of civil rights, substantiated Whitman's anxiety over the lack of adherence to "*democratic nationality*": "It is useless to deny it: Democracy grows rankly up the thickest, noxious, deadliest plants and fruits of all . . . needs newer, larger, stronger, keener compensations and compellers" (*PW* II, 422). The contradictions that plagued the continuance of federal hegemony, met only by the resistance of those unprepared for the extension of civil rights to ex-slaves, would be balanced only through the evolution of the constituted law into a political "common ground": "Law is the unshakable order of the universe forever; and the law over all, and law of laws, is the law of successions; that of the superior law, in time, gradually supplanting and overwhelming the inferior one" (*PW* II, 381). Surely the "feudal" past was no longer the sure footing it had been in antebellum America, with the overturning of such founding measures as the tolerance of slavery and black exclusion from both citizenship and the franchise. In a radicalized democracy, "Federal hegemony," "constituted law," and "common ground" come together as controvertible terms in their ability to move localized attachments toward the embrace of "strangers" in the citizenry of the Union.

Therefore Whitman's vista for postwar America challenged the divided past to begin to reconstruct its future as a network of collaborative social relations between races and sections: "The founders have pass'd to other spheres — but what are these terrible duties they have left us?" (*PW* II, 409). The "terrible duties" of Whitman's "Radical Democracy" constructed the future on the blurring of domestic social relations (formerly including master-slave relations) into "the divine, vast, general law" of the embrace of discarded strangers: "And topping democracy, this most alluring record, that it alone can bind, and ever seeks to bind, all nations, all men, of however various and distant lands, into a brotherhood, a family" (*PW* II, 381). Such a "binding" between competing cultures (recall the "religious" underpinning of such an endeavor) took the isolated individual (with sole reliance on "particular attachments") and submerged that individual in the democratizing pool of "adhesiveness, or love, that fuses, ties and aggregates, making the races comrades, and fraternizing all" (*PW* II, 381). Nowhere was Whitman's collaborative model of democracy more apparent than in his collapsing of the division between federalism and state autonomy, the superstructure that the government constructed over the racial divide, into a dialectical relation in which one always presupposed the cooperation of the other. As the representative of "Radical Democracy," Whitman was neutralizing the deepest ideological divide that blocked the realization of an interracial democracy: "There are, who, [*sic*] talking of the rights of The States, as in separatism and independence, condemn a rigid nationality, centrality. But to my mind, the freedom, as the existence of all, of The States, pre-necessitates such a nationality, an imperial Union" (*PW* II, 756). In short, Whitman's democracy meant the establishment of an "imperial Union" built on strong centralized government so that states, interest groups, and individuals could voluntarily pledge their allegiance to their common freedoms.

Supporting the construction of such an "imperial Union" identity, which brought "citizens" together "into a brotherhood, a family," Whitman's representations provided the nexus from which to project the movement from "comradeship" ("separatism and independence") to citizenship ("a rigid nationality, centrality"). As the legislative voice of "Radical Democracy," Whitman understood that the affections of localized "comrades" were not subject to the demands of communal law, but, in the reconstructive task of "making the races comrades," the law furnished its indispensable part toward the dismantling of the "noxious weeds" of racism and sectionalism. The Civil War amendments had attempted to pull the "isolate" states into the firmer configuration of an aggregated Union, founded on equal rights for black and white Americans. Whitman foresaw that these legislative amendments, though initially aborted in large-scale resistance, would eventually provide a precedent for an inclusive democracy: "Their politics [*sic*] the United States have, in my opinion, with all their faults, already establish'd, for good, on their own native, sound long-vista'd principles, never to be overturn'd, offering a sure basis for all the rest" (*PW* II, 409). In the "long-vista'd" evolution of cooperative American democracy, the unreconstructed resistance to a Union of "relative strangers" would be dismantled in the extension of cooperative citizenship, for "I say we can only attain harmony and stability by consulting ensemble and the ethic purports, and faithfully building upon them" (*PW* II, 409).

In his federalizing role, Whitman projected a three-stage process for the construction of this "ensemble" identity in the United States. First, the *Vistas* underscored the establishment of a collaborative governmental infrastructure founded on federal and state interdependence in the enactment of "Radical Democracy": "This is the American programme, not for classes, but for universal man, and is embodied in the compacts of the Declaration of Independence, and, as it began and has now grown, with its amendments, the Federal Constitution — and in the State governments . . . with general suffrage" (*PW* II, 410). Second, national identity would be consolidated through the diffusion of material prosperity in "produce, labor-saving machines, iron, cotton, local, State, and continental railways, intercommunication and trade with all lands . . . cheap appliances for comfort, numberless technical schools, books, newspapers, a currency for money circulation" (*PW* II, 410). Third, the "ensemble" identity of the Union would win out over sectionalized factions through the mechanism of the "native expression-spirit" of the "original authors and poets to come," who would manage the interests of competing voices in America "by a sublime and serious Religious Democracy sternly taking command, dissolving the old, sloughing off surfaces, and from its own interior and vital principles, reconstructing, democratizing society" (*PW* II, 410).

Therefore the primary mediating cultural agent for moving Reconstruction America from factionalized "comrades" to inclusive "citizens" was the voice of the poet who chanted "the great poems of death" (*PW* II, 420). The creators of such reconstructive cultural texts would sing songs of the "death" of discrimination, signaling not simply the dissolving of the individual self but also the dissolving of the outmoded social compact, which had constructed discriminatory practices, subjugated minorities, and perpetuated social hierarchies. Whitman's *Vistas* provided the representative poet with the legislative task of aggregating the Union against all the enemies of such a syntactic "common skeleton, knitting all close." Such an ameliorative vision of the poet as legislator had actually inaugurated Whitman's 1855 preface to the first edition of *Leaves of Grass*: "What is past is past. If [the new poet] does not expose superior models, and prove himself by every step he takes, he is not what is wanted" (*PW* II, 438). Sixteen years later, *Democratic Vistas* only elaborated such a representational need to "make it new" in an America that had thus far only been the "daughter of a physical revolution." After the appearance of poets who dismantled discrimination, America would promote the dissolution of the "feudal" vestiges of inequality and become the "mother of the true revolutions, which are of the interior life, and of the arts. For so long as the spirit is not changed, any change of appearance is of no avail" (*PW* II, 410). The "spirit" of reconciliation between the races remained at arm's length despite the "appearance" of the Fifteenth Amendment and *Democratic Vistas*, though such texts constructed an America as the "mother of the true revolutions" of social solidarity between strangers.

In *Democratic Vistas*, Whitman seemed to intuit that the discourse of law had the potential, through its autonomous force and punitive character, of checking the balkanized factions in society. While not promoting camaraderie, or transforming human rancor, such legislative restraint did empower black males to reach the ballot box across America in 1870 with the Fifteenth Amendment, and such restraint was reaffirmed through the Enforcement Acts of 1870–71, which punished Klan terrorism through federal surveillance south of the Mason-Dixon. The immediate effects of the Fifteenth Amendment's ratification in 1870, however, were confined to the enfranchisement of Northern blacks and to the prolongation of legislative majorities for the Republican Party. But neoabolitionists in the twentieth century were endowed with a weighty constitutional precedent when the Second Reconstruction for black civil rights gained its legislative victories in the 1950s and 1960s. Indeed, William Gillette has argued that the Fifteenth Amendment constitutes "both the source and vision of political equality — deduced by generally twentieth-century justices in their decisions and expressed by negro Americans casting their ballots at the polls."[39] A compromised amendment in the 1870s confronted the institutional racism of America almost a century later and thus constructs a compelling case for the Fifteenth Amendment as an installment in the enactment of Whitman's "Radical Democracy," which makes "the races comrades" and "fraternizes" strangers everywhere.

Notes

[1]   See chapter 1 of William Gillette's *Retreat from Reconstruction, 1869–1879* (Baton Rouge: Louisiana State U P, 1979), "Reveille for Reconstruction, 1867–1870," 1–24.

[2]   Gillette, 16.

[3]   Thomas Carlyle, "Shooting Niagara: And After?," was originally published in *Macmillan's Magazine* 16 (1867): 319–36, and reprinted in Horace Greeley's *New York Tribune*, 16 August 1867, and subsequently in *Works of Thomas Carlyle* (London: Chapman & Hall, 1869–72), vol. 30, 1–48.

[4]   The original issue, an eighty-four page pamphlet with a green paper cover, *Democratic Vistas* was printed by J. S. Redfield of New York. The title page read: "*Democratic / Vistas. /* Washington, D.C. / 1871." When this 1871 pamphlet was published, Gay Wilson Allen notes, it was met with "a conspiracy of silence" (*The Solitary Singer: A Critical Biography of Walt Whitman* (rev. ed., Chicago: U of Chicago, 1986) 427. There were, in fact, only two notices: Anon., "New Publications," *New York Times* (11 November 1870) 2:2; and Edward Dowden, [Review of *Leaves, Vistas,* and *Passage to India*], *Westminster Review* 96 (July 1871): 33–88. Dowden argues that Whitman makes "the people itself, in its undiminished totality" materialize in his poems and that the American nation is, in effect, the epic hero of his work. However, Allen's "conspiracy" theory rings true, in that such an intentional silence from a major author suggests that the document may have been too "radical" in its content for reviewers to stomach. Also, I would like to suggest that Whitman's argument so closely echoed the Radical Republican agitation in Congress during the Fifteenth Amendment debates, that editors may have felt Whitman's rhetoric recapitulated the indisputably dominant issue of 1870–71. Some twenty years later, when Whitman's revised *Vistas* was included in *Specimen Days* (1882), the essay did draw the critical notice of O. B. Frothingham, in "Democracy and Moral Progress," *North American Review* 137 (July 1883): 28. Frothingham called Whitman "perhaps the greatest democrat living" and called Whitman's diatribe against the diseases of American democracy "severe" because the poet "sees so much at stake in the experiment of liberty."

[5]   Michael Mosher, 588.

[6]   Richard Chase, 165. Chase's 1955 essay on *Democratic Vistas* was the first major twentieth-century recovery of the long neglected 1871 text, which inaugurated a critical upsurge of interest that has included the following competing positions: Robert J. Scholnick, "The American Context of *Democratic Vistas*," in ed. Joann P. Krieg, *Walt Whitman: Here and Now* (Westport, CT: Greenwood P, 1985) 147–156; Betsy Erkkila, *Whitman: The Political Poet* (New York: Oxford U P, 1989) 246–259; George Kateb, "Walt Whitman and the Culture of Democracy," *Political Theory* 18 (November 1990) 545–571; Responses to Kateb's article include: David Bromwich, "Whitman and Memory: A Response to Kateb," *Political Theory* 18 (November 1990) 572–76; Nancy L. Rosenblum, "Strange Attractors: How Individualists Connect to Form Democratic Unity," *Political Theory* 18 (November 1990) 576–86; Michael Mosher, "Jacobin" 587–95; Leo Marx, "George Kateb's Ahistorical Emersonianism," *Political Theory* 18 (November 1990) 595–600.

[7]   As ratified by the states on 30 March 1870, the text of the Fifteenth Amendment to the U.S. Constitution reads as follows:

Section 1. The right of citizens of the United States to vote shall not be denied or abridged by the United States or by any State on account of race, color, or previous condition of servitude.

Section 2. The Congress shall have power to enforce this article by appropriate legislation.

The textual compromises of the drafts of the Fifteenth Amendment, while it made its way through Congress, are best catalogued by William Gillette in *The Right to Vote*, 46–78. The major losses to the proposed amendment were, obviously, the ban on voter qualifications and the right to hold office irrespective of race. These legislative proposals did not survive the Congressional debates, because of the resistance of both Democrats and moderate Republicans, who opposed such legislation as against popular consent at that time (January–February 1869). The Radical Republicans, rather than have the amendment tabled in the Third Session of the 40th Congress and thereby consigned to legislative limbo, caved in to the opponents in order to pass the enfranchisement statute. Gillette is a primary research source for the legislative process that resulted in the Fifteenth Amendment, which, he argues, was passed primarily to enfranchise Northern blacks, whereas Southern blacks were already enfranchised de facto under the provisions of the Fourteenth Amendment. Two other discussions of the Fifteenth Amendment are located in Harold M. Hyman and William M. Wiecek, *Equal Justice Under Law: Constitutional Development, 1835–1875* (New York: Harper and Row,

1982) 463–72; and Michael Les Benedict, *A Compromise of Princi-ple: Congressional Republicans and Reconstruction, 1863–1869* (New York: Norton, 1974) 325–36.

[8] The ratification parades in Washington were chronicled in the *New York Herald*, 1 April 1870; *Washington National Republican*, 16 April 1870, and the *Washington New National Era*, 7 April 1870.

[9] Grant's message to Congress following the ratification of the Fif-teenth Amendment is found in James D. Richardson (comp.), *A Compilation of the Messages and Papers of the Presidents, 1789–1897*, 10 vols., (Washington, D. C.: Government Printing Office, 1897), VII, 56.

[10] Charles Sumner, *The Works of Charles Sumner*, 15 vols., (Boston: Lee and Shepard, 1870–1883), XIII (1880) 35–52.

[11] Carlyle *Works*, XXX, 5.

[12] Ibid., 7.

[13] Ibid., 6.

[14] In the original *Galaxy* publication of the first installment called "Democracy" (December 1867), Whitman explicitly denounced the racist elitism of Carlyle's abusive language about the so-called "Nigger Question." By adopting Carlyle's grandiloquent rhetoric with mock solemnity, Whitman in effect neutralizes its racism through satire: "How, then (for that shape forebodes the current del-uge)—how shall we, good-class folk, meet the rolling, mountainous surges of 'swarmery' that already beat upon and threaten to over-whelm us? . . . What under heaven is to become of 'nigger Cushee,' that imbruted and lazy being — now, worst of all, preposterously free? etc . . . . Ring the alarum bell! Put the flags at the half mast! Or, rather, let each man spring for the nearest loose spar or plank. The ship is going down!" (*PW* II, 749). Through satiric humor, Whit-man, in effect, appropriated the vocabulary of racism and elitism to rob it of its odious signification. Carlyle's feudal argument won the following response from the poet of "Radical Democracy": "Be not so moved, not to say distraught, my venerable friend. Spare those spasms of dread and disgust" (*PW* II, 749). Whitman goes on to dismiss Carlyle's racism as mere "cat-squalling," but he does so through positioning Carlyle at a black revival meeting in South Caro-lina: "But I must now affirm that such a comic-painful hullabaloo and vituperative cat-squalling as this about 'the Niagara leap,' 'swarmery,' 'Orsonism,' etc . . . . I never yet encountered; no, not even in ex-tremest hour of midnight, in whooping Tennessee revival, or Bedlam let loose in crowded, colored Carolina bush-meeting" (*PW* II, 750). By turning Carlyle's elitism on its head and effectively placing him in a "Bedlam" of stereotypical black religious frenzy, Whitman has

robbed Carlyle's racism of its critical edge. The fact that Whitman deleted this long passage from the completed *Democratic Vistas* in its 1871 pamphlet form suggests that between 1867 and 1871 Whitman found the passage anachronistic because of the successful ratification of the Fifteenth Amendment in 1870. With constitutional reform having enfranchised black males, and with federal enforcement of black civil liberties, I suggest such a deletion does not dilute Whitman's denunciation of racism and elitism, but the particular *occasion* of Carlyle's "Shooting Niagara" diatribe had receded from public consciousness.

[15] Two unpublished manuscript fragments by Whitman on the question of the black race have surfaced, and they are interpreted in the following two essays: Kenneth Price, "Whitman's Solutions to 'The Problem of the Blacks,'" *Resources for American Literary Study* 15 (1985): 205–08; and Geoffrey Sill, "Whitman on 'The Black Question': A New Manuscript," *Walt Whitman Quarterly Review* 8 (1990): 69–75. The arguments attempt to construct a biographical case, based on these two unpublished notebook entries, that Whitman himself was racist, and opposed to black equality. In the present chapter, such a conjecture is where I *begin*, not end, for I assume that Whitman's own attitudes were subjected to the same racism indelible in most of the white majority. Whatever Whitman's biographical attitudes were toward blacks (and the evidence is largely conjectural), my arguments suggest that the cultural work in his *Vistas* prescinds from any personal racist attitudes and performs the cultural work of the legislative poet who sang songs of the death of racial discrimination. Whitman not once published either of the two fragments discussed by Price and Sill, though he published his *Vistas*, in various formats, *four* times during his career (in the *Galaxy*, 1867–68; in pamphlet form, 1871; in *Two Rivulets*, 1876; and in *Specimen Days and Collect*, 1882).

[16] Gillette, *Right*, 81.

[17] *Congressional Globe*, 40th Congress, 3rd Session (1868–69), 561.

[18] Ibid.

[19] Ibid.

[20] Ibid. Senator Edmunds's comments on the suffrage amendment are found at 1303–08, 1313, 1316, 1318. The citation is from 1316.

[21] Ibid., 909–10.

[22] Ibid., 911.

[23] Ibid., 710.

[24] Walt Whitman's "General Notes" to *Democratic Vistas* appeared in the original pamphlet (New York: J. S. Redfield, 1871), 79–84. The citation is from page 83. They were reprinted in toto in *Two Rivulets*,

the second volume to the centennial edition of *Leaves of Grass* (Camden, N.J.: Author's Edition, 1876); and most of them survive in Walt Whitman's *Prose Works 1892*, Vol. II, *Collect and Other Prose*, ed. Floyd Stovall (New York: New York U P, 1964), see note following *Democratic Vistas*, 426.

[25] *Congressional Globe*, 40th Congress, 3rd Session (1868–69), 670.

[26] Ibid.

[27] *Congressional Globe*, 40th Congress, 3rd Session (1868–69), 710.

[28] Erkkila, 258.

[29] *Congressional Globe*, 40th Congress, 3rd Session (1868–69), 1440.

[30] Ibid.

[31] *Congressional Globe*, 40th Congress, 3rd Session (1868–69), 1441.

[32] Walt Whitman's, "General Notes," to *Democratic Vistas*, 83.

[33] *Congressional Globe*, 40th Congress, 3rd Session (1868–69), 705.

[34] *Congressional Globe*, 40th Congress, 3rd Session (1868–69), 706.

[35] Ibid.

[36] *Congressional Globe*, 40th Congress, 3rd Session (1868–69), 1311.

[37] Ibid.

[38] Ibid.

[39] Gillette, *Right*, 164.

3
"I'd sow a seed for thee of endless Nationality"

The 1871–72 *Leaves of Grass* and
the Construction of the Book of
Democratic Nationality

O N EASTER SUNDAY IN 1873, the most ruthless act of racist violence in the entire Reconstruction era took place in Grant Parish at the Colfax, Louisiana, parish seat. The 1872 gubernatorial race had produced both Republican and Democrat claimants to the contested election, and black citizens at Colfax, afraid that Democrats would seize the statehouse and reverse their newly acquired constitutional rights, laid siege to the parish's central township by digging trenches around the city limits and by engaging in paramilitary exercises under the command of black Civil War veterans. After three weeks of such black resistance in an effort to fortify the Fifteenth Amendment right to vote, armed whites massacred fifty freedmen after they had surrendered their rifles. In the random terror that followed, scores of innocent blacks were killed by the white mob.[1] Such a bloodbath was long remembered by blacks in Louisiana, and elsewhere, as a sobering reminder that armed resistance to white supremacy had disastrous potential for an unprincipled assault on blacks who dared to assert their political autonomy in an unreconstructed polity. By Easter 1873, blacks were besieged throughout the South by Klanism, and public knowledge of the penumbral violence wrought by white supremacists on numberless victims circulated widely in the North as well as the South soon after the 1870 ratification of the Fifteenth Amendment, the last Constitutional intervention in the Reconstruction legislative archive.

In an 1867 poem called "What Place Is Besieged?," Walt Whitman had proclaimed his solidarity with besieged victims of stronger forces everywhere. This text could have resonated with the murdered black resisters at Colfax, Louisiana, six years later: "What place is besieged, and vainly tries to raise the siege? / Lo! I send to that place a commander, swift, brave, immortal; / And with him horse and foot — and parks of artillery, / And artillerymen, the deadliest that ever fired gun" (*LG Var* II, 399). Though the fifty freedmen in Grant Parish were slaughtered with pitiless dispatch, Whitman's rhetorical gesture echoed with the ensuing Radical Republican agitation against the vigilante violence of the Ku Klux Klan in the recalcitrant South, which would give rise to the Enforcement Acts of 1870–71, designed to obliterate racist obstructions to the ballot box, as well as the

Ku Klux Klan Act of 1871, passed to impede lynchings. The Civil War Amendments had placed black Americans on the public map in a forceful way, and Whitman did not ignore this racial reckoning in his own public discourse.

Two years prior to the Colfax massacre, Whitman the "commander" had assembled his deadly "artillery" and enlisted in the raising of the siege against white racist violence by issuing a radically altered fifth edition of *Leaves of Grass* (1871–72). This new edition of *Leaves* intervened a de facto racial war south of the Mason-Dixon by recollecting the Civil War in anxiety, and also by constructing a network of nationalistic images that would justify the ways of federal authority to the unruly subjects of an inheritance of state sovereignty at all costs. The Enforcement Acts were the high-water mark for federal coercion of the states and were the legislative intervention that severely weakened the Klan and provided a greater black access to the ballot box than would be witnessed again until the 1960s. Whitman's publication of the 1871–72 *Leaves* effectively served as his representational reinforcement of such a coercive move in the welding together of disparate regions into an "imperial Union." The poet's textual preoccupation with a book of "Democratic Nationality," announced in the 1872 preface for the first time, offered his *Leaves* as the "perfect pilot" for a ragged nation of violent factions, a guide needed in the rough voyage of the states toward an interracial democracy. Whitman had presented his book as the earlier companion poem to "What Place is Besieged?," called in 1871 "Here, Sailor!": "Here, sailor! Here, ship! take aboard the most perfect pilot, / Whom in a little boat, putting off, and rowing, I hailing you, offer" (*LG Var* II, 398).

In effect, Whitman handed over his fifth edition of *Leaves*, "a little boat," to the beleaguered "Ship of State" as a poetic installment in his metaphorical abandonment of the shores of a racially divided past in order to set sail for a reconstructed future on the "oceans" of social solidarity. These two small poems were originally one composite "Calamus" poem in 1860 (no. 31), and their political signification had moved away from localized "comradeship" toward the solidarity between citizens en masse. Whitman's desire for "Radical Democracy" had not changed, but the implementation of the desire to federalize his poetic images occurred just when congressional legislation reached far beyond any coercive federal boundary before 1870; indeed, such a nationalization of civil rights enforcement was not witnessed again until President Lyndon Johnson signed the Civil Rights Act in 1964, which was followed by the Voting Rights Act in 1965.

As early as the summer of 1869, Whitman had been preoccupied with a revised edition of *Leaves of Grass* to follow the publication of the fourth (1867) edition. When the poet escaped the summer heat of Washington,

D.C., to return to New York on 27 July 1870, having secured a substitute in his clerkship in the attorney general's office, he was determined to publish the fifth edition with J. S. Redfield of New York. By the winter of 1870–71, the fifth edition of *Leaves* was on sale in New York, Boston, Philadelphia, and Washington.[2] Despite this signal moment, Whitman was virtually ignored by the critics, and the complicated publication history of the fifth edition included at least two other rearrangements of the book, perhaps signaling his restless displeasure over the absence of an audible response from the public to what, for him, was a major publishing event. In any case, Whitman reissued *Leaves* with the *Passage to India* annex, adding 120 pages with seventy-four poems, twenty-four of which were new texts, the others selected from earlier editions of his work. In 1872 this bifurcated edition was reissued directly from Washington, D.C., dated 1872 but copyrighted in 1870. Still another issue of the book contained *Passage to India*, with separate pagination, as well as the annexation of the supplement *After All Not to Create Only* with 24 additional pages, also published as a separate pamphlet with separate pagination. Additionally, Whitman issued a pamphlet publication from Washington called *As a Strong Bird on Pinions Free and Other Poems* in 1872, which introduced seven new poems, and the significant prose preface, announcing a departure from *Leaves* proper in favor of another book of "democratic nationality."[3] In short, the fifth edition of *Leaves of Grass* contained in its final format three separate books of poetry and, with the discrete supplement of *As a Strong Bird* and its preface, added up to a massive displacement of Whitman's work as the public had known it: Whitman was pointing to a reassessment of how his shifting project would speak to readers in the middle of the Reconstruction period.

The 1872 preface, though published as a prefix to *As a Strong Bird on Pinions Free*, belonged to the textual archaeology of the growth of *Leaves of Grass* insofar as Whitman announced in lucid terms that the book of "democratic nationality," signalled in 1867 by the supplement "Songs Before Parting" and further codified a year earlier in the separate book *Passage to India*, had been the inauguration of a new book to supplement his *Leaves* with a companion volume. All these supplementary texts still bore the imprint "Leaves of Grass" on their title pages, but their rhetorical energies were leading Whitman to the realization that "he had brought the *Leaves* to an end and was starting a new book."[4] As for *Leaves*, the preface declared, the poet had given utterance to "New World songs, and an epic of Democracy, having already had their publish'd expression . . . in 'Leaves of Grass,' the present and future pieces from me are really but the surplusage forming after that volume, or the wake eddying behind it" (*PW* II, 458–59). The preface affirmed that the poet had "the ambition of devoting yet a few years to poetic composition to continue to represent "America —

cities and states — the years, the events of our Nineteenth century" (*PW* II, 459).

This historical desire would result in the representation of an America not merely as a materialistic behemoth but also as "the grand producing land of nobler men and women — of copious races, cheerful, healthy, tolerant, free — to become the most friendly nation, (the United States indeed)—the modern composite nation, form'd from all, with room for all, welcoming all immigrants" (*PW* II, 460). As in the 1871 *Democratic Vistas*, the text articulated the desire for "social, literary, religious, or esthetic organizations" that would knit together the already vast material advantages of America, a "seething mass of *materials*" which were now "eligible to be used to carry towards its crowning stage, and build for good, the great ideal nationality of the future, the nation of the body and the soul" (*PW* II, 460–61). Such an "ideal nationality" would result from the jettisoning of "religion" from its ecclesiastical trappings and the binding of religion to "democracy *en masse*, and to literature." This loosening of religion from its feudal past, and its infusion in the masses of America, had its historical analogue in the erasure of the traumas of the "Four Years' War," to be superseded by "a young and lusty generation" whose energies were "obliterating the war, and all its scars, its mounded graves, and all its reminiscences of hatred, conflict, death" (*PW* II, 463). Then, with an unprecedented imprimatur to such a rupture of memory, Whitman stated; "So let it be obliterated."

While there was more than a little compensation to Whitman's pronouncements of "that strange, sad war" that was "hurrying even now to be forgotten," the poet's rhetoric had an even more important representational function: the desire for a departure from the divisive social balkanization between section and section, between races, or between federal authorities and unruly state and municipal authorities. In other words, Whitman was bidding a nostalgic farewell to the unbridled heterogeneity of America as a confederacy of states and welcoming the renovated compact of *United* States that Americans could enlist in their self-understanding as national citizens en masse: "I say the life of the present and the future makes undeniable demands upon us each and all, south, north, east, west. To help put the United States (even if only in imagination) hand in hand, in one unbroken circle in a chant." The poet had intervened in order to arouse "the thought of their great future, and the attitude conform'd to it — especially their great esthetic, moral, scientific future, (of which their vulgar material and political present is but as the preparatory tuning of instruments by an orchestra)" (*PW* II, 463).

In effect, Whitman had made the move from plural "United States" to the pluralized "citizens" within a singular nation. This Whitmanian ambition had crystallized by 1872 into the surpassing of the ambition of *Leaves of Grass* ("the song of a great composite *democratic individual*, male or female") through the movement toward "the thread-voice, more or less audible, of an aggregated, inseparable, unprecedented, vast, composite, electric *democratic nationality*" (*PW* II, 463). The construction of such a book of democratic nationality had already been well under way, for Whitman had made such an aggregating gesture in the 1867 *Songs Before Parting* annex as well as in the 1871 book *Passage to India*. Though critics have assumed that such a project was never truly accomplished because of the onset of ill health, Whitman's delivery of *Two Rivulets* as the companion volume to the 1876 *Leaves* conformed to all his representational criteria for legislating the "ideal nationality" he envisioned in the 1872 preface: in fact, Whitman included in *Two Rivulets* all the Reconstruction texts that had been his "preparatory tuning of instruments by an orchestra," including *Democratic Vistas, Passage to India*, and *As a Strong Bird on Pinions Free*.

The most significant innovation of the 1871–72 *Leaves of Grass*, aside from the obvious fact that Whitman took nearly a third of his published poems and shifted them into the *Passage to India* annex, was the poet's dispersal of the *Drum-Taps* cluster throughout the body of the *Leaves*. While *Drum-Taps* appeared as a cluster in *Leaves* for the first time in this fifth edition, the Civil War texts were reedited, and the number of thematic clusters focused on the war and Reconstruction jumped to three instead of one: "Drum-Taps," "Marches Now the War is Over," and "Bathed in War's Perfume." The "strange, sad war" that Whitman had willed "obliterated" in the 1872 preface was hardly demolished in his *Leaves* but rather had exploded out into the textual body of the poet's work, and its representational multiplication became the pivot on which revolved much of the democratic urge that motivated *Leaves* in the first place.[5] As an antebellum journalist, Whitman had shared in the state-sovereignty ideology that permeated the governmental structures of the states, but as Betsy Erkkila has persuasively put it, the war had forced Whitman to underscore the sometimes coercive value of federalism in the goal of Union preservation: "After years of defying the ever-stronger foot of federal power, Whitman during the war years found himself on the side of national, as opposed to state, sovereignty."[6] The fact that Lincoln, always Whitman's apotheosis, had resorted to flexing federalist muscle to enforce the indissolubility of the Union, and thereby to win the struggle, found its centralizing echo in these three "war" clusters in his 1871–72 *Leaves*.

The cluster "Marches Now the War Is Over" enlisted images of nationalism in the pursuit of civil restoration immediately after the war years. One of the *Drum-Taps* poems that pointed the way for the reconstruction of civil order, "Pioneers! O Pioneers!," reinforced this rhetorical containment of social disruption in its form, complete with trochaic meter and conventional stanzaic patterns. While the title echoes the westward migration, the signifier "pioneer" can be traced back to include among its roots the Old French *peonier*, for "foot soldier," and thus denotes an imagistic parallel to the martial images of the war troops. In fact, the text culminated in an explicitly soldier-like image: "Swift to the head of the army!—swift! spring to your places, / Pioneers! O pioneers!" (*LG Var* II, 478). Thus, while the "Pioneers!" poem pointed backward as an echo chamber of the war memory, it also pointed forward to the reconstructive energies of creating a future that recast "soldiers" as "pioneers."

Clearly, Whitman's pioneers were moving forward, as originators of a new social formation, to prepare the renovated social relations that would embrace regional and racial difference with a vigor that would surpass the outmoded feudal relations inherited from the Old World: "Have the elder races halted? / Do they droop and end their lesson, wearied, over there beyond the seas? / We take up the task eternal, and the burden, and the lesson, / Pioneers! O pioneers!" (*LG Var* II, 475). Whitman's "foot soldiers," like his conventional poetic "feet," were drafted into the Reconstruction urge of forging a future of social solidarity that stressed the extension of democratic identity beyond the neighborhoods, towns, and states that had donated self-understanding to Americans before the war. Such provincial identity formations had to include national allegiance as well, one of the desired products of the federal legislation that had marked the postwar decade at every turn: "All the past we leave behind; / We debouch a newer, mightier world, varied world; / Fresh and strong the world we seize, world of labor and the march, / Pioneers! O pioneers!" (*LG Var* II, 475). The loosening of the hold of past subjectivities in favor of "newer, mightier" subjects had had a rough passage since Appomattox. Whitman had to admit that just as his "pioneers" were making a metaphorical continental passage, the "venturing as we go the unknown ways" was not to be a vacation; the rhetorical march of the "Pioneers!" text had value only in the dynamic embrace of the risk on the open road of the future, "Through the battle, through defeat, moving yet and never stopping" (*LG Var* II, 476).

Perhaps the most unlikely of the "Marches Now the War Is Over" originated in 1856 as "Poem of the Propositions of Nakedness" and had transmuted in 1871–72 to "Respondez!," a theater of irrational exclamations that inverts conventional social roles and values into a carnival of unreason. The imperative title demands a response from the reader, now that "The war is completed — the price is paid — the title is settled beyond recall" (*LG Var* I, 260). The ironic pyrotechnics of this rather lengthy text have a performative function insofar as its rhetoric dissolves all the ideological notions informing social relations, only to point out how overdetermined they are by social institutions. In a line not present in 1856,

Whitman makes this proposition clear: "I pronounce openly for a new distribution of roles" (*LG Var* I, 260). Such a representational strategy claims persuasive power only in its empowerment of the reader to recreate social relations from the ground up because of the faulty dominations of the status quo. If social roles are bounded by attachment to autonomy rather than solidarity, then the poet orders, "Let the sympathy that waits in every man, wait! or let it also pass, a dwarf, to other spheres!" (*LG Var* I, 261). Like "Pioneers!," this march enables reconstructed readers to unmoor themselves from the past in order to set out for a better future built on solidarity with strangers: "Let freedom prove no man's inalienable right! Every one who can tyrannize, let him tyrannize to his satisfaction!" (*LG Var* I, 261).

In a newly added 1871 passage, Whitman's speaker discountenances the impediments to democratizing nationality that were manifested in the anti-Reconstruction sentiments prevalent in the North and the South: "Let the eminence of meanness, treachery, sarcasm, hate, greed, indecency, impotence, lust, be taken for granted above all! let writers, judges, governments, households, religions, philosophies, take such for granted above all!" (*LG Var* I, 261). The vehemence of Whitman's reversed rhetoric reveals the heart of a trenchant social critic, for the poem decries the "public and private corruption" that forced the poet to resort to this exclamatory performance in order to dismantle the performative line, "Let the theory of America still be management, caste, comparison!" (*LG Var* I, 261). The "caste" system of race relations constitutes the major stumbling block to implementing national citizenship, for the antagonism between blacks and whites had only worsened since the poet wrote, "Let the white person again tread the black person under his heel! (Say! which is trodden under heel, after all?)" (*LG Var* I, 264). The telling 1871 insertion of the word "again" demonstrates Whitman's awareness of the resurgence of racism in postslavery America, and the parenthetical reversal of racial dominance implies that blacks will rise to the top through their moral supremacy over white "management." By turning the world upside down on the page, Whitman was reconstituting the social system in his imagination to point the way to a democratic culture where social oppositions would not impede the cooperative social relations that he envisioned for postwar America.

Whitman's resistance to the perpetuation of hierarchical social relations, which blocked the realization of democratic liberty, reappears in another of the "Marches" called "Adieu to a Soldier," a brand-new text that furthers the nostalgic farewell that would appear in his eulogy to the war in the 1872 preface. The actual "rude campaigning" in the theater of war may have been over, and the soldier's "mission" may have been "fulfill'd," but the speaker of the poem declared himself "more warlike, / Myself and this contentious soul of mine," in order to engage in an unnamed battle with unnamed opponents: "Here marching, ever marching on, a war fight out — aye here, / To fiercer, weightier battles give expression" (*LG Var* III, 630–31).

In the next "march," "As I Walk These Broad, Majestic Days," Whitman named the referent ("Libertad") for his resistance and cast the reconstructive energies of the cluster squarely in the legislative theater of Reconstruction politics: "Libertad, and the divine average — Freedom to every slave on the face of the earth" (*LG Var* II, 328). The vertiginous energy that Whitman had released in this announcement of interracial liberty found its ecstatic voice in the final poem of this cluster, "O Sun of Real Peace": "O ample and grand Presidentiads! Now the war, the war is over! / New history! New heroes! I project you! / Visions of poets! only you really last! sweep on! sweep on!" (*LG Var* II, 292). In Whitman's postwar drama, only "New history" written by "New heroes" in their metrical march toward equality would suffice. Through the trajectory of this new cluster of postwar marches, Whitman had dissolved the prewar subject encased in webs of social division and had stepped to the boundary of a wholly new equalitarian subject who had not yet been constituted in the America of 1871.

The dominant image in the second of the displaced *Drum-Taps* clusters, "Bathed in War's Perfume," was Whitman's metonymic representation of the United States: the Stars and Stripes. In fact, the "delicate flag" represents the image washed in the perfume of conflict. The title poem engenders the seductive image of the flag "like the eyes of women" as it called "the sailors and the soldiers" (*LG Var* II, 493). Once again, the second text, called "Delicate Cluster," constitutes its composite force as the "flag of teeming life!" as well as the "Flag of death! (how I watch'd you through the smoke of battle pressing! / How I heard you flap and rustle, cloth defiant!)" (*LG Var* III, 631). Furthermore, the domestic images of maternity are enlisted in the rhetoric of public representation, for the flag is both "My matron mighty!" and "My sacred one, my mother" (*LG Var* III, 631). The intrusion of public representations on private relations bore more than a passing resemblance to contemporary political events: the Radical Republican agitation that culminated in the Enforcement Acts of 1870–71 intruded federal surveillance into state voting patterns, the latter roughly the rhetorical equivalent of "domestic" relations as understood by opponents of Washington's intervention. In validating the "matron mighty" in political terms, Whitman had blurred the gendered images inherited from the past, complete with the restrictions of womanhood to "hearth and home." As in "Respondez!," Whitman pointed to an innovative synthesis of public relations (federal hegemony) and private relations (state sovereignty) that might have constituted an alternative to the bitter racial bloodbath in the unreconstructed South. The march of democratic liberty had to continue within the shores of America, represented by "Thick-Sprinkled Bunting," for liberty was to infect all subjugated peoples everywhere who took the New World as their model: "For the prize I see at issue, at last is the world! / All its ships and shores I see, interwoven with your threads, greedy banner!" (*LG Var* II, 518).

The most significant text that appeared in "Bathed in War's Perfume" made its debut in the 1871–72 *Leaves* as Whitman's first attempt to address the subject of blacks since the 1855 edition of *Leaves* spoke, in "Song of Myself" and "The Sleepers," in the voice of the slave. "Ethiopia Saluting the Colors" represents the bewildered confrontation between a black "dusky woman, so ancient, hardly human," and a soldier in Sherman's army during the war. But the poem's aporia multiply to the point that its primary historical setting recedes into a secondary position and thus allows the text to emerge as an allegorical enactment of the racial anxieties prevalent in 1871–72, which had given birth to both the Enforcement Acts and the Ku Klux Klan's atrocities. Whitman's text opens with an interrogative, indicating that the uncertainty of the "hardly human" woman's identity had no constitution to the white soldier who doubled the poem's puzzlement with "Why rising by the roadside here, do you the colors greet?" (*LG Var* III, 631). Situated in a poetic cluster of "flag" texts, the affront of the black woman's salute to the Stars and Stripes takes on corrosive significance in that the "dusky" black woman had no subjectivity in the social network of white dominance in the arena of American ideology. In effect, she presents herself to Sherman's Yankee soldier as a "hardly human" object. The soldier-persona of the poem cannot even personalize the black "other" except through a competing national moniker: Sherman's underling calls her only "Ethiopia" and thus strips her of any representation within the boundaries of American civil liberties.

Whitman's representation of the faceless black woman is given a voice in the boundaries of the poem, but her words amount to reductive italicized doggerel: "*Me, master, years a hundred, since from my parents sunder'd, / As little child, they caught me as the savage beast is caught; / Then hither me, across the sea, the cruel slaver brought*" (*LG Var* III, 632). Syntactically, the text refuses to subjectify the black woman by choosing the objective pronoun "Me" rather than "I" and thus reinforces the identification of the woman as a mere object of the white male gaze. The woman "curtsies" to the passing troops with a determination to be recognized as a subject of the Union "flag," or rather as a legitimate citizen of the American culture in the wake of the Civil War amendments, but the dumbfounded soldier only widens the racial divide with three more interrogatives, which end the poem: "What is it, fateful woman — so blear, hardly human? / Why wag your head, with turban bound — yellow, red and green? / Are the things so strange and marvelous, you see or have seen?" (*LG Var* III, 632). The "Ethiopia" poem thus becomes a representation of the fissure between the white representation of the black woman and the woman's insistence on belonging to the metonymic "colors" that she claims with her posture and her gaze.

In effect, the black woman reaches out in a gesture of inclusion, interracial comradeship, and political citizenship in a newly interracial democracy. The white soldier's befuddlement, and his insistence on her "otherness," betrays the inability of white dominance to cede its social authority over blacks. By 1871 major concessions had been made to blacks, including emancipation, citizenship, and the black male's right to vote; but Whitman's text pointed to the persistence of racism, which manifested itself in the need to represent the black subject as an unassimilable "object," impenetrable in its aura of exotic difference. In the political arena, one of the only sites of rhetorical resistance to such colonial projections was the halls of Congress. Radical Republicans pushed ahead in 1870–71 with three revolutionary pieces of legislation that would result in the temporary curtailing of the scourge of Klanism and would provide federal protection laws for blacks brave enough to cast ballots.

The rampant Klanism in the South prompted Congress to reinforce the Fifteenth Amendment, even before it was ratified, with legislation designed to protect black voters. Just as Whitman's federalizing impulse had begun to percolate in his poems with more insistence, the Enforcement Acts of 1870–71 made the "force clauses" the centerpieces of their juridical power to nationalize the civil rights protection of black Americans as never before. After a bitter debate culminating in a nineteen-hour all-night session on 20 May 1870, President Ulysses S. Grant signed on 31 May the First Enforcement Amendment, a bulky treatise comprised of almost five thousand words spread out over twenty-three sections.[7] Titled "An act to enforce the Right of Citizens of the United States to Vote in the several States of this Union, and for other Purposes," the bill broke new legal ground in the relatively recent field of civil rights legislation: the First Enforcement Act offered to ensure protection of black voting under the Fifteenth Amendment, to ensure adherence by the states to the "privileges and immunities" clause of the first section of the Fourteenth Amendment, to extirpate Klanism and lynching, to stop voting fraud in congressional elections, to prevent former Confederate officials from holding elective office, and to specify federal mechanisms pursuant to these goals. Such a comprehensive package of social reforms would have perhaps been impossible to achieve in any context, but the overriding concern of the bill was to provide clear access to voting for blacks south of the Mason-Dixon line.

Democrats objected to the revisionist scope of the law, which subjected all citizens to the same prerequisites for voting (such as poll taxes, literacy tests, or property qualifications) irrespective of race, and violators of this impartial ruling would be subject to fines and imprisonment. Senator John Pool of North Carolina, the state that witnessed some of the most notorious Klan atrocities, drafted the two sections of the bill designed to stamp out the Klan. Pool's amendment made it a felony for "two or more persons [to] band or conspire together, or go in disguise upon the public highway or upon the premises of another" with the purpose of the denial to any citizen "of any right or privilege granted or secured to him by the Constitution or laws of the United States." Convicted felons faced the harshest sentences then provided by the law, fines up to five thousand dollars and sentences of up to ten years, after trial in the federal courts. This was an unprecedented ratification of federal police power.

Democrats were horrified at the far-reaching micromanagement of state election procedures by federal surveillance. Because the president was authorized by the bill to employ federal troops to patrol polling places, Senator Allen G. Thurman of Ohio declared that such measures threatened tyranny, for "here in a republic you propose to confer upon one man, who may be a candidate for election himself, the power to surround any poll he pleases . . . with troops to see that the election law is not violated."[8] Democratic thunder in Congress echoed with charges that the First Enforcement Act was patently unconstitutional, but Senator Pool countered, "If a state shall not enforce its laws by which private individuals shall be prevented by force from contravening the rights of the citizen . . . it is the duty of the United States government to supply that omission."[9] Because of the comfortable Republican majority, such Democrats' objections were subjugated to the radical view summarized by Senator George E. Spencer of Alabama: "Violence and blood are written in the history of reconstruction . . . . Nothing but the most stringent of all laws and regulations will check this era of bloodshed and dethrone this dynasty of the knife and bullet."[10]

This feudal "dynasty" had to be overturned through rhetorical strategies of egalitarianism, which the rattled Democrats opposed en bloc because of its potential for rescripting social relations on an impartial basis. Representative John D. Stiles of Pennsylvania thundered, "Under the guise and pretense of giving protection to the newly-enfranchised race, the negro, you strike at the very foundation of free government . . . . This is not a law to enforce the fifteenth amendment . . . . It is the entering wedge to a new order of things."[11] Racial terrorism had changed the language of representatives in 1870 (both literary and congressional), and indeed this "new order of things" demanded federal hegemony as its modus operandi if the boundaries of interracial democracy were to be widened. Senator Carl Schurz of Missouri responded in one of the most eloquent speeches of the whole debate: "We are charged with having revolutionized the Constitution . . . . Yes, the Constitution . . . has been changed in some most essential points; that change does amount to a great revolution, and this bill is one of its legitimate children." This "revolution" was not simply an upheaval but also a full turn in the legislative momentum of equal rights, the "legitimate children" of a renovated Constitution. Waving the "bloody shirt" with abandon, Schurz continued, "Democrats argued not for the liberty of all, but it is for the liberty of one to impair and restrict the liberty of another."[12] Such partisan wrangling consistently spoke to party interests, but also reflected the humanitarian concern for democratic liberty for blacks who risked life and limb in showing up to vote at polls throughout the South.

President Grant signed the Second Enforcement Act on 28 February 1871 and thereby reinforced the first mandate with more detailed duties for federal enforcement officers, more crimes that could be punished, and the stipulation that cities of at least twenty thousand inhabitants could request election supervisors to verify all poll results.[13] Thus federal hegemony had finally arrived at the arithmetic task of tabulating ballots. Whatever the partisan motives present in the drafting of the Second Enforcement Act, Everette Swinney has pointed out that there were two aims at work in its successful passage: first, the Second Enforcement Act was the culmination of the federal hegemonic movement in Washington since Appomattox; second, this bill was undeniably designed to affect the Northern cities in their voting patterns more than those of the South.[14] Republicans had tabulated the results of the national elections in 1870 nervously, for these elections were the first since 1860 in which all the states participated and also the first in which the enfranchised black freedmen had voted. Despite the landmark First Enforcement Act, there were widespread reports of fraudulent elections in Northern cities and discouraging reports of increased Klan intimidation in the South. Nevertheless, as Swinney points out, there were only seven Southern cities with inhabitants of twenty thousand or more (New Orleans, Louisville, Richmond, Charleston, Memphis, Salem, and Savannah), whereas there were sixty-one cities in the North subject to the second statute's restrictions.[15] Ultimately, the Second Enforcement Act was amended in the Enforcement Act of 10 June 1872 to provide for federal supervision of rural elections, and it was in this modified format that such federalizing force was used in the racially divided South.[16]

President Grant signed the Ku Klux Klan Act on 20 April 1871 and thus ratified the third sweeping federal statute in the Republican campaign to provide for civil rights supervision on behalf of black Americans. The Ku Klux Klan Act banned all terrorist organizations that used violence in their truncation of the civil liberties of others, gave the President the power to authorize martial law, and provided for the suppression of habeas corpus in the pursuit of vigilante thugs. Representative Samuel Shellabarger of Ohio wrote most of the succinct bill, and more than eighty representatives spoke in the House debate from 28 March to 6 April 1871. The bill significantly increased the penalties for violators and expanded the jurisdiction of the federal courts in hearing civil rights cases. Everette Swinney has evaluated the importance of the anti-Klan law in terms of its civil rights rhetoric: "Together with section six of the First Enforcement Act, it created a new federal crime — conspiracy to deprive of civil rights — and thereby brought the basic rights of American citizenship under the protection of the general government."[17] Democrats heaped charges on the Republicans for having caused the advent of Klanism in the South, "deemed a necessity for the protection of the life, property, and honor of the white race."[18] Republicans countered that racism was the motive for the Klan's crimes: "It originates in a fiendish conspiracy to deprive the colored race of the ballot. It seeks to strike down your reconstruction laws and reduce the newly-enfranchised race to a non-voting population."[19]

Furthermore, the Republicans justified their extension of civil rights protection to vulnerable blacks through federal power because, in the Southern states, "the enormity of the crimes constantly perpetuated there finds no parallel in the history of the Republic in her darkest days."[20] But, as Representative William E. Arthur of Kentucky countered, federal hegemony had gone too far for Democrats to tolerate, however humanitarian the goals. Arthur argued that "under the pretext of protecting the people, the people are being enslaved; under the pretext of establishing order, liberty is being overthrown; under the pretext of securing the rights of the voter, the voter is disfranchised."[21] While such partisan exchanges caricatured the moral subject of the ongoing enforcement program, namely the domestic protection of citizens from gross intimidation and violence, the actual adjudication of enforcement cases in the federal courts of the South numbered 3,382 between 1870 and 1874. It is no coincidence that 90 percent of the total number of convictions for violations against these Enforcement Acts were handed down in these same five years.[22] Such a meager number of convictions for untold numbers of maimings and deaths could have been viewed as a failure of the legislative avalanche of 1870–71, but as Eric Foner has correctively argued, "in terms of its larger purposes — restoring order, reinvigorating the morale of Southern Republicans, and enabling blacks to exercise their rights as citizens — the policy proved a success."[23]

During Reconstruction, the subjugation of the black race to white violence only escalated, though this "dynasty of knife and dagger" could not overcome the resistance of both black and white civil rights activists who demanded equal protection for freedmen. If federal domination succeeded in this egalitarian quest, then the former domination of master over slave would be nullified. Michel Foucault once reminded his students that the "insurrection of subjugated knowledges" spawned by political liberation movements of marginalized peoples (such as the movement for black civil rights) had given rise to another set of questions: "Is the relation of forces today still such as to allow these disinterred knowledges some kind of autonomous life? Can they be isolated by these means from every subjugating relationship? What force do they have in themselves?"[24] Foucault was seeking a loophole in Nietzsche's theorem that history was a continuous process of subjugation and rebellion, for that hypothesis meant that the human race "settles each one of its violences within a system of rules, and thus goes from domination to domination."[25] The ultimate knowledge, for Foucault a lifelong philosophical quest, amounted to imagining a way out of this endless repetition of violence through the advent of a "new form of right" liberated "from every subjugating relationship."[26]

Curiously, the 1871-72 *Leaves* struggled with this insurrectionary notion of liberation from domination, specifically in a cluster of poems that appeared in only this edition and was called "Songs of Insurrection." In a headnote to the original manuscript of these "Songs," Whitman wrote, "Not only are these States born offspring of Revolt against mere overweening authority — but seeing ahead for Them in the future a long, long reign of Peace with all the growths corruptions and tyrannies & formalisms of Obedience," the poet suggested "the ideas of the following cluster will always be needed, that it may be worth while to keep well up, & vital, such ideas and verses as the following (*WWW*, 229). In effect, Whitman, like Foucault, was attempting to imagine his way out of the struggles of power, contemporaneously in the battle between state sovereignty and federalism over interracial voting rights. In his textual production, Whitman came closest to surpassing the cycle of subjugation and revolt as the dialectic of history: within the syntax of his Reconstruction poems, Whitman enacted a model of the poet as the legislator of a kind of social solidarity America had not yet realized. Hence in 1871 Whitman accented the federalization of America, represented in the pastiche of mainly earlier "Insurrection" poems as well as in his project of a book of "democratic nationality."

In the only new poem in the insurrectionary cluster, "Still Though the One I Sing," such centralizing imagery had begun to cohere: "Still, though the one I sing, / (One, yet of contradictions made,) I dedicate to Nationality, / I leave him in Revolt, (O latent right of insurrection! O quenchless, indispensable fire!)" (*LG Var* III, 632). The incoherent "Nationality" uttered in this text had not sung its composition outside the Sisyphean struggle of domination succeeding domination, but its mode of delivery would arrive through the experience of "insurrection" on behalf of democratic liberty. Though originally an 1856 text that commemorated the failed European revolutions of 1848, "To a Foil'd European Revolutionaire" articulated the topical perdurance of the fight for liberty in the racial struggles of the postwar Union: "When liberty goes out of a place, it is not the

first to go, nor the second or third to go, / It waits for all the rest to go —
it is the last" (*LG Var* I, 251). Similarly, in another of these "Songs," called
"Europe, The 72nd and 73d Years of These States," Whitman's 1855 occasional poem also signifies its position as a Reconstruction text in its call in
the opening lines for the rescripting of hierarchical social relations:
"Suddenly, out of its stale and drowsy lair, the lair of slaves, / Like light-
ning it le'pt forth, half startled at itself, / Its feet upon the ashes and the
rags — its hands tight to the throats of kings" (*LG Var* I, 144). The liberation of subjugated persons (note: "slaves") from the "dynasty" of white
terrorism, for Whitman, could be deferred but not defeated: "Not the
grave of the murder'd for freedom, but grows seed for freedom, in its turn
to bear seed, / Which the winds carry afar and re-sow, and the rains and
the snows nourish" (*LG Var* I, 146). Effectively, in Whitman's Reconstruction project, the dissemination of the "seeds" of freedom is a historical
process not only in specific struggles but also in its discursive momentum
to overcome all setbacks to the democratization of liberty in any temporal
framework.

In 1871–72, the primary Union struggle for planting these libertarian
"seeds" was situated in the enforcement of black civil liberties. Whitman's
solidarity with freedom seekers had no boundaries: "Liberty! let others despair of you! I never despair of you" (*LG Var* I, 146). It was within the
boundaries of this quest for democratic freedom, then, that Whitman's famous dictum "Resist much, obey little," from another "Song" called "Walt
Whitman's Caution," had to be read. Resistance in the fight for liberty was
uppermost in the struggle for legislative protections against Klanism, too,
as veteran abolitionist Charles Sumner cried in Congress on 13 April 1872,
"Imperialism! Give me the centralism of Liberty! Give me the imperialism
of Equal Rights!"[27] Though still inscribed in Nietzsche's subjugation and
revolt model of history, the "insurrection" of equal rights for black Americans in the 1860s and 1870s still brought to light a hidden "knowledge"
that would not go away but rather had been manifested in the ongoing
demands for full "privileges and immunities" for blacks as American subjects. In the same way, Whitman's "Songs of Insurrection" sang within the
new federal "domination" that succeeded the older "domination" of slavery, for blacks had elected to remain inside the national household, as subjects of the United States, and Radical Republicans furnished their part in
legislating for an interracial democracy.

Whitman's construction of his book of "democratic nationality" took
coherent form in the first annex to the 1871–72 *Leaves, Passage to India*,
which contained seventy-five poems, mostly lifted from earlier editions,
with only twenty-three new texts.[28] The poet's centralizing imagery took
on added urgency just as the legislative workshop achieved its hegemony in
the juridical forum, though the federalization of civil liberties would lapse

for almost a century. Nevertheless, Whitman's jettisoning of former American representations that foregrounded the autonomous sovereignty of the individual in favor of a "composite" representation of federalized identity finds compelling referents in the annex's two central metaphors: voyaging ships and death. Mutlu Konuk Blasing has suggested that one of the major strategies in poetic representation is the metonymic trope, which "is a strategy of reducing the intangible to the tangible, the immaterial to material proofs, manifestations, signs."[29] This metonymic trope is expressed in allegorical texts, which "reduce" the vaporous nature of intangible language, by anchoring the transcendent in material events. As a theoretical strategy, this metonymic trope constitutes the historical nexus from which to read Whitman's two "intangible" concerns (voyaging and death) in his constitution of "democratic nationality." The title page combined these two images in its inscription: "Gliding o'r all, through all, / Through Nature, Time, and Space, / As a Ship on the waters advancing, / The Voyage of the Soul — not Life alone, / Death — many Deaths, I sing." Whitman's willingness to abandon the shoreline, evident in the *Passage* cluster called "Sea-Shore Memories," opened a new thematic preoccupation for a poet who had always stood on the shore. As Gay Wilson Allen has pointed out, "Heretofore, and especially in the great emotional poems of 1860, his imagination always returned to the seashore, where the fierce old mother incessantly moaned, whenever he was deeply moved by an experience or memory." However, Allen continues, "we find the poet venturing beyond the shore, even embarking on ships and vicariously sailing the oceans."[30]

Such a departure pointed to Whitman's willingness to discard older methods of self-understanding and, implicitly, to suggest that his book of "democratic nationality," as well as the "Ship of State," had to unmoor America from its resistance to centralization in its self-representation. Of course, the most recognizable image of the "Ship of State" had been published in the popular 1865–66 text "O Captain! My Captain!," which Whitman reprinted in *Passage to India* in the cluster called "President Lincoln's Burial Hymn": "The ship is anchor'd safe and sound, its voyage closed and done; / From the fearful trip the victor ship comes in with object won" (*LG Var* II, 541). Since the Union ship was rudderless without the federal implementation of equal rights, Whitman's model of "Radical Democracy" assimilates such centralizing demands for liberty in its poetic lines and clusters. In addition, the "Deaths" that Whitman was singing in *Passage* had less to do with the war dead or with the philosophical dimensions of finitude; rather, Whitman's *Passage* reinforces the growing nationalist ideology in the land by linking "death" to the dissolution of decentralized government, outmoded social relations, and interracial rivalries. Undeniably, Whitman's infatuation with death reaches new heights in his Reconstruction project, at the time when Civil War deaths were being mythologized as the "nutrient" for a reinvigorated Union. The temporal dimension of "death" as the passageway to the unwritten future was conducive to the general atmosphere of postwar representations of newer social relations founded on nationality and democratic citizenship. In the 1871 *Passage* text "Proud Music of the Storm," Whitman constructs the poet's role as the legislator of innovative songs that surpass all former musical compositions in their free embrace of the dissolution of the reified past in favor of the reconstructive energies of the future: "But, too a new rhythmus fitted for thee, / Poems, bridging the way from Life to Death, vaguely wafted in night air, / Which, let us go forth in the bold day and write" (*LG Var* III, 582). Such a dissolving of the crippled inheritance of the political past, in its liberation of democratic impulses for equal rights, signaled the desire to set out on the "open road" of reconstructing America.

The title poem, "Passage to India," opens with an encomium to three technological breakthroughs of the nineteenth century: the laying of the first transatlantic cable in 1866, the opening of the Suez Canal in 1869, and the joining of the Union Pacific and Central Pacific railroads at Promontory Point, Utah, in 1869. These historical events motivate the poet to declare that "Our modern wonders, (the antique ponderous Seven outvied,) / In the Old World, the east, the Suez canal, / The New by its mighty railroad spann'd, / The seas inlaid with eloquent, gentle wires," showed the evolutionary nature of human development; "For what is the present, after all, but a growth out of the past?" (*LG Var* III, 563–64). In the "deep diving bibles and legends" of past cultures, the text locates the global communication that would link all the continents for the first time: "Lo, soul! seest thou not God's purpose from the first? / The earth to be spann'd, connected by net-work, / The people to become brothers and sisters, / The races, neighbors, to marry and be given in marriage, / The oceans to be cross'd, the distant brought near" (*LG Var* III, 565). Such an assimilationist reading of interracial relations, through communication and social solidarity, must have sounded awfully jarring to the ears of unreconstructed readers. And yet, Whitman is suggestively imagining an evolutionary pathway toward what Foucault called a "new kind of right," in this case interracial equality, to represent what reconstructed American racial relations might look like. As the poem makes clear, the representative poet embodies this centralizing tendency to weld together competing cultures: "After the great captains and engineers have accomplish'd their work, / After the noble inventors — after the scientists . . . / Finally shall come the Poet, worthy that name; / The true Son of God shall come, singing his songs" (*LG Var* III, 568).

Thus the text of "Passage to India" turned out not to be primarily about technology at all or about the transhistorical dimensions of the godhead; rather, this major text argued that the poet represents the cosmopolitan legislator of social solidarity. For such a legislative poet would succeed in the following federative tasks: "All affection shall be fully responded to — the secret shall be told; / All these separations and gaps shall be taken up, and hook'd and link'd together; . . . /[and] shall be gloriously accomplish'd and compacted by the true Son of God, the poet" (*LG Var* III, 568). The poem then excavates its way through an archaeology of the evolutionary progress of civilization from ancient India to Columbus's discovery of the New World. Columbus, "the chief histrion," had awakened the demise of the "sunset splendor of chivalry" in his discovery of the continent that would give rise to America, the birthplace of revolutionary democracy. Though Columbus had set out to discover the Orient through a westward passage, it was not until Whitman's day that technology had spanned the globe, and thus Whitman's speaker can read these modern events retrospectively to Columbus's dream: "(Curious, in time, I stand, noting the efforts of heroes; / Is the deferment long? bitter the slander, poverty, death? / Lies the seed unreek'd for centuries in the ground? / Lo! to God's due occasion, / Uprising in the night, it sprouts, blooms . . .)" (*LG Var* III, 570).

Significantly, the "Passage to India" text has landed on the shores of America, not the shores of India. As the prototype of the Western migration to the New World, Columbus indeed represented the "chief histrion," inaugurating the historical narrative that would culminate in Whitman's dream of a reconstructed America. Like Columbus, the text itself has landed in America, and the "passage to India" has been diverted through the transcontinental passage across the continent to the Pacific shoreline. On 11 May 1869, the day after the transcontinental railroad had been finished, the *New York Evening Post* reporter covering the beat declared: "This is the way to India, telegraphed the directors of the Pacific Railroad, yesterday . . . . But, give us only half a century of peace and freedom . . . and we shall not cry out, This is the way to India; we shall stick up on our shores the sign, This is India."[31] Likewise, the subject of Whitman's passage surrendered to a passage to more than India because his destination turned out to be America ("This is India"), the site of the culmination of historical experiments in democracy, though not yet realized "democratic nationality." Therefore, the poet had to set out on a westward trek across the continental United States, already connected to global linkages through technology but not in fact: "Passage to more than India! . . . / Of you, woods and fields! Of you, strong mountains of my land! / Of you, O prairies! Of you, gray rocks! . . . / O day and night, passage to you!" (*LG Var* III, 573).

After such a continental passage, the social solidarity of Whitman's Reconstruction project would be accomplished through the departure of the

"Ship of State" from the "shores" of racism and sectionalism: "Away, O soul! hoist instantly the anchor! / Cut the hawsers — haul out — shake every sail! / Have we not stood here like trees in the ground long enough?" (*LG Var* III, 574). Only by cutting the "hawsers" of localized comradeship in favor of national self-understanding, in allegorical terms, would the nation cross the "deep waters" of assimilation of black Americans into the Union, "For we are bound where mariner has not yet dared to go, / And we will risk the ship, ourselves and all" (*LG Var* III, 574). Syntactically, Whitman has collapsed the plural "ourselves" into the singular "all." Betsy Erkkila has argued that Whitman's departure from the "shore" was simply "a push away from American democracy . . . . Like the ancient fables he describes in 'Passage,' he, too came to spurn and elude the 'hold of the known' in order to climb out of time and history and ascend to heaven."[32] On the contrary, Whitman's plunge into the uncharted waters of the reconstructed future represented his willingness to risk the legislative movement toward a centralized, interracial democracy that was under way (with much resistance) in the 1870s. The freedom of "farther, farther, farther" sailing within history, not outside of history, would validate or invalidate the construction of "democratic nationality."

As a nation-building text, the *Passage to India* volume returns again and again to the cultural work of the reinforcement of voluntary consent to march down the "open road" of the future. The *Passage* poem "O Living Always — Always Dying" voices this necessity of releasing the dead weight of the past in order to continually construct a freer future: "O me, what I was for years, now dead, (I lament not — I am content;) / O to disengage myself from those corpses of me, which I turn and look at, where I cast them! / To pass on, (O living! always living!) and leave the corpses behind!" (*LG Var* II, 396). As an allegorical text, this can be read to mean that the "corpses" of racism and state sovereignty had to be buried to avoid the shipwrecks recalled by the poet at a social gathering in "Thought (As I Sit . . .)," which trigger the same cultural resonance of a wrecked "Ship of State," "Sinking there, while the passionless wet flows on— . . . / Are Souls drown'd and destroyed so? / Is only matter triumphant?" (*LG Var* II, 428). The innovative cluster that made its debut in *Passage*, "Whispers of Heavenly Death," forecloses the possibility that such a national "shipwreck" would dash the democratic future of the United States. Despite the "measureless waters of human tears" in the title poem, the poet projects a resurrection of the national "Soul" in the dimness of the present: "(Some parturition, rather — some solemn, immortal birth: / On the frontiers, to eyes impenetrable, / Some Soul is passing over" (*LG Var* III, 583).

The "frontiers" of cooperative democracy may have been momentarily "impenetrable" through federal coercion, but such an intervention was simply the "parturition" of collaborative citizenship. The "waters" to be crossed may have been "measureless tears," but in grief over social divisions the Union could be reborn. In another new composition, "As I Watch'd the Ploughman Ploughing," the mournful task of sowing and reaping moves to an allegorical level of diction, suggesting that the nation needed to cast its lot with the future: "(Life, life is the tillage, and Death is the harvest according.)" (*LG Var* III, 587). Again, in the "Whispers" cluster, "Darest Thou Now, O Soul" articulates the uncertain but imperative passage into a consolidated national future: "Darest Thou now, O Soul, / Walk out with me toward the Unknown Region, / Where neither ground is for the feet, nor any path to follow?" (*LG Var* III, 584). Despite the unprecedented legislative push for centralization in social management as an emergency measure against further social deterioration, Whitman voices undeniable anxiety in this newly formed ideology, with "No map there, nor guide," where "all is a blank before us." But the "soul," which allegorizes the social solidarity of citizens, always situated beneath the surface "matter" of difference, pushes ahead in the poem until the "ties" of the past loosen: "Then we burst forth — we float, / In Time and Space, O Soul — prepared for them; / Equal, equipt at last—(Oh joy! O fruit of all!) them to fulfil O soul" (*LG Var* III, 584).

Again, in "The Last Invocation," the poet (as reconstructive cultural agent) sounds the call to move "From the walls of the powerful, fortress'd house" of the past in order to be "wafted" into the ameliorative future: "Let me glide noiselessly forth; / With the key of softness unlock the locks — with a whisper, / Set ope the doors, O Soul!" (*LG Var* III, 586). In another new composition, "A Noiseless, Patient Spider," Whitman casts the agency for social reform in the future. The "spider" represents a compelling emblem for the Reconstruction poet (and Congress) standing "isolated," casting forth "filament, filament, filament" into an unpromising future. Nevertheless, the text expresses the hope that the egalitarian "bridge you will need, be form'd" through the representational mission of "seeking the spheres to connect them" (*LG Var* III, 585). Only after the voluntary movement away from America's inherited self-understanding of ethnic-racial rivalry and a voluntary embrace of the federal hegemony of equalized civil rights would the postwar nation be able to bid "finale to the shore" of systematic social breakdown.

It is thus fitting that Whitman entitled his final *Passage* cluster "Now Finale to the Shore," wherein the poet enacts such a reconstructionist desire with radicalized daring that has not been seen in his impressive arsenal of publications to that date. In the title poem, the poet departs from the boundaries of self-identity in declaring a complete breakage with such attachments to the past: "Now finale to the shore! / Now, land and life, finale, and farewell! / Now Voyager depart! (much, much for thee is yet in store;)" (*LG Var* III, 608). After making many return voyages to the port of inherited social relations, the allegorical "Voyager" is metonymically called out to "obey thy cherish'd, secret wish, / Embrace thy friends — leave all in order; / To port, and hawser's tie, no more returning,/ Depart upon thy endless cruise, old Sailor!" (*LG Var* III, 608). Whitman explicitly endorses this federalizing intention in this last cluster of reconstructive poems, for when speaking of "what underlies the precedent songs — of my aims in them" in "Thought (As They draw ...)," the poet states that his purpose had been "To compact you, ye parted, diverse lives! / To put rapport the mountains, and rocks, and streams . . . / With you, O soul of man" (*LG Var* III, 609).

The rapprochement of "parted, diverse" citizens with the continental sprawl of the Union shows Whitman's "Radical Democracy" writ large in its capacity to hold multitudes. Furthermore, in "The Untold Want," this desire to "compact" social divisions through voluntary agreement rather than through involuntary squeezing becomes a national mandate in the reconstructed future if read as an allegorical text in the unreconstructed present: "The untold want, by life and land ne'r granted, / Now, Voyager, sail thou forth, to seek and find" (*LG Var* III, 610). The cultural work of such imperatives to follow through on the promises of Reconstruction reaches its joyous culmination in the final poem of the *Passage* annex, "Joy, Shipmate, Joy!": "Joy! shipmate — joy! / (Pleas'd to my Soul at death I cry;) / Our life is closed — our life begins; / The long, long anchorage we leave, / The ship is clear at last — she leaps! / She swiftly courses from the shore; / Joy! shipmate — joy!" (*LG Var* III 611).

The second annex appended to the 1871–72 *Leaves of Grass* extends Whitman's construction of his book of "democratic nationality" in its celebration of the technological ingenuity of American industry. "After All, Not to Create Only" (later "Song of the Exposition") was recited by Whitman himself at the fortieth annual exhibition of the American Institute in New York on 7 September 1871 and was printed in Boston by Roberts Brothers. The text provides a kind of coda to "Passage to India" in that Columbus's abrupt landing in 1492 on the shores of America had provided the opportunity for the "muse" of invention to import the cultural products of the Old World and imprint them with native genius: "After all, not to create only, or found only, / But to bring, perhaps, from afar, what is already founded, / To give it our own identity, average, limitless, free" (*LG Var* III, 612). The nativist poet invites the "muse" to "migrate from Greece and Ionia" and elsewhere to America, "a better, fresher, busier sphere where a wide, untried domain awaits, demands you" (*LG Var* III, 613).

The inspirational force of westward evolutionary expansion, from the Old World to the New, makes a space for the poetic function of text-making in an unlikely place: "By thud of machinery and shrill steam-whistle undismay'd, / Bluff'd not a bit by drain-pipe, gasometers, artificial fertilizers, / Smiled and pleased, with palpable intent to stay, / She's here, install'd amid the kitchen ware!" (*LG Var* III, 615). The legislative American poet welcomes the "muse" of inspiration "in liberty's name" and extols the energetic laborers and materials of American industry as worthy subjects of representation: "Here shall you trace in flowing operation, / In every state of practical, busy movement, / The rills of civilization. // Materials here, under your eye, shall change their shape, as if by magic" (*LG Var* III, 617).

By 1871 Whitman represented such industrial products as agents of rehabilitation from the trauma of the revolutions of the cultural vertigo induced by the Civil War. Hence the poet intervenes in his catalogue of economic productivity to dispel the war past with no qualification: "Away with themes of war! away with War itself! / Hence from my shuddering sight, to never more return, that show of blacken'd mutilated corpses! / That hell unpent, and raid of blood — fit for wild tigers, or for loptongued wolves — not reasoning men" (*LG Var* III, 619). Turning away from the "blacken'd mutilated corpses" of the past, Whitman's cultural poetics underscore the centralized energies released in the nation through Reconstruction legislation: "And thou, high-towering One — America! / Thy swarm of offspring towering high — yet higher Thee, above all towering, / With Victory on thy left, and at thy right hand Law; / Thou Union, holding all — fusing absorbing, tolerating all" (*LG Var* III, 621).

The Union ideology, which had reached a legislative zenith shortly before Whitman recited this text at the American Institute, receives an allegorical encomium that transmits the same hegemonic zeal voiced in the halls of Congress: "All thine, O sacred Union! / Ship, farm, shop, barns, factories, mines, City and State — North, South, item and aggregate, / We dedicate, dread Mother, all to thee!" (*LG Var* III, 623). This elaboration of a foundational Union, which precedes all other constructs of identity, has been undeniably ratified as "Protectress absolute, thou! Bulwark of all! / For well we know that while thou givest each and all, (generous as God,) / Without thee, neither all nor each, nor land, home, / . . . nor any here this day secure, / Nor aught, nor any day secure" (*LG Var* III, 623). In the closing section of this federalizing text, Whitman chooses to focus on the flag as the visible emblem of this imperial Union — "None separate from Thee — henceforth one only, we and Thou" and the "measureless wealth" of the industrial exhibition constitutes only a byproduct of the federalized identity that was under construction in 1871: "Think not our chant, our show, merely for products gross, or lucre — it is for Thee, the Soul, electric, spiritual! / Our farms, inventions, crops, we own in Thee! Cities and States in Thee! / Our freedom in Thee!" (*LG Var* III, 624).

Once again, Whitman is stylistically enacting his centralizing strategy by the movement from the plural ("Our freedom") to the singular ("Thee"). As the newly self-appointed arbiter of civil liberties, this "Protectress" represents radical Reconstruction with a metonymic enthusiasm that has hardly been noticed by either Whitman's readers or critics. Perhaps the strange critical silence surrounding this fifth edition of *Leaves*, when it appeared, can be read as a symptom of Whitman's egalitarian position against the "majority." Indeed, Whitman qualifies as an "unacknowledged legislator" of the world of Reconstruction society. Most Americans were not ready to admit that the dismemberment of "domestic" security in the Enforcement Acts, through federal surveillance in a time of civil crisis, could be justified by the establishment of interracial fraternity.

The third installment of Whitman's book of "democratic nationality," *As a Strong Bird on Pinions Free and Other Poems*, was published as a separate pamphlet in Washington, D.C. in 1872. This booklet contained seven new poems as well as the 1872 preface and had an unbridled federal rhetoric that was never surpassed in Whitman's poetic output. The title poem, later called "Thou Mother with Thy Equal Brood," was delivered at the 1872 commencement exercises at Dartmouth College, and Whitman thought enough of the piece to publish it almost immediately as the centerpiece of this small pamphlet of shorter works. Whitman enlisted his already impressive arsenal of centralized imagery in the projection of a cohesive nation in the first poem, "One Song, America, Before I Go," which he dedicates "For thee — the Future": "I'd sow a seed for thee of endless Nationality; / I'd fashion thy Ensemble, including Body and Soul; I'd show, away ahead, thy real Union, and how it may be accomplish'd" (*LG Var* III, 633). The accent on the "Future" accomplishment of his "endless nationality" suggests an implicit repugnance to the contemporary resistance to "Ensemble" identity, as manifested by the systematic violence of Klanism, and leads Whitman to declare: "(The paths to the House I seek to make, / But leave to those to come, the House itself.)" (*LG Var* III, 633).

In the poem "As a Strong Bird," the cultural work of federalizing the self-representation of America takes on its most transcendental form. The poet of "endless Nationality" registered his anxiety over the uncertain future ["How can I pierce the impenetrable blank of the future?" (*LG Var* III, 638"] but appropriates to his own poetic rhetoric the representation of the kind of federated union that had hardly begun to cohere in 1871-72: "(Thy soaring course thee formulating, not in thy two great wars, nor in thy century's visible growth, / But far more in these leaves and chants, thy chants, great Mother!)" (*LG Var* III, 639).

Thus the poet becomes the legislator of a "Land tolerating all, accepting all," in a manner analogous to the legislative outpouring of the Enforcement Acts, which handed over the surveillance of civil rights from the state to the federal government: "(Lo, where rise three peerless stars, / To be thy natal stars my country, Ensemble, Evolution, Freedom, / Set in the sky of Law.)" (*LG Var* III, 640). But Whitman also forecasts a rough passage for the voluntary self-understanding of an interracial democracy, for the "storm shall dash thy face, the murk of war and worse than war shall cover thee all over, / (Wert capable of war, its tugs and trials? be capable of peace, its trials, / For the tug and mortal strain of nations come at last in prosperous peace, not war;)" (*LG Var* III, 640). Whitman's voluntary surrender to a consolidated future has turned full circle despite the peacetime resistance to national identity (based on equal rights) by the majority, for the resistance itself produced the vehement demands by blacks and radicals for full inclusion of blacks as progeny of the "Mother" Union's household.

Whitman's book of "democratic nationality" was not complete, for he had merely constructed the "paths" to the reconstructed "House" of the future, but these texts intervened in a time of national emergency, when social solidarity had deteriorated on the racial divide to its lowest ebb since the war. The plural "paths" had not found their termination at the doorstep of the singular "House." The "mystical Union" that Whitman projected in "As a Strong Bird" lay down the "open road" of greater action on behalf of subjugated races, but Whitman had pointed the way for the Second Reconstruction of the 1950s and 1960s: "The present holds thee not — for such vast growth as thine, / For such unparallel'd flight as thine, such brood as thine, / The FUTURE only holds thee and can hold thee" (*LG Var* III, 641). It was surely no accident that the federative poet chose Washington, D.C., as the locale of the last poem in this pamphlet, which announced his book of "democratic nationality." In "By Broad Potomac's Shore," Whitman invokes with a liturgical fervor the capitol's benediction: "Perfume this book of mine O blood-red roses! / Lave subtly with your waters every line Potomac!" (*LG Var* III, 649). The pluralized "waters" of social antagonism had not flowed into the singular "Potomac" except through "every line" of Whitman's poems, washed in the "blood-red" perfume of egalitarian democracy.

Notes

1   Eric Foner, *Reconstruction*, 437.

2   Gay Wilson Allen, *The Solitary Singer: A Critical Biography of Walt Whitman* (rev. ed., Chicago: U of Chicago P, 1967) 430. For the finest biographical treatment of Whitman's life during the publication of the 1871–72 *Leaves of Grass*, the annexes *Passage to India* and *After All, Not the Create Only*, and the 1872 pamphlet *As a Strong Bird on Pinions Free and Other Poems*, see chapter 9, "Ships at Sea," 378–448.

3   Allen, *The New Walt Whitman Handbook* (New York: New York U P, Rev. ed., 1986) 132–41.

4   Allen, *Handbook*, 139.

5   Allen, *Handbook*, 133–34.

6   Betsy Erkkila, *Whitman: The Political Poet* (New York: Oxford U P, 1989) 196.

7   On 25 May 1870 the Senate passed the First Enforcement Act by a vote of 48 to 11; on 27 May 1870 the House passed the bill by a vote of 133 to 58. The text of the bill can be found in *Statutes at Large*, volume 16, 140–46. The respective congressional votes can be found in the *Congressional Globe*, 41st Congress, 2nd Session (25 May 1870), 3809; and (27 May 1870), 3884.

8   *Congressional Globe*, 41st Congress, 2nd Session (1870), 3566.

9   *Congressional Globe*, 41st Congress, 2nd Session (1870), 3613.

10 *Congressional Globe*, 41st Congress, 2nd Session (1870), 3668–69.

11 *Congressional Globe*, 41st Congress, 2nd Session, (1870), 3881.

12 *Congressional Globe*, 41st Congress, 2nd Session (1870), 3607–9.

13 The Second Enforcement Act was introduced in the *Congressional Globe*, 41st Congress, 3rd Session (1870–71), 9 January 1871. The full text of the Second Enforcement Act appears in *Statutes at Large*, volume 16, 433–40.

14 Everette Swinney, *Suppressing the Ku Klux Klan: The Enforcement of the Reconstruction Amendments, 1870–77* (New York: Garland, 1987) 118.

15 Swinney, 118.

16 Ibid., 118.

17 Ibid., 162.

18 *Congressional Globe*, 42nd Congress, 1st Session (1871), 336.

[19] *Congressional Globe*, 42nd Congress, 1st Session (1871), Appendix 195 (20 March 1871).

[20] *Congressional Globe*, 42nd Congress, 1st Session (1871), 393.

[21] *Congressional Globe*, 42nd Congress, 1st Session (1871), 364.

[22] Swinney, 317.

[23] Foner, 458.

[24] Michel Foucault, "Course of January 7, 1976," in *Power/Knowledge: Selected Interviews and Other Writings, 1972–1977*, ed. Colin Gordon (New York: Pantheon, 1980) 78–79.

[25] Foucault, "Nietzsche, Genealogy, and History" *in Language, Counter-Memory, Practice*, trans. Donald F. Bouchard and Sherry Simon (Ithaca, NY) 150–51.

[26] Foucault "Course of January 14, 1976" in *Power/Knowledge: Selected Interviews and Other Writings*, 1972–1977, ed. Colin Gordon (New York: Pantheon, 1980) 108.

[27] *Congressional Globe*, 42nd Congress, 1st Session (1871), 651.

[28] The new texts introduced in the 1871 *Passage to India* volume for the first time are the following: "Passage to India," "Proud Music of the Storm," "This Dust Was Once a Man," "Whispers of Heavenly Death," "Darest Thou Now O Soul," "A Noiseless Patient Spider," "The last Invocation," "As I Watch'd the Ploughman Ploughing," "Pensive and Faltering," "On the Beach, At Night," "The Return of the Heroes," "The Singer in the Prison," "Warble for Lilac Time," "Sparkles from the Wheel," "Brother of All, With Generous Hand (Outlines for a Tomb)," "Gods," "Lessons," "Now Finale to the Shore," "Thought (As they draw to a close...)," "The Untold Want," "Portals," "These Carols," and "Joy, Shipmate, Joy!."

[29] Mutlu Konuk Blasing, *American Poetry: The Rhetoric of Its Forms* (New Haven: Yale U P, 1987) 4,6.

[30] Allen, *Handbook*, 133.

[31] *New York Evening Post*, 11 May 1869, 2. Cited in Erkkila, 266.

[32] Erkkila, 273.

4
"The cold and bloodless electrotype plates of History"

The 1876 Centennial Edition of
Leaves of Grass and *Two Rivulets,*
or How the Real War Got into the Books

O N 31 DECEMBER 1875, the New Year's Eve edition of the *New York Evening Post* trumpeted that "the great work of the century is finished." In 1865, so the *Post* declared, "the old and dangerous subject" of slavery had died, and "not until now have the questions which grew out of slavery been fully and finally settled; not until now have the echoes of the war died out of our politics and our lives."[1] The legacy of emancipation had wearied the majority of white Americans past patience, and the country eagerly embraced the centennial festivities as a distraction from the racial hatred that continued to erupt into violence everywhere, irritating the ears of patriotic revelers with the "echoes of the war" despite their willed optimism. On the Fourth of July 1876, the town of Hamburg, South Carolina, became the site of the bloody massacre of a black militia on parade, committed by whites who were fed up with public displays of black Reconstruction solidarity.[2] The Hamburg Massacre shared space in the nation's newspapers with the reports of Richard Henry Lee's reading of an original copy of the Declaration of Independence near Independence Hall in Philadelphia to a cheering crowd of five thousand spectators. It was clearly not the end of the presence of the "old and dangerous subject" of ex-slaves in the "lives" of Americans, though there had been decisive setbacks to black civil rights in the "politics" of Reconstruction's legislative retreat from interracial cooperation.

The Civil Rights Bill of 1875 had been signed into law by President Ulysses S. Grant on 1 March 1875, in theory guaranteeing blacks free access to public transportation and accommodations; but this last major legislative act by Radical Republicans to bring blacks closer to cultural equality was virtually stillborn on delivery, was rarely enforced, and was vilified in the Northern and Southern press.[3] In addition, the 1876 Supreme Court struck down key provisions of the 1870–71 Enforcement Acts, arguing that the Fourteenth and Fifteenth amendments applied to states' racist policies but not to individuals' racist attitudes and actions. Disgruntled whites found myriad means to circumvent federalist pressures toward integration at every turn, and Jim Crow's strange career would only grow more routine with the passing decades.

What Walt Whitman would call "the cold and bloodless electrotype plates of History" (*MDW*, 65), an image of the subjection of marginalized experience to the domination of official representations of memory, seemed destined to inter the radical rhetoric of black civil rights after most white Americans sought to anesthetize Civil War memories through accommodation to the status quo. Millions of Americans had more pressing patriotic matters to attend to, such as the ten million (one-fifth of the population of the United States) who trooped through the International Centennial Exhibition from 10 May to 19 October 1876 on its 450-acre expanse in Philadelphia's Fairmount Park.[4] One of those millions was Whitman. Though he was always enthralled with public manifestations of American ingenuity, he traveled to the Exhibition only once and, quite surprisingly, seemed not to appreciate the fairground as much as the ferry ride back home to Camden, New Jersey (*PW* I, 203–4). Gay Wilson Allen has speculated that Whitman's lackadaisical attitude toward the Centennial Exhibition may have resulted either from his not being chosen as the official poet for the fair (an honor that went to Bayard Taylor) or from his paralysis, which had made him less agile since his stroke in 1874.[5]

In any case, Whitman did make an extraordinary contribution to the nation's Centennial through his publication of the 1876 "Author's Edition" (or in one case, "Centennial Edition") of his works, composed of *Leaves of Grass* (a reissue of the fifth, 1871–72 edition) and the companion volume *Two Rivulets*.[6] Though there were only five short poems added to the previous Leaves, the *Two Rivulets* volume marked a unique moment in Whitman's Reconstruction project and has been relegated to the dungeon of footnotes in Whitman studies ever since. Undeniably, Whitman himself had contributed to its lukewarm reception by declaring in the 1876 preface his frustrated desire to "compose a further equally needed Volume" in addition to *Leaves*, "based on those convictions of perpetuity and conservation" that would "make the unseen Soul govern absolutely at last . . . . But the full construction of such a work (even if I lay the foundation, or give impetus to it) is beyond my powers, and must remain for some bard in the future" (*PW* II, 466). But Whitman made a significant qualification to this deprecation, which nullifies much of his assertion of incapacity. The representative poet refused "entirely to give the go-by to my original plan, and far more to avoid a mark'd hiatus in it, than to entirely fulfill it." He asserted, "I end my books with thoughts . . . on Death, Immortality, and a free entrance into the Spiritual World" (*PW* II, 467). Whitman's 1876 compilation of his prose and poetry, in short, accomplished far more than his unsteady intention, for the "Soul" of a reconstructed America, "immortal" in its capacity for continual shedding of the "dead" weight of past errors and in its reinvention of American representations, radiated throughout *Two Rivulets*.

Contrary to the critical impression of its unimportance, *Two Rivulets* gathered together all of Whitman's discrete Reconstruction projects between two covers (*Democratic Vistas, Centennial Songs—1876, As a Strong Bird on Pinions Free, Memoranda During the War*, and *Passage to India*) as well as a new prose preface and a strange cluster of poetry and prose called *Two Rivulets*, printed respectively on the top half and bottom half of the same pages so as literally to resemble two rivulets of discourse. Just as radical Reconstruction was breaking apart into a surrender to the forces of racist violence and segregation, Whitman issued his summa of reconstructive poetics, dominated by images of a radical democracy that dismantled discrimination in all its forms and of a nationality that promoted the change from localized comrades' social barriers to the federalized identity of cooperative citizens. Though *Two Rivulets* has been dismissed as a "contrived assemblage"[7] of autonomous texts with "centrifugal impulses, held together not organically from within but by binding from without,"[8] the poet's effort to construct a book of "democratic nationality," announced in the 1872 preface, had arrived for the Centennial. Critical dismissals do not account for its singularity (*Two Rivulets* was not published again) or for its reconstructive density (never again were Whitman's major Reconstruction texts represented in such a federation).

In *Two Rivulets* Whitman had published a centripetal representation of the unifying strategies of social solidarity he had imagined from 1871 to 1876, texts that projected the second century of the United States as an era of desire for cooperation between ethnic and racial factions rather than as a repetition of the violence and revolt against subjugation that had marked the first. Though such collaborative social relations were not to find their historical analogue in Whitman's textual performance of comradeship with strangers, the rediscovery of buried Reconstruction legislation from the 1860s and 1870s was to give rise to the Second Reconstruction legislation of the 1950s and 1960s, which was enlisted as a means toward what Whitman had only imagined in the 1876 text "In Former Songs": an America dedicated "To you, O FREEDOM, purport of all! / (You that elude me most — refusing to be caught in songs of mine,) / I offer all to you" (*LG Var* III, 672).

Whitman opened the *Two Rivulets* volume with the prose "Preface, 1876, to the two-volume Centennial Edition of L. of G. and 'Two Rivulets,'" in which the poet represents his centenary mission to the nation in terms of cultural poetics: "I have not hesitated to embody in, and run through the volume, two altogether distinct veins, or strata — politics for one, and for the other, the pensive thought of immortality" (*PW* II, 465). The cultural work that Whitman's two volumes was to perform in 1876 parses out as his "contribution and outpouring" for the Centennial of "New World nationality — and then as chyle and nutriment to that moral, indissoluble union, equally representing all, and the mother of many coming centennials" (*PW* II, 464). Thus the political impetus of Whitman's 1876 preface rose out of his conviction that "indissoluble union" between states and between citizens had to be ratified in the cooperative social relations that had always disintegrated into pitched battles between factions. The three points that Whitman had enlisted in his ideological projection of the future republic bore out his mission as the representative of a "Radical Democracy": first, the textual production of "superior literary, artistic and religious expressions, far more than in its republican forms, universal suffrage, and frequent elections, (though these are unspeakably important)"; second, the resolution of the ongoing battle between advocates of state autonomy and federal intrusion on states' rights, "with the indispensable necessity of centrality and Oneness — the national identity power — the sovereign Union, relentless, permanently comprising all, and over all, and in that never yielding an inch"; and third, the supersession of the current "morbid facts of American politics and society everywhere" through the promise of the open road of the future of the United States, of which "their first century, has been but preparation, adolescence — and that this Union is only now and henceforth, (i.e., since the secession war,) to enter on its full democratic career" (*PW* II, 467–68).

Whitman's invocation of the Civil War at the time of the Centennial Exhibition shows a surprising lack of political diplomacy, given the popular desire to forget the trauma of the 1860s. But the "strange, sad war revolving" turned out to be the raison d'être of his entire writing project. As he stated in a centenary footnote, "the whole book, indeed, revolves around that four years' war, which, as I was in the midst of it, becomes, in 'Drum-Taps,' pivotal to the rest entire" (*PW* II, 469). The upheaval of social relations that had ensued after the war, with the incorporation of black Americans through federal hegemony over their civil liberties, represents an unprecedented validation of the poet's desire for an extension of "this never-satisfied appetite for sympathy, and this boundless offering of sympathy — this universal democratic comradeship — this old, eternal, yet ever-new interchange of adhesiveness, so fitly emblematic of America" (*PW* II, 471). This desire for "democratic comradeship" finds its voice in the "political significance" of the "Calamus" cluster ("and more or less running through the book"), which performs the cultural work of representing "comradeship" with strangers beyond the boundaries of localized blood ties. Whitman's federalist project is clear: "In my opinion, it is by a fervent, accepted development of comradeship, the beautiful and sane affection of man for man, latent in all the young fellows, north and south, east and west," that would produce the "national identity power" that he had earlier invoked in *Democratic Vistas*, so that "the United States of the future, (I cannot too often repeat,) are to be most effectually welded together, intercalated, anneal'd into a living union" (*PW* II, 471).

Though such a federalizing impulse was undeniably always present in Whitman's work, the camaraderie he described had hardly begun to be manifested in the nation by 1876, and Whitman's assimilation of most of his postwar project into *Two Rivulets* demonstrates his determination to keep Reconstruction rolling. Indeed, by the Centennial much of the Radical Republicans' legislative legacy of equal rights for blacks had already begun to break apart. But the representative poet promotes the "national identity power" unleashed in his poetry and prose as a counterstatement to the recalcitrance of racial hatred: "I bequeath poems and essays as nutriment and influences to help truly assimilate and harden" the needed imaginative texts that would further the realization of "a compacted Nation" (*PW* II, 469). Invoking the plenitude of the open road of national comradeship, Whitman turns to the renovated future for validation, away from the fratricidal hatred that had terrorized the country for fifteen years: "I count with such absolute certainty on the great future of the United States — different from, though founded on, the past — that I have always invoked the future, and surrounded myself with it" (*PW* II, 469). Whitman insists that his representations are grounded in the historical events of his time but that even the war's unruly reverberations are only the inauguration of a fuller network of "universal democratic comradeship" among competing American cultures, and thereby "to enter upon their real history — the way being now, (i.e., since the result of the Secession War,) clear'd of death-threatening impedimenta, and the free areas around and ahead of us assured and certain" (*PW* II, 473).

Such an optimistic shedding of former confederate rivalries in favor of a fuller federative social cohesiveness had been billed as the object of the second strata of Whitman's *Two Rivulets*, namely death and immortality. "With cheerful face estimating death," Whitman had joined his texts together in a federative volume so that the rupture with outmoded social relations would only push his readers farther out into a democracy purged of ethnic hatred and the book could enter on its "immortal" voyage of "Comradeship": "For, in my opinion, it is no less than this idea of immortality, above all other ideas, that is to enter into, and vivify, and give crowning religious stamp, to democracy in the New World" (*PW* II, 466). The chattel economics of the slavocracy were an aberration in the evolutionary equality at work in American politics, and the shedding of this history of subjugation was only the first step toward "FREEDOM — purport of all!" sung in "former songs" of the first century of America.

After 1876 Whitman's representations foresaw another century that would dismantle the discriminatory heritage inherited from the past, "the past century being but preparations, trial voyages and experiments of the ship, before her starting out upon deep water" (*PW* II, 473). *Two Rivulets* was an intervention in the troubled social history of subjugation and revolt, in which the poet's texts sang of the "deep water" of a federation of "comradeship" with those outside the familiar neighborhoods of power. The *Two Rivulets* volume compressed between two covers the following books: *Democratic Vistas, Centennial Songs—1876, As a Strong Bird on Pinions Free, Memoranda During the War*, and *Passage to India*. In "The Beauty of the Ship," an 1876 poem that appeared only in the Centennial *Leaves of Grass*, Whitman's Reconstruction "Ship of State" manifests a tenacious hold on the fuller promise of "the national identity power" that the poet announced in the 1876 preface: "When, staunchly entering port, / After long ventures, hauling up, worn and old, / Batter'd by sea and wind, torn by many a fight, / With the original sails all gone, replaced or mended, / I only saw, at last, the beauty of the Ship" (*LG Var* III, 651). For the representative poet, the "original sails" of the Constitution could no longer provide the legislative matrix for an unreflective adherence to racial inequality.

When President Grant signed the Civil Rights Act of 1875 on 1 March, he ended the legislative wrangling that John Hope Franklin has called one of the longest foregrounds to a bill in congressional history.[9] Senator Charles Sumner of Massachusetts had first introduced the bill on 13 May 1870 as a "supplementary" bill to the Civil Rights Act of 1866, reinforcing the legislative muscle of the Thirteenth Amendment. In Sumner's original version, the bill would have safeguarded blacks with federal protection to "equal rights in railroads, steamboats, public conveyances, hotels, licensed theatres, houses of public entertainment, and cemetery associations . . . also in jury duties, national and state."[10] As the capstone to an impressive legislative archive on behalf of black Americans' civil rights, the bill that Sumner envisioned marked the limit of federal intervention: "I know of nothing further to be done in the way of legislation for the security of equal rights in this Republic."[11]

Horrified legislators, aghast at the possibility of integration in schools, churches, and cemeteries in particular, left the bill to languish in the committee caucus rooms and hoped it would go away. President Grant did not display any favor toward the bill's audacious social agenda and therefore did not make the integrationist cause an executive priority. In the five intervening years, the bill was subject to labyrinthine analysis in successive debates in the halls of Congress and in the popular press. The intransigence of the bill's opponents indicated what was at work in its rhetoric: not simply a shifting of objective legal sanctions, such as the Thirteenth, Fourteenth, and Fifteenth Amendments had been, but rather a shift in the social relations that had remained largely segregated even after the legal inroads black Americans had made into the forum of public citizenship.

Bouts of illness between 1872 and 1874 prevented Sumner from an all-out rhetorical campaign for his integrationist bill; he died in March 1874. Largely as a tribute to his single-mindedness, the Senate passed the Civil Rights Bill in May 1874. The *Chicago Tribune* decided on 29 May 1874, "It is the dying struggle of Radicalism. Whom the gods destroy they first make mad." In the November 1874 elections, the House Republicans' two-thirds majority plummeted to a deficit of seventy votes, more than half of the House Republicans losing their races. Thus, when the lame-duck Second Session of the Forty-Third Congress reconvened in December 1874, Representative Benjamin Butler of Massachusetts appended the Civil Rights Act of 1875, shorn of its school integration clause, to an army appropriations measure, and the measure was passed by the House on 4 February by a vote of 162 to 100.[12] On 27 February the Senate adopted the measure by a vote of 38 to 26,[13] and Grant did not veto this controversial bill, which potentially would mandate the first forced integration of the races in American history.

The text of the Civil Rights Bill of 1875, titled "An act to protect all citizens in their civil and legal rights," contained a preface that was copied from the Democratic Party platform of 1872, much to the chagrin of embarrassed Democrats who voted against the measure: "Whereas, it is essential to just government we recognize the equality of all men before the law, and hold that it is the duty of government in its dealings with the people to mete out equal and exact justice to all, of whatever nativity, race, color, or persuasion."[14] In section 1, the new statute mandated integration of public transportation, public accommodations, public amusements, and jury duty (but not of burial sites or of public schools), "applicable alike to citizens of every race and color, regardless of any previous condition of servitude." Section 2 legislated that convictions obtained by those bringing suit for racial offenses would "be deemed guilty of a misdemeanor, and, upon conviction thereof, shall be fined not less than five hundred nor more than one thousand dollars, or shall be imprisoned not less than thirty days nor more than one year." Section 3 placed the enforcement of the statute under the exclusive purview of the federal courts, which were required to bring to trial "every person who shall violate the provisions of this act, and cause him to be arrested and imprisoned or bailed . . . for trial before such court of the United States." Section 4 prohibited discrimination against the selection of jurors "on account of race, color, or previous condition of servitude," and Section 5 placed the review of discrimination cases under the aegis of the Supreme Court.

However, this valedictory legislation in the decade of radical reform was openly mocked in its day,[15] was seldom enforced,[16] and was declared unconstitutional by the Supreme Court eight years later, on 15 October 1883, in the *Civil Rights Cases*.[17] In his majority opinion, ironically mandated by section 5 of the 1875 bill, Justice Joseph Bradley held that the Fourteenth Amendment only prohibited state interference in individual rights and that the Civil Rights Act of 1875 had erroneously tried to regulate private social relations, which were effectively outside the boundaries of Congressional authority. So sternly was this 1883 rebuttal to federal authority in civil rights upheld that not until the Civil Rights Act of 1964 would Congress restore the 1875 statute's integrationist provisions to the purview of the law.

During the 1876 Centennial year, the Supreme Court had already begun its judicial reversal of the radical Reconstruction legacy in two decisions that effectively emasculated the civil rights advances of 1865–75, including the Thirteenth, Fourteenth, and Fifteenth Amendments, the Enforcement Acts of 1870–71, and the Civil Rights Act of 1875. In *United States v. Cruikshank*,[18] the alleged white murderers of over one hundred blacks in the Colfax Massacre of 1873 were exonerated from violations of the First Enforcement Act of 1870, which forbade armed conspiracies against citizens in the exercise of civil rights. On 27 March 1876 the Court decided that the unrepentant whites were not subject to federal review, for the Fourteenth Amendment limited actions only by states and not by individuals. Therefore the defendants were remanded to the state courts for a decision in unreconstructed Southern courtrooms. In another influential reversal, the Supreme Court heard its first case testing the limits of the voting rights provisions of the Fifteenth Amendment. In *United States v. Reese*,[19] the Court decided on 27 March 1876 that a Kentucky electoral official was within his rights to refuse to register a black freedman's vote because the voter's poll tax had not been paid prior to the local election. In this decision for state sovereignty, the Court effectively returned the regulation of suffrage predominantly to state jurisdictions, exempted states from Congressional authority over suffrage rights and qualifications, and placed the legislators outside the boundaries of the electoral forum.

Responding to all these decisive legislative reversals of a decade of Radical Republican agitation on behalf of equal rights, it was with unusual gravity that Frederick Douglass addressed the 1876 Republican Party's presidential convention: "You say you have emancipated us. You have: and I thank you for it. You say you have enfranchised us. You have; and I thank you for it. But what is your emancipation? —what is your enfranchisement?" Douglass asked rhetorically, "What does it all amount to, if the black man, after having been made free by the letter of your law, is unable to exercise that freedom, and, having been freed from the slaveholder's lash, he is subject to the slaveholder's shot-gun?"[20] Such a rhetorical chal-

lenge to a largely hostile white culture performed the cultural work of re-
calling the ineradicable racism of Reconstruction America to the minds of
politicians and newspaper readers. *The New York Evening Post* of 15 June
1876 reported, "It is to be regretted that Frederick Douglass will not teach
the colored people the lesson of self-dependence, instead of always demanding for them fresh guarantees . . . of the rights which they must
largely maintain for themselves." Such rhetoric of self-reliance masked the
subtext of a massive resistance to racial integration, but it reflected the en-
trepreneurial thinking dominant in all sections of the country. In any case,
clearly the civil rights legislation of the previous decade, in its movement
toward what Whitman called "universal democratic comradeship," had
been delivered into an inhospitable social environment.

Whitman's paradigm of "universal democratic comradeship" becomes
most clearly enacted in his *Memoranda During the War* (1875–76),
wherein the poet performs his vision of the "national identity power" in
the inhospitable environment of the Civil War hospitals, camps, and battle-
fields. Much earlier, in 1863, Whitman had proposed to publisher James
Redpath a volume to be called *Memoranda of a Year*, which would contain
"something considerably beyond mere hospital sketches" and include
"memoranda of incidents, persons, places, sights, the past year (mostly
jotted down either on the spot or in the spirit of seeing or hearing what is
narrated)" (*Corr* I, 171). Redpath was not able to underwrite this pro-
spectus, but the poet did contribute several newspaper columns on his
firsthand experiences at the war front,[21] and he subsequently edited his war
notebooks to produce the self-financed *Memoranda* in 1875, of which not
more than a hundred bound copies seem to have been printed.[22] In his
Memoranda, Whitman presents himself ostentatiously as the icon of the
democratic "comrade" who reaches out beyond the borders of his circle of
friends to embrace between eighty thousand and a hundred thousand sick
and wounded soldiers (black as well as white) from all sections of the Union. As the representative "wound-dresser," Whitman intercalated two
portraits of himself at the opening of the book as well as a biographical précis of his life up to that point.[23]

The poet's network of comrade making represents the kind of performative gesture that would materialize, in a socially divided society, the
"national identity power" that his ministrations made real in the world of
social relations. Indeed, Whitman's *Memoranda* performs the cultural work
of a counterstatement to the rolling back of federalist surveillance over
democratic equal rights evident in Klanism and in the nonenforcement of
radical legislation: "Is there not, behind all, some vast average, sufficiently
divine, uniform and unswervable Purpose, in the development of America,
(may I not say divine purpose? only all is divine purpose,) which pursues its
own will, maybe unconscious of itself" (*MDW*, 66). This democratic

"average," which levels discrimination in favor of cooperative fellow feeling with strangers, constitutes the representative poet's mission in his recording of "the living heat and excitement" of the war years, before such federative actions were "getting ready to be cast into the cold and bloodless electrotype plates of History" (*MDW*, 65). Eight years later, when Whitman reedited most of the *Memoranda* material in his autobiography *Specimen Days*, he added the famous phrase "the real war will never get into the books" (*PW* I, 115). In fact the "real war" had gotten into the books through Whitman's performative embodiment of the "national identity power" in his daily hospital visits from 1862 to 1865. It had also been inscribed through the legislative texts of black civil inclusion, though the "bloodless" resistance of white "History" to such fruits of the war would make equal rights unrecoverable for almost a century.

Whitman's nondiscriminatory memoranda consistently refuse to justify the human toll of the war, and they do not pretend to be a totalized narrative of the conflict. Rather, the fratricidal violence unleashed on millions of citizens represents an aberration to the vision of "universal democratic comradeship" on which Whitman founded his whole literary project: "Future years will never know the black infernal background of countless minor scenes and interiors, (not the few great battles) of the Secession War; and it is best they should not" (*MDW*, 5). The poet's narrator ("I"), partly a fictional invention and partly autobiographical, turns instead to the vast network of hospitals around Washington, D.C., to situate the fraternal heart of the war: "I know not how it may have been, or may be, to others — to me the main interest of the war, I found, (and still, on recollection, find,) in those specimens [of the 'Common People'], and in the ambulance, the Hospital, and even the dead on the field" (*MDW*, 4). It is the wounded and diseased veterans of the armies that the narrator chooses as the conveyors of "the Personal Character and eligibility of These States," for the "marrow of the tragedy concentrated in those Hospitals," and indeed "it seem'd sometimes as if the whole interest of the land, North and South, was one vast central Hospital, and all the rest of the affair but flanges" (*MDW*, 4–5). Whitman's narrator has chosen the recuperative site of the medicinal places where Union energies were being bound up for a reconstructed Union, rather than the battlefield where there ruled "every lurid passion, the wolf's, the lion's lapping thirst for blood — passionate, boiling volcanoes of human revenge for comrades, brothers slain" (*MDW*, 36).

Thus Whitman's *Memoranda* serve as a countermemory to the official "electrotype" histories that focused their rhetorical strategies on the valor of the battlefield. Instead, Whitman proposes to write "the Untold and Unwritten History of the War" in the wounded and diseased who are "infinitely greater" than "the few scraps and distortions that are ever told or written" (*MDW*, 5–6). Even the dead "buried in the grave, in eternal darkness" fall within the boundaries of this narrative, and thus the narrator places the representational accent on the resistance to forgetting. Among the "fruits of the War," comradeship had been forged between strangers on such a vast scale that the "national identity power" had a chance to bring about such fraternal self-identification in the social relations of the future. In fact, Whitman's narrator dedicates the whole *Memoranda* project to the war dead with the closing utterance: "And now, to thought of these — on these graves of the dead of the War, as on an altar — to memory of these, or North or South, I close and dedicate my book" (*MDW*, 58).

By founding the act of cultural remembrance on those who were voiceless, Whitman's *Memoranda* articulates their reconstructive strategies on the absence of language, that is, on the part of those who could not speak in the grave. By implication, Whitman's voice also speaks for all others who were marginalized in the network of power relations. Thus these notebook memoranda form an insurrectionary counterstatement by reconstituting the voices of all the slain "comrades" and those deemed outside the roster of full citizenship "privileges and immunities," such as black Americans. Through widening the boundaries of social relations to include strangers, and even the "dead," Whitman's text points out that after the war, antebellum rivalries, local allegiances, and racial hatreds had been reconfigured in the "heat and excitement" of the war's traumas; and this "revisionist" past, while hardly "buried in the grave," had given legislative traces of "a new birth of freedom" that would be better reaped only after the "darkness" of Jim Crow, far into the twentieth century. Indeed, the "hospital" of postwar Reconstruction strategies constitute the historical site of Whitman's *Memoranda*, and the "convulsiveness" of the war itself ranks as a secondary character in its cultural work of recuperation.

As a plank in Whitman's representational strategy of nondiscrimination, the *Memoranda* narrator neutralizes the hierarchical distinctions among social strata and focuses instead on the rank and file who were not only casualties in battle but also casualties in historiographical memory's focus on leaders and officers. For instance, Whitman valorizes the obscure twenty-two-year-old Yankee sergeant who refused to surrender at Fort Steadman: "When I think of such things, all the vast and complicated events of the War on which History dwells and makes its volumes, fall indeed aside, and for the moment at any rate I see nothing but young Calvin Harlowe's figure in the night disdaining to surrender" (*MDW*, 46). Even the pecking order of the army hierarchy had to be reconfigured in the narrator's new patterns of social relations. In a section called "A New Army Organization Fit for America Needed," the narrator argues for overturning current military practices that were "adopted from Europe from the feudal institutes" and "not at all consonant with the United States, nor our people, nor our days," which called out for "democratic premises" (*MDW*, 31). If the kind of military ranking practiced in the army on soldiers resulted in such slaughter, then comradeship had lost its agency: "In the present struggle . . . probably three-fourths of the losses, men, lives &c., have been sheer superfluity, extravagance, waste" (*MDW*, 32).

Resisting subjugations that lead to violence, the narrator constructs a whole platoon of democratic comrades among the common soldiers, who connect with the stranger-narrator with an immediacy that solidifies the social bonds that would reconstruct the Union. For instance, Whitman's narrator signals such acts of social solidarity for "Marcus Small, Co. K, Seventh Maine — sick with dysentery and typhoid fever — pretty critical, too — I talk with him often — he thinks he will die — looks like it indeed." In order to relieve the stranger stranded among strangers, the poet's "I" serves as a bridge for him between the capitol and his home in Maine: "I write a letter for him home to East Livermore, Maine — I let him talk to me a little, but not much, advise him to keep very quiet — do most of the talking myself — stay quite a while with him as he holds on to my hand — talk to him in a cheering, but slow, low, and measured manner" (*MDW*, 17). Armed with writing paper, books, preserves, money, and even ice cream, the representative poet concentrates an unflagging devotion on this "universal democratic comradeship." Indeed, the descriptions of such ministrations multiply across the pages of these memoranda to provide most of the material for remembrance in reclaiming dozens of disposable lives for posterity, among them Charles Miller, bed No. 19, Company D, Fifty-Third Pennsylvania; Thomas Haley, Co. M, Fourth New York Cavalry; Thomas Lindly, First Pennsylvania Cavalry; Amer Moore, Second U.S. Artillery; Oscar F. Wilbur, Company G, One Hundred and Fifty-Fourth New York; Stewart G. Glover, Co. E, Fifth Wisconsin. By circulating among the living, the comrade-narrator rescued these national citizens from the fate of "thousands or tens of thousands, the significant word UNKNOWN" (*MDW*, 57).

But offering more than the gifts, the narrator positions himself inside a cultural text of reconstructive social solidarity, at the heart of these newly configured social relations: "In my visits to the Hospitals I found it was in the simple manner of Personal Presence, and emanating ordinary cheer and magnetism, that I succeeded and helped more than by medical nursing, or delicacies, or gifts of money" (*MDW*, 18). In the performance of solidifying bonds between strangers from every state in the Union, this federalizing narrator enables the reader to transcend even the sectional antagonism that had not died out by 1875 but rather had become more virulent in its racist practices: "I have myself, in my thought, deliberately come to unite the whole conflict, both sides, the South and North, really into One, and to view it as a struggle going on within One Identity," in order to give rise to "deeper harmony, freer and larger scope, completer homogeneousness and power" (*MDW*, 65). Refusing to discriminate even among Yankees and Rebels, in "Two Brothers, One South, One North" the poet brings his "Personal Presence" indiscriminately to both: "It was in the same battle both were hit. One was a strong Unionist, the other Secesh; both fought on their respective sides, both badly wounded, and both brought here after absence of four years. Each died for his cause" (*MDW*, 53).

In "Calhoun's Real Monument" the narrator overhears a Secesh soldier describing the monument to the adamantly proslavery John C. Calhoun that he had seen somewhere in the South. The Connecticut soldier-audience replies, "I have seen Calhoun's monument . . . . It is the desolated, ruined South; nearly the whole generation of young men between seventeen and fifty destroyed or maim'd." This representation of the postwar revolution in social relations refuted the legacy of slave economics: how "all the old families [are] used up — the rich impoverish'd, the plantations cover'd with weeds, the slaves unloos'd to become the masters, and the name of the Southerner blacken'd with every shame — all *that* is Calhoun's *real* monument" (*MDW*, 54). But another memorandum reminds readers that the desire to retain slavery had been too exclusively identified with the South, for "the North had at least been just as guilty, if not more guilty; and the East and West had" also: "*the Secession cause had numerically just as many sympathizers in the Free as in the Rebel States*" (*MDW*, 64). By locating the racist desire for subjugation in all sections of the nation, these memoranda provided a corrective utterance to those who exempted themselves from its odious traces. The "completer homogeneousness and power" of federalized social relations had to pass through the upheaval of destabilized social relations in both the North and the South.

In Whitman's *Memoranda*, the disruption of formerly settled patterns of citizenship represent one of the fruits of Union victory: "The War itself with the temper of society preceding it, can indeed be best described by that very word, *Convulsiveness*" (*MDW*, 59). The dislocation of social relations ensuing from the war had originated from the misdirected passions and interests of the "Slaveholders, the Calhounites, to carry the States' Rights portion of the Constitutional Compact to its farthest verge, and nationalize Slavery, or else disrupt the Union, and found a new Empire, with Slavery for its corner-stone" (*MDW*, 65). But because of its complicity, the North would have been defeated by these states' rights enthusiasts as well, for the extension of slavery had been supported by Yankees insofar as the "perfect equality of slavery with freedom was flauntingly preach'd in the North — nay, the superiority of slavery" (*MDW*, 64). Thus the turning of social relations topsy-turvy, in the grim but carnivalesque image of

"Calhoun's real monument," had rendered a rupture with states' rights hegemony and provided a reconstructive opportunity for formulating social relations anew. Ironically, the social disruption of the war had given rise to more than carnage, for the traumas had ratified the "national identity power" as no transformative event had before: "That our national-Democratic experiment, principle, and machinery, could triumphantly sustain such a shock, and that the Constitution could weather it, like a ship at storm, and come out of it as sound and whole as before, is by far the most signal proof yet of that experiment" (*MDW*, 65). The "soundness" of the Constitution does not contradict the accretion of the Civil War amendments but rather confirms the Constitution as a reconstructed agent for postwar social relations.

The vertiginous energies of pluralizing American democracy across ethnic and racial boundaries became a possibility for the Ship of State "at storm," although the racist impulses that had divided the antebellum nation had only deepened: "The Slavery contest is settled — and the War is over — yet do not those putrid conditions, too many of them, still exist? still result in diseases, fevers, wounds — not of War and Army Hospitals — but the wounds and diseases of peace?" (*MDW*, 64). In contrast, Whitman's narrator points the way to a cure for these "wounds and diseases" in his socializing with strangers in the hospitals of the nation's capitol. As the medicinal "wound-dresser," Whitman best articulates his transformative mission in the memorandum called "Soldiers and Talks": "I find men here from every State in the Union, without exception . . . . I now doubt whether one can get a fair idea of what this War practically is, or what genuine America is, and her character, without some such experience as this I am having" (*MDW*, 25). The war's disruption, in short, makes the pluralistic democracy of the future possible: "It is certain to me that the United States, by virtue of the Secession War and its results, and through them and them only, are now ready to enter, and must certainly enter, upon their genuine career in history," not as "torn and divided in their spinal requisites" but rather as "a great Homogeneous Nation" (*MDW*, 65). The federalizing tendency of national identity had still to endure "the confusion, chaos, and measureless degradation and insult of the present" conditions in the South, "viewed as a temporary, deserv'd punishment for their Slavery and Secession sins." Whitman's narrator thus authorizes the Radical Republican intervention as a needed but temporary measure in the voyage of the Union to true "comradeship." Indeed, the four-year conflict had justified such a federal intervention because of the "signal triumph of Nationalism" it brought about so that the open road of the future could inaugurate a history not "cold and bloodless" but rather "grandly developing, exfoliating, stretching through the future" (*MDW*, 66).

The reversal of the unfolding civil liberties for American blacks, however, gave Whitman's narrator pause: it was apparent that the "terrible and deeply complicated problem" of slavery in the nation's first century served only as a prelude to more racial unrest in the second: "But how if the mass of the blacks in freedom in the U.S. all through the ensuing century, should present a yet more terrible and more deeply complicated problem?" (*MDW*, 66). The stillborn delivery of the Civil Rights Act of 1875, coupled with the dismantling of the Enforcement Acts and Civil War amendments by the Supreme Court, were troubling precedents in the occlusion of Whitman's "universal democratic comradeship." Along with the widespread Klan terrorism and the growing consensus that segregation was the law of the land, the "great convulsive struggle for Unity" would reveal that the "real war" had gotten into the books only if America performed gestures of social solidarity like the Whitmanesque "I" of his *Memoranda*: "And fortunately, to-day, after the experiments and warnings of a hundred years, we can pause and consider and provide for these problems, under more propitious circumstances, and new and native lights, and precious even if costly experiences" in order to "now launch the United States fairly forth . . . on the seas and voyages of the Future" (*MDW*, 68).

In *Two Rivulets* Whitman prepared a cluster of poems called *Centennial Songs—1876*, which intervened in the "shipwreck" of the "national identity power" that had run ashore in the retreat from Reconstruction. Such an intervention attempts to project an image of social cohesiveness in all the texts: "Song of the Exposition" (formerly "After All, Not to Create Only"), "Song of the Redwood-Tree," "Song of the Universal," and "Song for All Seas." These *Centennial Songs* have typically been read as proof of the diminution of Whitman's poetic ability, but Gay Wilson Allen has qualified this statement in a significant manner; he notes that "as [Whitman's] inspiration slackens and his vigor ebbs away, [the poet] turns more resolutely than ever to critical commentary and editorial revision of his life's work."[24] Even Betsy Erkkila's similar argument has been mitigated by the revealing comment that "in his centennial poems he seems content to be the poet of public policy."[25] Unintentionally, these critical statements have opened the way for a revisionist reading that situates Whitman's *Two Rivulets* squarely in the poetics of "public policy" because of its representational resistance to the disintegrative tensions on the racial front. In the midst of America's centennial celebration of the dictum "all men are created equal," these reconstructive texts offer a counterstatement to the Klan terrorism that had been unleashed in the revolution of the war and in the retreat from a public policy push for an inclusive democracy.

In February 1874 *Harper's Monthly* had printed "Song of the Redwood-Tree," and Whitman reprinted the text, which in the "death-chant" of a California redwood allegorically represents the rupture of antiquated social relations in favor of the "hidden national will" that would solidify the nation in the future: "*Farewell, my brethren, / Farewell, O earth and sky — farewell ye neighboring waters; / My time has ended, my term has come*" (*LG Var* III, 674). In the "Redwood forest dense" the poet hears a chant unheard by the "quick-ear'd teamsters" and thus remedies the deafness of the lumberjacks to an italicized utterance, projected only to the "reconstructed" ears of social solidarity, which had progressed from the feudal cultures of Asia and Europe to "*These virgin lands — Lands of the western Shore, / To the new Culminating Man — To you, the Empire New, / You, promis'd long, we pledge, we dedicate*" (*LG Var* III, 676). Thus the giant tree takes on the metonymic role of the national ancestors, who had to be "felled" (recall the Ship of State's "original sails all gone") to give way to "a superber race" that would ratify the "unseen moral essence of all the vast materials of America" (*LG Var* III, 676). In superseding the flawed social relations of division, the American landscape could be cleared to fulfill its moral destiny: "*You hidden National Will, lying in your abysms, conceal'd, but ever alert, / Your past and present purposes, tenaciously pursued, may-be unconscious of yourselves, / Unswerv'd by all the passing errors, perturbations of the surface . . . / Here build your homes for good*" (*LG Var* III, 676–77).

Whitman's performative text gets enlisted in the social renovation project of giving utterance to a "hidden National Will" that was at work in the foundational documents of America but that had experienced "perturbations of the surface," or the contingent events of an evolving nation of "equalizers." Thus the deferral of such social networks of citizens in a communal quest for a "National Will" is temporally positioned in an interstitial space, but a voluntary surrender to federal alliances invites citizens to "*Here climb the vast, pure spaces, unconfined, uncheck'd by wall or roof*" (*LG Var* III, 677). However, the reconstructed democracy of these cooperative citizens had been heard only by the representative poet, who nonetheless prophesies: "I see in you, certain to come, the promise of thousands of years, till now deferr'd, / Promis'd, to be fulfill'd, our common kind, the Race" (*LG Var* III, 678). Because of the recalcitrant social factions of 1876, the "New Society at last" could be heard only by the narrator-poet of his *Memoranda During the War*, who had been long "Clearing the ground for broad Humanity, the true America, heir of the past so grand, / To build a grander future" (*LG Var* III, 678–79).

Likewise, in "Song of the Universal" the poet assumes the privileged position of federalizer above bickering factions, accepting the Muse's invitation to "Sing me a song no poet yet has chanted, / Sing me the Universal" (*LG Var* III, 679). Once again the "grossness and the slag" of the present had to be relativized in the inexorable advance of democratic comradeship, for the dismantling of social partitions in "this broad earth of ours" nevertheless held out the potential that "Enclosed and safe within its central heart, / Nestles the seed perfection" (*LG Var* III, 679). Rather than absolutize such "perfection," for "the seed is waiting" after all, Whitman seems to have relied on the etymological sense of perfection as "the action or process of making perfect" (*Oxford English Dictionary*). Such a "mystic evolution" always held out the chance to defeat social divisions in its federalizing force: "Out of the bulk, the morbid and the shallow, / Out of the bad majority — the varied, countless frauds of men and States, / Electric, antiseptic yet — cleaving, suffusing all, / Only the Good is universal" (*LG Var* III, 680). The referent for "universal" as a figure for America becomes clear in section 4, where the nation represents "the scheme's culmination" insofar as "Thou too surroundest all, / Embracing, carrying, welcoming all." One of most clarifying federalist images in all of *Two Rivulets* projects America's perfection as being enacted only by "absorbing, comprehending all, / All eligible to all" (*LG Var* III, 681). If America's social factions disrupt this nationalization of comradeship ("Give me — give him or her I love, this quenchless faith / In Thy ensemble"), then "Health, peace, salvation universal" would remain an illusion, "And, failing it, life's lore and wealth a dream, / And all the world a dream" (*LG Var* III, 682).

The last of these *Centennial Songs*, called "Song for All Seas, All Ships," transports Whitman's unitive cultural work, with its ameliorative unfolding of a freer future, onto the oceans of the world: "Flaunt out O Sea, your separate flags of nations! / Flaunt out, visible as ever, the various ship-signals!" (*LG Var* III, 683). The pervasive sea imagery dominates the poems of the *Two Rivulets* cluster, which was printed on the top half of the pages, with the prose sections printed below. The epigraph to these interwoven prose-poetry sections reads, "*For the Eternal Ocean bound, / These ripples, passing surges, streams of Death and Life*"; and in the context of the fuller poem "Two Rivulets," the poet continued, "Object and Subject hurrying, whirling by, / The Real and Ideal, // Alternate ebb and flow the Days and Nights, / (Strands of a Trio twining, Present, Future, Past)" (*LG Var* III, 655). The fluidity of these images suggests the instability of the political alliances in 1876 . . . "but it also opens up new ways of making sense of the "Two Rivulets" cluster, ways that allow Centennial readers to rethink their social bonds in a reconstructed future: "In You whoe'er you are, my book perusing, / In I myself — in all the World — these ripples flow, / All, all, toward the mystic Ocean tending" (*LG Var* III, 655). Such a reconstructive mission had produced the impetus for the construction of this book of "democratic nationality" in the first place, for as the poet declares in "Or From That Sea of Time," "These thoughts and Songs — waifs from the deep — here, cast high and dry, / Wash'd on America's shores" (*LG Var* III, 656). The poet's reconfigured Union texts were "waifs," however, in that the political reversals of "universal democratic comradeship," quite visible in 1876, had the potential of dismantling Whitman's vision of a cooperative pluralistic society: "(Not safe and peaceful only — waves rous'd and ominous too, / Out of the depths, the storm's abysms — Who knows whence? Death's waves, / Raging over the vast, with many a broken spar and tatter'd sail.)" (*LG Var* III, 656).

Again, the uncertainty of Reconstruction's destiny as the social translator of a movement from divisive factions toward a "national identity power" undergirds Whitman's "Prayer of Columbus." This "Columbus" text takes the form of a dramatic interior monologue by the discoverer at his lowest ebb, after the Jamaican shipwreck in 1503 that marked his last voyage to the New World: "A batter'd, wreck'd old man, / Thrown on this savage shore, far, far from home, / Pent by the sea, and dark, rebellious brows . . . / I take my way along the island's edge, / Venting a heavy heart" (*LG Var* III, 661-62). Whitman's Columbus, formerly the "chief histrion" of the evolutionary voyage of democracy to the New World, now finds only failure and physical breakdown, and he even verges on madness: "Is it the prophet's thought I speak, or am I raving? / What do I know of life? what of myself? / I know not even my own work, past or present, / Dim, ever-shifting guesses of it spread before me, / Of newer, better worlds, their mighty parturition,/ Mocking, perplexing me"(*LG Var* III, 664).

While the nation focused on reading the Declaration of Independence in Philadelphia and sought to suture the racial wounds that were still festering in both North and South, Whitman's representation of Columbus registers only "ever-shifting guesses" about the possibility of greater social solidarity in the near future. The supplication of Columbus, however, foresees that the present "parturition" would deliver to the United States "some miracle" of social unity through the signal of "anthems in new tongues saluting me" (*LG Var* III, 664).

Despite this qualified hope, Whitman's representation of the political vista in 1876 contains "gloomy thoughts," as evident in "Wandering at Morn," wherein the poet returns to the image of the "singing thrush," which had opened his decade of Reconstruction texts in "When Lilacs Last in the Dooryard Bloom'd," as the inaugurator of his songs of universalized comradeship: "Yearning for thee, harmonious Union! thee, Singing Bird divine! / Thee, seated coil'd in evil times, my Country, with craft and black dismay — with every meanness, treason thrust upon thee" (*LG Var* III, 669). Refusing to succumb to these political currents that sought to silence his songs of freedom, the poet locates consolation in "the singing thrush, whose tones of joy and faith ecstatic, / Fail not to certify and cheer my soul" (*LG Var* III, 669). Despite the reversal of the Reconstruction project through the intransigence of racism and sectional divisions, in the natural images of the poem, the "worms, snakes, loathsome grubs" are transmuted into "sweet spiritual songs" when fed by "the parent thrush" to its off-spring. Thus the "wandering" poet has found a referent to prophesy an end to antidemocratic resistance afoot in the country, which sought to quench his "yearning for thee, harmonious Union!"

Whitman's narrator achieves similar consolation in *Memoranda During the War* when he positions the "convulsive" political forces as steps on the evolutionary ladder toward the "national identity power": "What is any Nation, after all — and what is a human being — but a struggle between conflicting paradoxical, opposing elements — and they themselves and their most violent contests, important parts of that One Identity, and of its development" (*MDW*, 65). Thus the social dislocation produced by the war, which demanded a reconfiguration of national identity, could actually contribute to a more pluralistic future: "Then may I trust in you, your fortunes, days, my country; / —Who knows but these may be lessons fit for you? / From these your future Song may rise, with joyous trills, / Destin'd to fill the world" (*LG Var* III, 669–70). One of the proleptic discourses that contributed to such a pluralistic democracy had been the legislative traces of interracial equality (though it was under seige in 1876), which would furnish their part to the struggles of the Second Reconstruction in the mid-twentieth century.

By exposing these social threats to the amelioration of democracy in Centennial America, Whitman's *Two Rivulets* cluster avoids the elision of the darker forces of division in order to offer a corrective vision to the national inundation of patriotic propaganda. The possibility that such a jingoistic but ultimately vacuous display of national unity masked the ideology of white dominance forces the poet to offer a sober caveat in the poem "In Former Songs": "In former songs Pride have I sung, and Love, and passionate, joyful Life, / But here I twine the strands of Patriotism and Death" (*LG Var* III, 672). Such an utterance subverted the empty patriotic rhetoric of 1876 through its coupling of "Patriotism" with "Death," which again suggests the allegorical dissolution of the inherited politics of social division: "'Tis not for nothing, Death, / I sound out you, and words of you with daring tone — embodying you, / In my new Democratic chants — keeping you for a close, / For last impregnable retreat — a citadel and tower, / For my last stand — my pealing final cry" (*LG Var* III, 673).

In the prose "rivulet" of this cluster, Whitman elaborates this counter-statement to empty patriotism. In "Democracy in the New World," the poet stated that America had "justified itself" but had "now to be seriously consider'd also in its pronounc'd and already developt dangers" (*PW* II, 529). The settlement of the war had only given rise to "new responsibilities," which demanded more than white cultural elision of the factions that were still seceding from the Union of "comrades" that the poet was prefiguring: "I can conceive of no better service in the United States, henceforth, by democrats of thorough and heart-felt faith, than boldly exposing the weakness, liabilities, and infinite corruptions of democracy" (*PW* II, 529). Through the exposure of the "infinite corruptions" of contemporary democracy, which suggests the persistence of hierarchical subjugation of marginalized citizens, Whitman was resurrecting a hidden "knowledge" in danger of being unheard in the Centennial self-congratulation industry. Whitman's "Thoughts For the Centennial" was written as a text allowing readers to escape "from all narrow and merely local influences — and also from the coloring and shaping through European feudalism — and still to be averaged by the scale of Centuries" (*PW* II, 765). In "Foundation Stages — Then Others," Whitman summarized the matrix of his desire for a neutralization of violent factions in America: "In nothing is there more evolution than in the American mind" (*PW* II, 530).

Whitman's contribution to this calibrated evolution of the democratic "average" rather than the unending struggle of domination and rebellion was constituted in *Two Rivulets* in his position as the representative poet who gave voice to "universal democratic comradeship" out of contesting voices. The heart of his argument was a demand for more writers of "Radical Democracy" in poetry and prose beyond his own contributions: "Where is America's art-rendering, in any thing like the spirit worthy of herself and the modern . . . ? So far, our Democratic society (estimating its various strata, in the mass, as one,) possesses nothing" to compare with the "indescribably beautiful charm and hold which fused the separate parts of the old feudal societies together" (*PW* II, 533). The social divisions in America were not simply racial, for Whitman deplored the "want and mutuality of love, belief, and rapport of interest" between the rich and the poor, a division that also proved calamitous in the production of a first-class nation of reconstructed comrades. Always first to place the accent on the non-feudal democratic "average," which equalized social relations in a pluralistic society, Whitman continued to counterpose "feudal" social relations of Europe and Asia, replicated in the master-slave relations in the American South — "(In the Southern States, under slavery, much of the same.)" (*PW* II, 533)—with the encircling desire for America to surpass these outmoded dominations: "Other times, other lands, have had their missions — Art, War, Ecclesiasticism, Literature, Discovery, Trade, Architecture, &c., &c. — but that grand future is the enclosing purport of the United States" (*PW* II, 536).

America's cultural work had to do with the federalization of such Old World cultural inheritances: "What we have to do to-day is to receive them cheerfully, and to give them ensemble, and a modern American and democratic physiognomy" (*PW* II, 537). The "national identity power" that had left its traces in the amalgamation of sections, races, and civil rights in Reconstruction legislation found its analogue in Whitman's "Thoughts for the Centennial": "Though These States are to have their own Individuality, and show it forth with courage in all their expressions, it is to be a large, tolerant, and all-inclusive Individuality" (*PW* II, 766). This "grand and universal Nation" of comrades would have to meet the prerequisites of "the power to take in and assimilate all the human strata, all kinds of experience, and all theories, and whatever happens or occurs, or offers itself, or fortune, or what is call'd misfortune" (*PW* II, 766).

The dilation of "all-inclusive" democracy, though trumpeted in the public displays of patriotism at the Centennial Exhibition in 1876, had never been enacted in the praxis of American politics. Whitman's medicinal prognosis for the inevitably rough passage of Reconstruction into the "redemption" era of Jim Crow was his proposal of a truce between the enthusiasts of federal sovereignty and those of state sovereignty. Each civic-government paradigm became inextricably bound up in the other to prevent the return of anarchy: "As the centripetal law were fatal alone, or centrifugal law deadly and destructive alone, but together forming the law of eternal kosmical action, evolution, preservation, and life — so, by itself alone, the fullness of individuality, even the sanest would surely destroy itself" (*PW* II, 513). But because of the disastrous war which rose out of the absolutizing of state sovereignty, Whitman shifts the rhetorical balance slightly toward the cause of federalism: "This is what makes the importance to the identities of these States of the thoroughly fused, relentless, dominating Union — a moral and spiritual idea, subjecting all the parts with remorseless power, more needed by American democracy than by any of history's hitherto empires or feudalities" (*PW* II, 513). As an expedient in time of civic emergency, Whitman suggested that the Radical Republican actions of the 1860s and 1870s had enlisted the federalizing force of law in their pursuit of a more just national polity.

In the second century of its democratic identity, Whitman's United States would have to face its deepest challenge in reconstructing national comradeship as a voluntary embrace of such federalizing legal measures, following the odium of punishment in the Enforcement Acts: "We need this conviction of nationality as a faith, to be absorb'd in the blood and belief of the people everywhere . . . to emanate in their life, and in native literature and art. We want the germinal idea that America . . . is the custodian of the future of humanity" (*PW* II, 513). If both the federal government and the state governments were unable to strike a truce in their supervision of civil liberties, then Whitman's reconstructed Union of national comrades was doomed to extinction: "I say the loss or abdication of one set, in the future, will be ruin to democracy just as much as the loss of the other set. The problem is, to harmoniously adjust the two, and the play of the set" (*PW* II, 514). This paradoxical dialectic would fall into disrepair throughout the retreat from Reconstruction, for states' rights in the forum of civil liberties would harden the systematic segregation of the races into an ideology that has yet to be completely dismantled. In fact, the continual fact of white dominance in post-Reconstruction America has forced Whitman's ministerial role as mediator between partisans back into the textual site it sprang from. In the pages of *Two Rivulets*, Whitman redrew the social map to open the social relations of his day to "universal democratic comradeship "; but the United States has yet to fully emerge from the racial wounds of Reconstruction, which Eric Foner has soberly called, in the subtitle of his exhaustive history, "America's Unfinished Revolution."

Not surprisingly, the last prose text in Whitman's *Two Rivulets* cluster of prose and poetry constituted his Centennial thoughts on freedom. The poet of nationalized comradeship recognized that the concept of freedom had been misrecognized by partisans of differing ideologies, but his reconstructive program struck its keynote in the discourse of law: "The whole Universe is absolute Law. Freedom only opens entire activity and license *under the law*" (*PW* II, 537–38). The knowledge of limits, legislated to promote the highest good for individuals and for nations, paradoxically promotes "that law as absolute as any — the Law of Liberty" (*PW* II, 538). Such a knowledge of subjection leading to personal and communal freedom provoked two responses: the "shallow" chose liberty as "a release from all law, from every restraint," but the "wise" chose liberty as "the potent Law of Laws, namely, the fusion and combination of conscious will, or partial individual law, with those universal, eternal, unconscious ones, which run through all Time, pervade history," and donate "moral purpose" and "dignity" to human social relations (*PW* II, 538).

Whitman's performative *Two Rivulets* represents a legislative summa of his Reconstruction strategies for binding up the Union in its "national identity power" through the stress on "universal democratic comradeship" or the voluntary surrender of localized social relations to the pull of identification with strangers in our midst as well as from the far-flung corners of the nation. By publishing his *Rivulets* during the centenary of the Declaration of Independence, which was not a legislative document, Whitman was circulating a text that, in effect, *constituted* the Declaration (as a reconstructed "constitution") with a revolutionary plenitude that had been compromised through tolerance for slavery at the Constitutional Convention. Though black Americans were voiceless in the nation's charter, Supreme Court Justice Thurgood Marshall reminded the nation in 1987 that the approaching bicentennial would celebrate a flawed Constitution and that its currency could be validated not by Founding Fathers but rather by "those present who refused to acquiesce in outdated notions of 'liberty,' 'justice,' and 'equality,' and who strived to better them. The true miracle of the Constitution was not the birth of the Constitution, but its life."[26]

Walt Whitman's Reconstruction texts, too, refused to surrender to "outdated" forms of feudal subjection, including the peculiar institution; and his striving for an inclusive democracy in these poems and essays can deservedly receive Marshall's benediction. The "strange, sad War revolving" in Whitman's reconstructive cultural poetics continued its revolutions far beyond the edges of the 1870s. Kathleen Diffley has effectively argued that the "waning command of the household as a model for political change" was further weakened in the 1896 Supreme Court case *Plessy v. Ferguson*, wherein the Court continued to roll back the civil rights of blacks through a decision in favor of state regulation of "separate but equal" public accommodations for the races.[27] The primary alliances of family ties had given way to a kind of depersonalized "citizenship" that had promoted racist discrimination, cloaked beneath the rhetoric of "separate but equal" but not social solidarity.

The erasure of familial images of a national household was further constituted in the interdiction of segregated schools for "citizens," not progeny, in the 1954 *Brown v. Board of Education of the City of Topeka*.[28] But the movement toward a representational model of nationalized "citizens" was not exclusively a model of decline. The replacement of primary legislative identification with one's own familiars in favor of identification with strangers in the communal social compact had helped to establish the more inclusive "national identity power" that Whitman predicted would provide freer access to the "Law of Liberty." The Second Reconstruction of the 1950s and 1960s turned the legislative diction of "citizens" to its political advantage in the civil rights struggle that led to more revolutionary legislative victories for American blacks in their bid for equal rights.

The Civil Rights Act of 1964, which was signed by President Lyndon Johnson on 2 July 1964, provided even stronger federal and judicial remedies to racial discrimination in public accommodations and employment than Charles Sumner's integrationist Civil Rights Bill of 1875.[29] Contrary to its Reconstruction precedents, the 1964 statute, as Hugh Davis Graham notes, established "with surprising speed and virtually self-executing finality" the end to Jim Crow's strange career in its surveillance of public accommodations: "The Civil Rights Act of 1964, following upon a decade of paralysis in school desegregation since the *Brown* decision, would within another decade help transform the South into the most desegregated region in the country."[30] The Fifteenth Amendment also received a reconstructive recovery the next year in the Voting Rights Act of 1965,[31] which Lyndon Johnson signed on 6 August 1965, for this sweeping statute reinstated federal authority over the supervision of impartial voting regulations and procedures on behalf of citizens in state jurisdictions. The shadow of the Enforcement Acts of 1870–71 fell across this medicinal federal inter-vention, which was enlisted in the fight against the widespread disenfran-chisement of blacks since the 1870s and placed the burden of proof on white perpetrators of discrimination rather than on the victims.

Though initially unsettling, these two statutes provided the most drastic federal intrusions into state jurisdictions imaginable, but they assured the kind of legal inclusiveness that the Radical Republican agitators of a hun-dred years before could only have dreamed of. When the Supreme Court upheld the 1965 statute a year later, the Justices praised this federal inter-vention, for "after enduring nearly a century of widespread resistance to the Fifteenth Amendment, Congress has marshalled an array of potent weap-ons against the evil" of discrimination on the basis of color. The majority opinion in *South Carolina v. Katzenbach* continued: "Hopefully, millions of non-white Americans will now be able to participate for the first time on an equal basis in the government under which they live."[32] On 4 June 1965, in his famous Howard University commencement address, President Lyndon Johnson spoke of the kind of performative interdependence be-tween antagonistic factions that Whitman had advocated over ninety years before. Johnson stunned his audience with the words "We seek not just freedom but opportunity — not just legal equity but human ability — not just equality as a right and a theory but equality as a fact and as a result."[33]

Walt Whitman had already legislated such a "universal democratic com-radeship" in his Reconstruction "workshop" from *Drum-Taps* (1865) to *Two Rivulets* (1876), but many of these reconstructive texts have not been recovered with the same rhetorical vigor by literary scholars as that with which the Reconstruction legislative workshop has been recovered by the federal government in the Second Reconstruction of civil liberties. How-ever, both representational workshops have furnished their federative parts toward a more interracial Union, though the revolutions of the wheels of the Civil War may not be halted on the racial divide for decades to come. In his *Memoranda During the War*, Whitman predicted, "And the real History of the United States — starting from that great convulsive struggle for Unity, triumphantly concluded . . . is only to be written at the remove of hundreds, perhaps a thousand, years hence" (*MDW*, 68).

Notes

[1] *New York Evening Post*, 31 December 1875. Cited in William Gillette, *Retreat from Reconstruction*, 300.

[2] Eric Foner, *Reconstruction*, 571.

[3] For a concise reading of the passage and repudiation of the Civil Rights Act of 1875, see Gillette, *Retreat from Reconstruction*, chapter 12, "Insignificant Victory: The Civil Rights Act of 1875," 259–79.

[4] For a useful discussion of the proceedings of the Centennial Exhibition of 1876, see Louise L. Stevenson's *The Victorian Homefront: American Thought and Culture, 1860–1880* (New York: Twayne, 1991), chapter 8, "Centennial Milestones: 1876 and Beyond," 182–99.

[5] Gay Wilson Allen, *Solitary Singer*, 477. The finest biographical account of the events in Whitman's life during the composition of the Centennial Edition of *Leaves of Grass* and *Two Rivulets* can be found in Allen, *Solitary Singer*, chapter 10, "Ebbing Tide," 449–500.

[6] For a brief formal analysis of the 1876 Centennial Edition of *Leaves of Grass* and *Two Rivulets*, see Allen, *Handbook*, "'Author's Edition,' 1876," 141–46. The title pages of the two volumes both stated: "Author's Edition / Camden, New Jersey / 1876." The five new poems added to the 1876 edition of the first volume, *Leaves of Grass*, are the following: "Come, Said My Soul" (title-page epigraph), "As in a Swoon," "The Beauty of the Ship," "When the Full-grown Poet Came," and "After an Interval."

[7] Allen, *Handbook*, 145.

[8] Betsy Erkkila, 288.

[9] John Hope Franklin, "Enforcement," 225.

[10] *Congressional Globe*, 41st Congress, 2nd Session, 3434 (13 May 1870).

[11] *Congressional Globe*, 41st Congress, 2nd Session, 3434 (13 May 1870).

[12] *Journal of the House*, 43rd Congress, 2nd Session, 4 February 1875, 1633 and 402–03.

[13] *Congressional Globe*, 43rd Congress, 2nd Session, 27 February 1875, 1870.

[14] *United States Statutes at Large*, volume 18, 335–36.

[15] Gillette, 259–79.

[16] Franklin, 225–35.

[17] *Civil Rights Cases*, 109 U.S. 3 (1883), argued 29 March 1883, decided 15 October 1883 by vote of 8 to 1; Bradley for the Court, Harlan in dissent. See Robert J. Kaczorowski, 318–24.

[18] *United States v. Cruikshank*, 92 U.S. 542 (1876), argued 30–31 March and 30 April 1875, decided 27 March 1876 by vote of 9 to 0; Waite for the Court, Clifford concurring. See Kaczorowski, 300–318.

[19] *United States v. Reese*, 92 U.S. 214 (1876), argued 13–14 January 1875, decided 27 March 1876 by vote of 8 to 1; Waite for the Court, Hunt in dissent. See Kaczorowski, 321.

[20] Frederick Douglass, quoted in *Proceedings of Republican National Convention, 1876*, 26–27. Cited in Gillette, 304.

[21] Relating to his war experiences, Whitman published the following newspaper columns: "The Great Army of the Sick," *New York Times*, 26 February 1863; "Washington in the Hot Season," *New York Times*, 16 August 1863; "Our Wounded and Sick Soldiers," *New York Times*, 11 December 1864; "The Soldiers," *New York Times*, 28 February 1865; and "'Tis But Ten Years Since," a series of six columns in the *New York Weekly Graphic*, 24 January; 7, 14, 21, 28 February; and 7 March 1874. See *PW* I, 22–23n.

[22] Allen, *Handbook*, 141, *Solitary Singer*, 457.

[23] See Walt Whitman, *Walt Whitman's Memoranda During the War [&] Death of Abraham Lincoln*. The biographical précis (called "Personal — Note") and the two portraits are reproduced on the pages following 48, and Whitman's footnote describing the portraits reads as follows: "The picture in shirt-sleeves was daguerreotyped from life, one hot day in August 1833, by my friend Gabriel Harrison, in Fulton St., Brooklyn — and here drawn on steel by McRae— (was a very faithful and characteristic likeness at the time.) The head that follows was photographed from life, Washington, 1872, by Geo. C. Potter, here drawn on wood by W. J. Linton." These two portraits were republished in the Centennial Edition of *Leaves of Grass*, respectively facing the poem "Walt Whitman" (later "Song of Myself") and facing the poem "The Dresser" (later "The Wound-Dresser").

[24] Allen, *Handbook*, 146.

[25] Erkkila, 287.

[26] Thurgood Marshall, "Reflections on the Bicentennial of the United States Constitution," *Harvard Law Review* 101 (1987): 1–5. The citation is from 5.

[27] Kathleen Diffley, *Where My Heart Is Turning Ever*, 186–87.

[28] Diffley, 187–88.

[29] The Civil Rights Bill of 1964 was passed by the Senate on 19 June 1964 by a vote of 73–27. The House passed the measure on 2 July 1964 by a vote of 289–126, and President Johnson signed it post-

haste on the same day. For an exhaustive study of the intricate politics and passage of the Civil Rights Act of 1964, see Hugh Davis Graham, chapter 5, "The Civil Rights Act of 1964," 125–52. Perhaps the most striking notation records that the Senate filibuster to prevent passage of the 1964 statute broke all Senate records, having consumed "82 working days, 63,000 pages in the Congressional Record, and ten million words" (151).

[30] Graham, 152.

[31] The Voting Rights Act of 1965 passed the House on 3 August 1965 by a vote of 328–74, and passed the Senate by a vote of 79–18. President Johnson traveled to Capitol Hill to sign the revolutionary federal statute on 6 August 1965. Again, for an exhaustive study of the intricacies of the passage of the 1965 mandate, see Graham, chapter 6, "From the Civil Rights Act to the Voting Rights Act: The Johnson White House at Flood Tide, 1964–1965," 153–76. According to his autobiography, *Vantage Point*, President Johnson is reported to have said to Attorney General Nicholas Katzenbach, "Write the god-damnedest, toughest voting rights act that you can devise" (Johnson 161).

[32] *Public Papers of the Presidents:* Johnson, 1965, I, 636.

Coda:
"Approach strong deliveress"

Why Lilacs First in Whitman's
Dooryard Bloomed

FOR WHITMAN, ABRAHAM LINCOLN was the dominant political figure who embodied the binding of the Union's wounds, whether inflicted by secession or by slavery. In his lecture "The Death of Lincoln," Whitman declared that the president's death on 15 April 1865 represented "that seal of the emancipation of three million slaves — that parturition and delivery of our at last free Republic, born again, henceforth to commence its career of genuine homogeneous Union, compact, consistent with itself" (*PW* II, 508). While Whitman was underplaying the dismal record of resistance to Reconstruction legislation designed to help ex-slaves, he clearly thought that Lincoln had broken with the scourge of slavery inflicted by generations of Americans who had done little and had resisted abolitionist activism at every turn. In addition, Whitman featured Lincoln's death as the implied center of what has become one of his most widely-read poems, "When Lilacs Last in the Door-yard Bloom'd," which was advertised as the title poem of the *Sequel to Drum-Taps* (1865–66).

However, Whitman refused to name Lincoln explicitly in this or any other of his Lincoln poems, much as he refused to feature black subjects in *Drum-Taps*, which suggests that *Sequel's* representational purposes were in tying such highly charged cultural figures to broader ideological concerns such as emancipationist images enlisted in the construction of a reconstructed Union. As Betsy Erkkila has pointed out, Whitman's elision of Lincoln's name in "Lilacs" opens up the elegy to its representative function as a cultural text: "Lincoln is embedded in the poem as a figure of the American people. The one is continually balanced with the many, the separate person with the en-masse, as Whitman places Lincoln and the particularities of his death in a poetic pattern that is at once national and universal."[1] Once again, from behind the camouflage of words, Whitman was addressing the "open road" of Reconstruction and singing a song of unimpeachable democracy founded on Union and emancipation.

While the nation was wrestling with the Thirteenth Amendment, Whitman memorialized Lincoln in "Lilacs" as the deliverer of emancipation to ex-slaves, but he did not record the president's reluctant enlistment in any proclamation of emancipation. Critics have failed to pose the question of *which* representation of Lincoln Whitman embedded in this luxuriant elegy, which has become synonymous with the poet's experience of Lincoln's assassination. In fact, Whitman's Lincoln in "Lilacs" represents the Reconstruction Lincoln, a subject who responded to the crisis of the Union by federal coercion that centralized national authority and by his slow conversion to the role of the great but reluctant emancipator. As the representative of the Union "en-masse," the Lincoln image in "Lilacs" validates the postwar federal hegemony that sought to overtake the states' resistance to the enforcement of black civil rights. Whitman's "Lilacs" elegized the "Great Emancipator" but also the reluctant "Emancipator" whose sympathy for slaves only gradually found its representations in executive policy. Like most Americans, the early Lincoln was imbued with the principle of "popular sovereignty" and routinely placed common consent above his own personal views with regard to public policy, including the policy of slaveholding in America. In an 1854 Peoria speech, which concerned the extension of slavery in the territories, he declared, "The doctrine of self-government is right — absolutely and eternally right, but it has no just application, as here attempted. Or perhaps I should say that whether it has such application depends upon whether the negro is not or is a man" (*Lincoln* II, 265).

This exemplary citation demonstrates Lincoln's willingness to compromise on the slavery extension question if the democratic will ruled the Negro a nonperson. But Lincoln also inserted the oppositional position of the full stature of black humanity to demonstrate that if "the negro is a man, why then my ancient faith teaches me that 'all men are created equal;' and that there can be no moral right in connection with one man's making a slave of another . . . . What I do say is, that no man is good enough to govern another man, without that other's consent" (*Lincoln* II, 265–66). Because "popular sovereignty" was, for Lincoln, "the sheet anchor of American republicanism" (*Lincoln* II, 266), his deferral of speaking out forthrightly in favor of unqualified emancipation submitted the question to be put to the white majority.

However, after the secession of the South began in earnest, Lincoln shifted the representational value of "popular consent," which, of course, the South invoked as its charter for leaving the Union. For the first time, Lincoln had to invent a legal boundary beyond which "sovereignty" could not march. In his first inaugural address 1861, Lincoln circumscribed states' rights through an incipient federal dominance and thus formulated a less-than-universal model of "consent," which forbade the dissolution of civil ties between one section and another: "A majority held in restraint by constitutional checks and limitations, and always changing easily with deliberate changes of popular opinions and sentiments, is the only true sovereign of a free people" (*Lincoln* IV, 268). With or without consent, in other words, the Union was indissoluble.

In 1861 Lincoln did not refer to the implicit sanction of slavery in those hoary "constitutional checks and balances" but rather offered a domestic image to illustrate the stakes in keeping the Union whole: "A husband and wife may be divorced and go out of the presence and beyond the reach of each other; but the different parts of our country cannot do this. They cannot but remain face to face, and intercourse, either amicable or hostile, must continue between them" (*Lincoln* IV, 269). The interdiction of divorce in the Union "household" stoked the fires of reunion, but Lincoln's domestic rhetoric also underscored the presence in that "amicable or hostile" cultural household of the alienated slave population and of the historical approbation of slavery in both the North and the South. Once again, the specter of "consent" rose up in the equivocation over extending the rights of slaveholders, to prevent sectional "divorce" in 1861 and to check the darker specter of anarchy. Lincoln's domestic image held coercive resonance that would only deepen through the radical Reconstruction years. Despite the waffling, Lincoln's rhetorical linkage of Union with emancipation, beginning in May 1862, would result in the uneven allegiances to two "fruits of victory," Union and emancipation, instead of one.

In December 1862 Lincoln informed Congress that his impending Emancipation Proclamation had a reflexive purpose: "In giving freedom to the slave, we assure freedom to the free" (*Lincoln* V, 537). When the Proclamation was issued in January 1863, Lincoln insisted to his cabinet that emancipation was "a military necessity, absolutely essential to the preservation of the Union. [Since the slaves are] undeniably an element of strength to those who had their service . . . we must free the slaves or ourselves be subdued."[2] Privately, Lincoln held that his Proclamation would alter "the character of the war" in order to subjugate the South, which "is to be destroyed and replaced by new propositions and ideas."[3] Thus the ascendancy of federalism was initiated even before the adoption of the Thirteenth Amendment in 1865, for consent of the governed (and state sovereignty) had lost some of its sheen even in the midst of the war. In other words, Lincoln had furnished his part in the founding of a reconstructed Union household with emancipation as its legislative foundation, and Whitman's presidential hero helped make Washington the arbiter of social relations before the Constitution codified the "revolution in federalism" that was to follow Lincoln's assassination.

However, blacks were not unambiguously welcomed into the national household despite the ascendancy of the abolitionists' agenda in the public forum. For instance, in August 1862, shortly before the issuance of the Proclamation, Lincoln told a delegation of freed blacks at the White House to consider colonization as an alternative to American citizenship: "Your race suffer greatly by living among us, while ours suffer from your presence . . . . If this is admitted, it affords a reason, at least, why we should be separated" (*Lincoln* V, 371). Lincoln's attempt to eject blacks from American shores was denounced by Frederick Douglass, who declared that the president had "no sincere wish to improve the condition of the oppressed . . . . [Lincoln] expresses merely the desire to get rid of them, and reminds one of the politeness with which a man might try to bow out of his house some troublesome creditor or the witness of some old guilt."[4] Once again the issue of "separation" arose in the war context, only this time Lincoln attempted to "divorce" blacks from whites, in contradistinction to his assertions that the North and South were inalienably wedded to each other. The "old guilt" of the constitutional tolerance of slavery, however, plus the tenacity with which blacks determined to remain within the national culture, helped to discredit any notion that Union was more significant than emancipation as a war aim.

On 19 August 1864 Lincoln rhetorically enacted his emancipatory promise to ex-slaves in an interview with two Republican senators when he stated, "There have been men who proposed to me to return to slavery the black warriors"; however, he countered, "I should be damned in time and in eternity for so doing. The world shall know that I will keep my faith to friends and enemies, come what will" (*Lincoln* VII, 507). A few days later, Lincoln even suggested that he was willing to lose his reelection bid rather than abandon emancipation, and the presence of over a hundred thousand black Union soldiers had, more than almost any other cultural renovation, nailed the lid on the peculiar institution's coffin.[5] Lincoln had slowly awakened to the moral demand for discontinuity with the Revolutionary household which had held America in thrall since 1787, and he demonstrated his willingness to renovate the Constitution by making the passage of the Thirteenth Amendment one of his 1864 reelection pledges.

Likewise, Walt Whitman wrote his "Lilacs" elegy as a testament to the cultural discontinuity with the Founders' inscription of slavery. In effect, the Lincoln that Whitman elegizes represented the unnamed terminator of the "old guilt" over the barbarity of slavery, which the states confronted with the ratification of emancipation in December 1865. The new foundation of Union-with-emancipation gave the nationalization of American identity an energetic (if contested) boost, and Lincoln's murder, for Whitman, consolidated this new interracial social contract as nothing else: "Strange, (is it not?) that battles, martyrs, agonies, blood, even assassination, should so condense — perhaps only really, lastingly condense — a Nationality" (*PW* II, 508). This "condensation" of democratic nationality would evolve into the raison d'être of Whitman's Reconstruction project, and "Lilacs" served as its preface, for the occasional poem of Lincoln's passing expanded its ideological scope to become the "coffin" of the country's continuity with the Revolutionary past. As Mutlu Blasing has argued, Whitman realized in "Lilacs" that the "terrorism of history" in the wake of Lincoln's death forced the poet to let go of "the fiction of natural continuity, the grandest of fictions."[6]

The disruption of historical continuity with the American past arrives early in the poem, for in section 2, the representative speaker apostrophizes: "O powerful, western, fallen star! / O shades of night! O moody, tearful night! / O great star disappear'd! O the black murk that hides the star! / O cruel hands that hold me powerless! O helpless soul of me! / O harsh surrounding cloud that will not free my soul!" (*LG Var* II, 529). The "star" had its biographical basis in Whitman's experience (the planet Venus had appeared luminously at the time of Lincoln's second inauguration in 1864), but its representational value lies in its denotation as an embodiment of the Union, embedded in the "black murk" of its collaboration with slaveholding. The "cruel hands" that had held blacks "powerless" for centuries on American soil also had enslaved the "soul" of white Americans (as Lincoln had said, "In giving freedom to the slave, we assure freedom to the free").

The appearance of the coffin (of the unnamed Lincoln) in sections 5 and 6 obviously had its parallel in Lincoln's cortege, which went from Washington to Springfield, Illinois, for burial on 4 May 1865; but the images of the text also suggest the cultural work of the dissolving of disabling alliances with the past in favor of the promise of a reconstructed future: "Over the breast of the spring, the land, amid cities, / . . . Carrying a corpse to where it shall rest in the grave, / Night and day journeys a coffin" (*LG Var* II, 530). In section 6 such reconstructive cultural work of the "coffin" becomes more apparent with the mournful citizens who flock to greet the death train, featured as "the States themselves," greeting the "coffin" of an antebellum constitutional democracy: "Coffin that passes through lanes and streets, / Through day and night, with the great cloud darkening the land / . . . With the show of the States themselves, / . . . With dirges through the night, with the thousand voices rising strong and solemn" (*LG Var* II, 531). The ritualized mourning that accompanied such a representational vehicle of cultural "death" through the Union landscape suggested more than the individual Lincoln: indeed, the "show of the States themselves" became manifest, at the same time Whitman wrote "Lilacs," in the ratification of the constitutional abolition of slavery, which came about through the "dirge" of national guilt over its violent past and through the Union will to subjugate the South through the erasure of one of its cherished social institutions.

But the mournfulness of the past, which had been ruptured by the intrusion of the "coffin" into the "Burial-chamber" of the revolutionary legacy, Whitman soon festoons with a celebratory gesture to commemorate this historical dissolution: "(Not for you, for one, alone; / Blossoms and branches green to coffins all I bring: / For fresh as the morning — thus would I chant a song for you, O sane and sacred death)" (*LG Var* II, 531). The sanity of erasing the ideology of the slave economy enables the speaker, in section 8, to unlock finally the significance of the "western orb," introduced earlier in section 2, which held all the racist resonances of the Union's antebellum self-understanding: "As I saw you had something to tell, as you bent to me night after night, / . . . As I watched where you pass'd and was lost in the netherward black of the night, / As my soul in its trouble, dissatisfied, sank, as where you, sad orb, / Concluded, dropt in the night, and was gone" (*LG Var* II, 532). The end of historical "continuity" with the past (weighted down with the incubus of slavery) then enables Whitman to emerge with his face set toward the reconstructive "open road" of the future. Whitman's elegy commences its movement toward social consolation at the tomb, just as the text interrogates its own interpretive mission: "O what shall I hang on the chamber walls? / And what shall the pictures be that I hang on the walls, / To adorn the burial-house of him I love?" (*LG Var* II, 533). The only "pictures" to be hung on the burial-chamber of the past, as a prelude to the representation of the postemancipation Union, are the images of the continental geography of a reunited nation. In effect, this postwar text permits an effusive catalogue of national identity, which aligns the poem with the federalist ascendancy in Washington, manifested in its superintendence of individual liberties in the several states: "The varied and ample land — the South and the North in the light — Ohio's shores, and flashing Missouri, / And ever the far-spreading prairies, cover'd with grass and corn" (*LG Var* II, 534).

In section 14 the consolatory mission of "Lilacs" culminates in the shift away from the "star" and the "lilacs" images, which had signaled the "disappearance" of historical continuity, and moves toward the song of the "hermit thrush," the representative singer of the "Death" of the Union's disabling legal attachment to slavery. While the speaker gazes at the vista of postwar Union material prosperity, there "Appear'd the cloud, appear'd the long black trail; / And I knew Death, its thought, and the sacred knowledge of death" (*LG Var* II, 535). The juxtaposition of the accumulated material benefits of a century of slave economics had interdicted the thrush's song with the intrusion of the "trail" of whites' atrocities against their black chattels. The "thought" and "sacred knowledge" of death, denoting the ever present threat of national dissolution in the "half-slave, half-free" Republic, and the *actual* dissolution of slavery in 1865 respectively, both products of the "terrorism of history," accompany the speaker to hear the song of the thrush, "the song of death": "Come, lovely, and soothing Death, / Undulate round the world, serenely arriving, arriving, / In the day, in the night, to all, to each, / Sooner or later, delicate Death. // Prais'd be the fathomless universe, / . . . O praise and praise / For the sure-enwinding arms of cool-enfolding Death" (*LG Var* II, 536).

The cultural work of the poem, in the mobilization of "Death" as the agent that sheds the political errors of the past, thus celebrates the dissolution of the dastardly inheritance of slavery; but, of course, it also recalls the heavy human toll of war dead that had purchased emancipation as well as reunion: "I saw the vision of armies, / And I saw, as in noiseless dreams, hundreds of battle-flags; / . . . And at last but a few shreds of the flags left on the staffs, (and all in silence,) / And the staffs all splinter'd and broken" (*LG Var* II, 538). The Union had been shattered, primarily through its adherence to its foundational discourse on race relations, but the representation of the Union in the text ("hundreds of battle-flags") was figured oxymoronically as "noiseless" in the sense that the "silence" suggested the legislative impotence of antiemancipationist voices in the Republican fight to secure emancipation. Likewise, the human bodies littered on the battle-fields illustrated the "burial-chamber" of the still reconstructing Union: "I saw battle-corpses, myriads of them, / And the white skeletons of young men . . . / I saw the debris and debris of all dead soldiers; / But I saw they were not as was thought; / They themselves were fully at rest . . . / The living remain'd and suffer'd" (*LG Var* II, 538). The "debris" left by the descendants of the Constitutional Convention graphically pointed up the "terrorism of history" catching up to an inheritance of institutionalized injustice, and such a fatalistic "rest" of Union casualties only makes a nearly nihilistic gesture, the "dead" better off than the "living," even bleaker. In fact, the "living" are the inheritors of the cultural "ruin" of the Union, and the survivors "suffer'd" through the postwar remodeling work of Reconstruction: their legislative decisions, and their enforcement of these decisions, would constitute one representational mark in judging whether the casualties were worth the cost or not. The cultural consolation of the Union would arrive only in leaving behind the antebellum failure of an "imperfect union" ("Must I leave thee, lilac with heart-shaped leaves?" [*LG Var* II, 539]), and advancing toward the "song" of the dissolution of the past: "Lilac and star and bird, twined with the chant of my soul, / With the holders holding my hand, nearing the call of the bird, / There in the fragrant pines, and the cedars dusk and dim" (*LG Var* II, 539).

The challenges of the early period of Reconstruction were to be monumental, for there was no antecedent to an interracial democracy, and there was no end to the ineradicable racism of whites toward blacks in virtually every place in the Union. But the legislative momentum of the Thirteenth Amendment had initiated a decade of legislative reform and built up a renovated foundation for the national household that included the greater civic homogeneity with which Americans represented themselves. Through Republican agitation, the stirrings of a national representation of identity were felt in every ratification of civil rights legislation in the 1860s and 1870s. The jubilation that followed the passage of the

Thirteenth Amendment so intoxicated the Radical Republicans that they declared the amendment the conclusion of an abolitionist campaign that had begun in the *Liberator* in 1831. William Lloyd Garrison himself called the amendment's ratification the peroration of the abolitionist movement: "With our own hands we have put in type this unspeakably cheering and important official announcement that, at last, the old 'covenant with death' is annulled, and the 'agreement with hell' no longer stands."[7] In hindsight, such jubilation seems naive at best, but in the *Sequel to Drum-Taps*, Walt Whitman also enacted the quickened call for an end to divisions in the Union, particularly in the poem "Reconciliation," a term he called the "Word over all, beautiful as the sky! / Beautiful that war, and all its deeds of carnage, must in time be utterly lost" (*LG Var* II, 555–56).

Whitman's impetus for this kind of cultural amnesia suggests a desire to forget the massive death toll and destruction of the war years, but it also implies tribute to the achievement of emancipation. While hardly an ideological ally of Garrison, Whitman joined in the shortsighted praise for the amendment's ratification in a poem aptly titled "Spirit Whose Work is Done" (" — Spirit of hours I knew, all hectic red one day, but pale as death next day" [*LG Var* II, 542]). However, the elegiac tone of the text turned disruptive with the concluding lines: "Touch my mouth, ere you depart — press my lips close! / Leave me your pulses of rage! bequeath them to me! fill me with currents convulsive! / Let them scorch and blister out of my chants, when you are gone; / Let them identify you to the future in these songs" (*LG Var* II 542–43). Whitman's "pulses of rage" suggest that he could not have unalloyed joy in the emancipation victory, for he had absorbed the "convulsive" currents of white resistance to black equality that were present in the land. The task of reconstructing a Union household on the base of emancipation would require representatives of a counter-resistance, who would have to reassert their legislative authority over and over again in the work of overturning a century of racial antagonism.

Tensions on the racial divide were multiplying despite William Lloyd Garrison's announcement that the abolitionist movement could disband its efforts for further agitation. Whitman's *Sequel to Drum-Taps* poems deployed images that were far less conclusive, and far more realistic, in their implications of the endurance of ongoing racial warfare. For example, in "Ah Poverties, Wincings, and Sulky Retreats," the poet's prognosis for healing the unburied racial fractures in the wake of the war sounds pessimistic: "(For what is my life, or any man's life, but a conflict with foes — the old, the incessant war?) / . . . You smarts from dissatisfied friendships, (ah wounds, the sharpest of all;) / You toil of painful and choked articulations — you meannesses; / . . . You broken resolutions, you racking angers, you smother'd ennuis" (*LG Var* II, 548). The fate of national stability lay in the political reversal of these discredited "choked articulations" of the Revolutionary heritage. On 6 May 1866, Thaddeus Stevens of Pennsylvania made clear in Congress just how far the revolutionary household had fallen in its credibility to sustain Reconstruction: "In rebuilding, it is necessary to clear away the rotten and defective portions of the old foundations, and to sink deep and found the repaired edifice upon the firm foundation of eternal justice."[8] Whitman's *Sequel* registers the same representational anxiety over the unwritten future in "As I Lay With My Head in Your Lap, Camerado," wherein the cultural work of abolitionist activism resonates in the lines "For I confront peace, security, and all the settled laws, to unsettle them; / I am more resolute because all have denied me, than I could ever have been had all accepted me; / I heed not, and have never heeded, either experience, cautions, majorities, nor ridicule" (*LG Var* II, 549).

Such textual echoes resist the dominant white culture's neglect to enforce the civil liberties for blacks. Ensuing emancipation, these "broken resolutions" had a decisive reversal in the passage of the Thirteenth Amendment despite its opponents' "cautions," "majorities," and "ridicule" toward any remodeling of the nation's charter. The amalgamation of the goals of Union and emancipation constituted, as yet, merely a parchment victory and had to confront "peace, security, and all the settled laws" in the political forum of a ruined past and an uncertain future. Despite the Thirteenth Amendment, the cultural work of rebuilding a national homestead on land seeded with racial strife had, like Appomattox, been only the beginning of the end of such a war on the racial divide. Casting a cold eye on the prospects for reconstructive cultural energies, Whitman had to concede to his troubled fellow comrades, who, like him, desired a cooperative democratic domicile for the Union, " . . . Dear camerado! I confess I have urged you onward with me, and still urge you, without the least idea of what is our destination, / Or whether we shall be victorious, or utterly quell'd and defeated" (*LG Var* II, 549).

Notes

1   Betsy Erkkila, 228.
2   See James McPherson, *Battle Cry of Freedom: The Civil War Era* (New York: Oxford U P, 1988), 504. See also Gideon Welles, "The History of Emancipation" 14 *Galaxy* 842–43 (December 1872), quoted in McPherson, *Abraham Lincoln and the Second American Revolution* (New York: Oxford U P, 1990), 83–84.
3   See McPherson, *Battle Cry*, 558.
4   Quoted by David Brion Davis, "The White World of Frederick Douglass," *New York Review of Books*, 16 May 1991, 12. See also William McFeeley, 229.
5   See McPherson, *Abraham Lincoln*, 89. "Even though the President was convinced in August 1864 that he would not be re-elected, he decided that to give the appearance of backing down on emancipation 'would be worse than losing the Presidential contest.'" (89).
6   See Mutlu Blasing, "Whitman's 'Lilacs' and the Grammars of Time," *PMLA* 97 (1982): 31–39. The citation is from 38.
7   Garrison is quoted in Kathleen Diffley, 27.
8   Stevens is quoted in the *Congressional Globe*, 39th Congress, 1st session (1865), 2459. Cited in Diffley, 65.

Works Consulted

Aaron, Daniel. *The Unwritten War: American Writers and the Civil War*. New York: Knopf, 1973.

Abbott, Richard H. *The Republican Party and the South, 1855-1877*. Chapel Hill: U of North Carolina P, 1986.

Allen, Gay Wilson. *The New Walt Whitman Handbook*. New York: New York U P, 1975.

———. *A Reader's Guide to Walt Whitman*. New York: Farrar, 1970.

———. *The Solitary Singer: A Critical Biography of Walt Whitman*. Rev. ed. Chicago: U of Chicago P, 1985.

Anderson, Quentin. *The Imperial Self: An Essay in American Literary and Cultural History*. New York: Knopf, 1971.

Arvin, Newton. *Whitman*. New York: Macmillan, 1938.

Aspiz, Harold. *Walt Whitman and the Body Beautiful*. Urbana: U of Illinois P, 1980.

Asselineau, Roger. *The Evolution of Walt Whitman: The Creation of a Book*. Cambridge: Belknap-Harvard U P, 1962.

———. *The Evolution of Walt Whitman: The Creation of a Personality*. Cambridge: Belknap-Harvard U P, 1960.

Baer, Judith A. *Equality Under the Constitution: Reclaiming the Fourteenth Amendment*. Ithaca: Cornell U P, 1983.

Bauerlein, Mark. "The Written Orator in 'Song of Myself': A Recent Trend in Whitman Criticism." *Walt Whitman Quarterly Review* 3 (1986): 1–14.

Belz, Herman. "The Constitution and Reconstruction," in *The Facts of Reconstruction: Essays in Honor of John Hope Franklin*, 189–218. Eds. Eric Anderson and Alfred A. Moss, Jr. Baton Rouge: Louisiana State U P, 1991.

———. *A New Birth of Freedom: The Republican Party and Freedmen's Rights, 1861–1866*. Westport, Conn.: Greenwood Press, 1976.

———. "The New Orthodoxy in Reconstruction Historiography." *Reviews in American History* 1 (March 1973) 106–13.

———. *Reconstructing the Union: Theory and Policy during the Civil War*. Ithaca: Cornell U P, 1969.

Benedict, Michael Les. *A Compromise of Principle: Congressional Republicans and Reconstruction, 1863–1869*. New York: Norton, 1974.

Berger, Raoul. *Government by Judiciary: The Transformation of the Fourteenth Amendment*. Cambridge: Harvard U P, 1977.

Berlin, Ira, Barbara J. Fields, Thavolia Glymph, Joseph P. Reidy, and Leslie S. Rowland. *The Destruction of Slavery*. Cambridge: Cambridge U P, 1985.

Berlin, Ira, Thavolia Glymph, Steven F. Miller, Joseph P. Reidy, Leslie S. Rowland, and Julie Saville, eds. *Freedom: A Documentary History of Emancipation, 1861–1867.* Cambridge: Cambridge U P, 1990.

Berlin, Ira, Barbara J. Fields, Steven F. Miller, Joseph P. Reidy, and Leslie S. Rowland. *Slaves No More: Three Essays on Emancipation and the Civil War.* Cambridge: Cambridge U P, 1992.

Bernstein, Richard B., and Jerome Agel. *Amending America: If We Love the Constitution So Much, Why Do We Keep Trying to Change It?* New York: Times Books, 1993.

Brasher, Thomas L. *Whitman as Editor of the Brooklyn Daily Eagle.* Detroit: Wayne State U P, 1970.

Brest, Paul. "The Misconceived Quest for the Original Understanding." *Boston University Law Review* 60 (1980) 204–38.

Buchanon, G. Sidney. "The Quest for Freedom: A Legal History of the Thirteenth Amendment." *Houston Law Review* 12 (October 1974): 1–34.

Campbell, Karlyn Kohrs, and Kathleen Hall Jamieson. *Deeds Done in Words: Presidential Rhetoric and the Genres of Governance.* Chicago: U of Chicago P, 1990.

Carter, Dan T. *When the War Was Over: The Failure of Self-Reconstruction in the South, 1865–1867.* Baton Rouge: Louisiana State U P, 1985.

Cell, John. *The Highest Stage of White Supremacy: The Origins of Segregation in South Africa and the American South.* Cambridge: Cambridge U P, 1982.

Chase, Richard. *Walt Whitman Reconsidered.* New York: Sloane, 1955.

Cox, Lawanda F. *Lincoln and Black Freedom: A Study in Presidential Leadership.* Columbia, S.C.: U of South Carolina P, 1981.

Coyle, William, ed. *The Poet and the President: Whitman's Lincoln Poems.* New York: Odyssey, 1962.

Crawley, Thomas Edward. *The Structure of Leaves of Grass.* Austin: U of Texas P, 1970.

Croushore, James H., and David Morris Potter. Introduction to John W. DeForest, *A Union Officer in the Reconstruction,* v–xxvi. New York: Arcon Books, 1968.

Curtis, Michael Kent. *No State Shall Abridge: The Fourteenth Amendment and the Bill of Rights.* Durham: Duke U P, 1986.

Dan, Martin E., ed. *The Black Press, 1827–1890: The Quest for National Identity.* New York: Putnam, 1971.

Diffley, Kathleen. "The Roots of Tara: Making War Civil." *American Quarterly* 36 (1984): 359–72.

_____. *Where My Heart Is Turning Ever: Civil War Stories and Constitutional Reform, 1861–1876.* Athens: U of Georgia P, 1992.

Ditsky, John. "'Retrievements out of the Night': Approaching Whitman Through the 'Lilacs' Elegy." *Calamus: Walt Whitman Quarterly International* 7 (1973): 28–37.

Eby, Edwin Harold. *A Concordance of Walt Whitman's Leaves of Grass and Selected Prose Writings.* Seattle: U of Washington P, 1949–54. Reissue. New York: Greenwood Press, 1969.

Erkkila, Betsy. *Whitman: The Political Poet.* New York: Oxford U P, 1989.

Fairman, Charles. *History of the Supreme Court of the United States, Volume 6: Reconstruction and Reunion, 1864–88.* New York: Macmillan, 1971.

Farber, Daniel A., and John E. Muench. "The Ideological Origins of the Fourteenth Amendment." *Constitutional Commentary* 1 (Summer 1984): 235–79.

Faust, Drew Gilpin. *The Creation of Confederate Nationalism: Ideology and Identity in the Civil War South.* Baton Rouge: Louisiana State U P, 1988.

Ferguson, Robert A. *Law and Letters in American Culture.* Cambridge: Harvard U P, 1984.

Fields, Barbara J. "Ideology and Race in American History." In *Region, Race, and Reconstruction: Essays in Honor of C. Vann Woodward,* 142–77. Eds. J. Morgan Kouseer and James M. McPherson. New York: Oxford U P, 1982.

———. "The Nineteenth-Century American South: History and Theory." *Plantation Society in the Americas* 2 (April 1983); 7–27.

Finkelman, Paul. "Rehearsal for Reconstruction: Antebellum Origins of the Fourteenth Amendment." In *The Facts of Reconstruction: Essays in Honor of John Hope Franklin,* 1–28. Eds. Eric Anderson and Alfred A. Moss, Jr. Baton Rouge: Louisiana State U P, 1991.

———. "Slavery and the Constitutional Convention: Making a Covenant with Death" In *Beyond Confederation: Origins of the Constitution and American National Identity,* 188–225. Eds. Richard Beeman, Stephen Botein, and Edward C. Carter II. Chapel Hill: U of North Carolina P, 1987.

Folsom, Ed. "Leaves of Grass, Junior: Whitman's Compromise with Discriminating Tastes." *American Literature* 63 (1991); 641–63.

———. "The Whitman Project: A Review Essay." *Philological Quarterly* 61 (1982); 369–94.

———. "'This Heart's Geography's Map': The Photographs of Walt Whitman." *Walt Whitman Quarterly Review* 3 (1986–87): 1–76.

Foner, Eric. *Nothing But Freedom: Emancipation and Its Legacy.* Baton Rouge: Louisiana State U P, 1983.

———. *Reconstruction: America's Unfinished Revolution, 1863–1877.* New York: Harper and Row, 1988.

———. "Reconstruction Revisited." *Reviews in American History* 10 (December 1982): 82–100.

———. "Slavery, the Civil War, and Reconstruction." In *The New American History,* 73–92. Philadelphia: Temple U P, 1990.

———. *Politics and Ideology in the Age of the Civil War.* New York: Oxford U P, 1980.

Foner, Philip S. *History of Black Americans, Volume 3: From the Compromise of 1850 to the End of the Civil War.* Westport, Conn.: Greenwood Press, 1983.

Foucault, Michel. "Course of January 7, 1976." In *Power/Knowledge: Selected Interviews and Other Writings, 1972–1977.* Ed. Colin Gordon (New York: Pantheon, 1980), 78–92.

_____. "Nietzsche, Genealogy, and History." In *Language, Counter-Memory, Practice,* Trans. Donald F. Bouchard and Sherry Simon (Ithaca, N.Y.: Cornell U P), 139–64.

Franklin, John Hope. "The Enforcement of the Civil Rights Act of 1875." *Prologue* 6 (Winter 1974): 225–35.

_____. *Reconstruction After the Civil War.* Chicago: U of Chicago P, 1961.

Frederickson, George M. *The Black Image in the White Mind.* New York, Harper and Row, 1977.

_____. *The Inner Civil War: Northern Intellectuals and the Crisis of the Union.* New York: Harper, 1965.

Genovese, Eugene D. *Roll, Jordan, Roll: The World the Slaves Made.* New York: Random House, 1974.

_____. *The World the Slaveholders Made: Two Essays in Interpretation.* Middletown, Conn.: Wesleyan U P, 1988.

Giantvalley, Scott. *Walt Whitman, 1838–1939: A Reference Guide.* Boston: G. K. Hall, 1981.

_____. "Walt Whitman, 1838–1939: A Reference Guide, Additional Annotations." *Walt Whitman Quarterly Review* 4 (1986): 24–40.

Gillette, William. *Retreat from Reconstruction, 1869–1879.* Baton Rouge: Louisiana State U P, 1979.

_____. *The Right to Vote: Politics and Passage of the Fifteenth Amendment.* Baltimore: Johns Hopkins U P, 1965.

Glatthaar, Joseph T. *Forged in Battle: The Civil War Alliance of Black Soldiers and White Officers.* New York: Free Press, 1990.

Golden, Arthur, ed. *Walt Whitman's Blue Book: The 1860–61 Leaves of Grass Containing His Manuscript Additions and Revisions,* 2 Vols. New York: New York Public Library, 1968.

Graham, Howard Jay. *Everyman's Constitution: Historical Essays on the Fourteenth Amendment, the "Conspiracy Theory," and American Constitutionalism.* Madison: State Historical Society of Wisconsin, 1968.

Graham, Hugh Davis. *The Civil Rights Era: Origins and Development of National Policy.* New York: Oxford U P, 1990.

Hindus, Milton, ed. *Walt Whitman: The Critical Heritage.* London: Routledge, 1971.

Hollis, C. Carroll. "Is There a Text in This Grass?" *Walt Whitman Quarterly Review* 3 (1986): 15–22.

_____. *Language and Style in Leaves of Grass.* Baton Rouge: Louisiana State U P, 1983.

_____. "Rhetoric, Elocution, and Voice in *Leaves of Grass.*" *Walt Whitman Quarterly Review* 2 (1984): 1–21.

Hubbell, Jay B. *The South in American Literature, 1607–1900.* Durham: Duke U P, 1954.

Hyman, Harold M. *A More Perfect Union: The Impact of the Civil War and Reconstruction on the Constitution.* New York: Knopf, 1973.

Hyman, Harold M, and William M. Wiecek. *Equal Justice Under the Law: Constitutional Development, 1835–1875.* New York: Harper and Row, 1982.

Kaczorowski, John A. "Searching for the Intent of the Framers of the Fourteenth Amendment." *Connecticut Law Review* 5 (Winter 1972–73): 368–98.

Kaczorowski, Robert J. *The Nationalization of Civil Rights: Constitutional Theory and Practice in a Racist Society, 1866–1883.* New York: Garland, 1987.

Kaplan, Justin. *Whitman: A Life.* New York: Simon & Schuster, 1980.

Kateb, George. "Walt Whitman and the Culture of Democracy." *Political Theory* 4 (November 1990) 545–71.

Kerber, Linda K. "The Republican Mother" In *Women's America: Refocusing the Past,* 83–91. Eds. Linda K. Kerber and Jane De Hart-Mathews. New York: Oxford U P, 1987.

Killingsworth, M. Jimmie. *The Growth of Leaves of Grass: The Organic Tradition in Whitman Studies.* Columbia, S.C.: Camden House, 1993.

_____. *Whitman's Poetry of the Body: Sexuality, Politics, and the Text.* Chapel Hill: U of North Carolina P, 1989.

Klumpp, James F., and Thomas A. Hollihan. "Rhetorical Criticism as Moral Action." *Quarterly Journal of Speech* 75 (1989): 84–97.

Krieg, Joann P., ed. *Walt Whitman: Here and Now.* Westport, Conn.: Greenwood Press, 1985.

Kummings, Donald D. "Walt Whitman Bibliographies: A Chronological Listing, 1897–1982." *Walt Whitman Quarterly Review* 1 (1984): 38–45.

_____. *Walt Whitman, 1940–1975: A Reference Guide.* Boston: G. K. Hall, 1982.

Levinson, Stanford. "Law as Literature." *Texas Law Review* 60 (March 1982): 373–403.

Lincoln, Abraham. *Collected Works of Abraham Lincoln.* 9 volumes. Ed. Roy P. Basler. New Brunswick, N.J.: Rutgers U P, 1953.

Linderman, Gerald F. *Embattled Courage: The Experience of Combat in the American Civil War.* New York: Free Press, 1987.

Litwack, Leon F. *Been in the Storm So Long: The Aftermath of Slavery.* New York: Knopf, 1979.

Lively, Robert A. *Fiction Fights the Civil War.* Chapel Hill: U of North Carolina P, 1957.

Mandle, Jay R. *The Roots of Black Poverty: The Southern Plantation Economy After the Civil War.* Durham: Duke U P, 1978.

Marx, Leo. "*Democratic Vistas:* Notes for a Discussion." *Emerson Society Quarterly* 22 (1961) 12–15.

____. "George Kateb's Ahistorical Emersonianism." *Political Theory* 18 (November 1990): 595–600.

McKitrick, Eric L. *Andrew Johnson and Reconstruction.* Chicago: U of Chicago P, 1960.

McPherson, James M. *Abraham Lincoln and the Second American Revolution.* New York: Oxford U P, 1990.

____. *Battle Cry of Freedom: The Civil War Era.* New York: Oxford U P, 1988.

____. "The Civil Rights Act of 1875." *Journal of American History* 52 (December 1965): 493–510.

____. *The Negro's Civil War: How American Negroes Felt and Acted During the War for the Union.* New York: Knopf, 1965.

____. *The Struggle for Equality: Abolitionists and the Negro in the Civil War and Reconstruction.* Princeton: Princeton U P, 1964.

Michaels, Walter Benn, and Donald E. Pease, eds. *The American Renaissance Reconsidered: Selected Papers from the English Institute, 1982–83.* Baltimore: Johns Hopkins U P, 1985.

Michaels, Walter Benn. "Romance and Real Estate." In *The American Renaissance Reconsidered: Selected Papers from the English Institute, 1982–83.* Walter Benn Michaels and Donald E. Pease, Eds., 156–184.

Miller, Edwin Haviland, ed. *A Century of Whitman Criticism.* Bloomington: Indiana U P, 1969.

____. *Walt Whitman's "Song of Myself": A Mosaic of Interpretations.* Iowa City: U of Iowa P, 1989.

Mitchell, Reid. *The Vacant Chair: The Northern Soldier Leaves Home.* New York: Oxford U P, 1993.

Montgomery, David. *Beyond Equality: Labor and the Radical Republicans, 1862–1872.* Urbana: U of Illinois P, 1981.

Moon, Michael. *Disseminating Whitman: Revision and Corporeality in Leaves of Grass.* Cambridge: Harvard U P, 1991.

Mosher, Michael. "Walt Whitman: Jacobin Poet of American Democracy." *Political Theory* 18 (November 1990): 587–95.

Nagel, Paul C. *This Sacred Trust: American Nationality, 1798–1898.* New York: Oxford U P, 1971.

Neely, Mark E., Jr. *The Fate of Liberty: Abraham Lincoln and Civil Liberties.* New York: Oxford U P, 1991.

Nieman, Donald G. *To Set the Law in Motion: The Freedmen's Bureau and the Legal Rights of Blacks, 1865–1868.* Millwood, N.Y.: KTO, 1979.

Oakes, James. *Slavery and Freedom: An Interpretation of the Old South.* New York: Knopf, 1990.

Pearce, Roy Harvey. *The Continuity of American Poetry.* Princeton: Princeton U P, 1961.

Pease, Donald E. *Visionary Compacts: American Renaissance Writings in Cultural Context.* Madison: U of Wisconsin P, 1987.

Pennock, J. Roland. *Democratic Political Theory.* Princeton: Princeton U P, 1979.

Perman, Michael. *Reunion Without Compromise: The South and Reconstruction, 1865–1868.* Cambridge: Harvard U P, 1973.

Pratt, Mary Louise. *Toward a Speech Act Theory of Literary Discourse.* Bloomington: Indiana U P, 1977.

Rabinowitz, Howard N. *Race Relations in the Urban South, 1865–1890.* Urbana: U of Illinois P, 1980.

_____, ed. *Southern Black Leaders of the Reconstruction Era.* Urbana: U of Illinois P, 1982.

Renner, Dennis K. "Walt Whitman's Religion of the Republic." Ph.D. Diss., University of Iowa, 1975.

Reynolds, David S. *Beneath the American Renaissance: The Subversive Imagination in the Age of Emerson and Melville.* New York: Knopf, 1988.

Roark, James L. *Masters Without Slaves: Southern Planters in the Civil War and Reconstruction.* New York: Norton, 1977.

Robinson, Armistead L. "The Difference Freedom Made: The Emancipation of Afro-Americans." In *The State of Afro-American History.* Ed. Darlene Clark Hine. Baton Rouge: Louisiana State U P, 1986.

Rose, Willie Lee, ed. *A Documentary History of Slavery in North America.* New York: Oxford U P, 1976.

Rubin, Joseph Jay. *The Historic Whitman.* University Park: Pennsylvania State U P, 1973.

Sanchez-Eppler, Karen. "Bodily Bonds: The Intersecting Discourses of Feminism and Abolition." *Representations* 24 (Fall 1988): 28–59.

Scholnick, Robert J. "The American Context of *Democratic Vistas.*" In *Walt Whitman: Here and Now,* 147–56. Ed. Joann P. Krieg. Westport, Conn.: Greenwood Press, 1985.

_____. "*The Galaxy* and American Democratic Culture, 1866–1878." *Journal of American Studies* 16 (1982): 69–80.

Shulman, Robert. *Social Criticism and Nineteenth-Century American Fictions.* Columbia, Mo.: U of Missouri P, 1987.

Smith-Rosenburg, Carroll. *Disorderly Conduct: Visions of Gender in Victorian America.* New York: Knopf, 1985.

Sollors, Werner. *Beyond Ethnicity: Consent and Descent in American Culture.* New York: Oxford U P, 1987.

Spencer, Benjamin T. *The Quest for Nationality: An American Literary Campaign.* Syracuse: Syracuse U P, 1957.

Stampp, Kenneth M. *The Era of Reconstruction, 1865–1877.* New York, 1965.

Swinney, Everette. *Suppressing the Ku Klux Klan: The Enforcement of the Reconstruction Amendments, 1870–1877.* New York: Garland, 1987.

Taylor, Arnold H. *Travail and Triumph: Black Life and Culture in the South Since the Civil War.* Westport, Conn.: Greenwood Press , 1976.

Taylor, Joseph H. "The Fourteenth Amendment, the Negro, and the Spirit of the Times." *Journal of Negro History* 45 (1960); 21–37.

Taylor, William R. *Cavalier and Yankee: The Old South and American National Character.* New York: Harper and Row, 1961.

tenBroek, Jacobus. *Equal Under Law: The Antislavery Origins of the Fourteenth Amendment.* New York: Collier Books, 1965.

Thomas, Emory M. *The Confederate Nation: 1861–1865.* New York: Harper and Row, 1979.

Thomas, M. Wynn. *The Lunar Light of Whitman's Poetry.* Cambridge: Harvard U P, 1987.

Tomkins, Jane. *Sensational Designs: The Cultural Work of American Fiction, 1790–1860.* New York: Oxford U P, 1985.

Trachtenburg, Alan. *The Incorporation of America: Culture and Society in the Gilded Age.* New York: Hill, 1982.

Traubel, Horace. *With Walt Whitman in Camden.* Vol. 1, Boston: Small, 1906. Vol. 2, New York: Appleton 1908. Vol. 3, New York: Kennerly, 1914. Vol. 4, ed. Sculley Bradley, Philadelphia: U of Philadelphia P, 1953. Vol. 5, ed. Gertrude Traubel, Carbondale: Southern Illinois U P, 1964. Vol. 6., eds. Gertrude Traubel and William White, Carbondale: Southern Illinois U P, 1982. Vol. 7, eds. Jeanne Chapman and Robert Macisaac, Carbondale: Southern Illinois U P, 1992.

Tourgee, Albion W. *A Fool's Errand.* Ed. John Hope Franklin. Cambridge: Belknap-Harvard U P, 1961.

U.S. Congress. *The Ku-Klux Conspiracy: Testimony Taken by the Joint Select Committee to Inquire into the Conditions of Affairs in the Late Insurrectionary States* 13 vols. Washington, 1872.

U.S. Congress. *Report of the Joint Committee on Reconstruction.* Washington, 1866.

White, James Boyd. *When Words Lose Their Meaning: Constitutions and Reconstitutions of Language, Character, and Community.* Chicago: U of Chicago P, 1984.

Whitman, Walt. *An American Primer.* Ed. Horace Traubel, 1904. Reprint, Stevens Point: Holy Cow!, 1987.

_____. *The Correspondence of Walt Whitman.* Ed. Edwin Haviland Miller. 6 vols. New York: New York U P, 1961–77.

_____. *Daybooks and Notebooks.* Ed. William White. 3 vols. New York: New York U P, 1978.

_____. *The Early Poems and the Fiction.* Ed. Thomas L. Brasher. New York: New York U P, 1963.

_____. *The Gathering of the Forces.* Ed. Cleveland Rodgers and John Black. 2 vols. New York: Putnam's, 1920.

_____. *I Sit and Look Out: Editorials from the Brooklyn Daily Times.* Ed. Emory Hollo-way and Vernolian Schwartz. New York: Columbia U P, 1932.

_____. *Leaves of Grass: Comprehensive Reader's Edition.* Harold W. Blodgett and Sculley Bradley, Eds. New York: New York U P, 1985.

_____. *Leaves of Grass: A Textual Variorum of the Printed Poems.* Eds. Sculley Bradley, Harold W. Blodgett, Arthur Golden, and William White. 3 vols. New York: New York U P, 1980.

_____. *Notebooks and Unpublished Prose Manuscripts.* Ed. Edward F. Grier. 6 vols. New York: New York U P, 1984.

_____. *Prose Works 1892.* Ed. Floyd Stovall. 2 vols. New York: New York U P, 1963–64.

_____. *Uncollected Poetry and Prose of Walt Whitman.* Ed. Emory Holloway. 2 vols. Garden City: Doubleday, 1921.

_____. *Walt Whitman of the New York 'Aurora,' Editor at Twenty-Two: A Collection of Recently Discovered Writings.* Eds. Joseph J. Rubin and Charles H. Brown. State College, PA: Bald Eagle, 1950.

_____. *Walt Whitman's Memoranda During the War and Death of Abraham Lincoln.* Ed. Roy B. Basler. Reproduced in facsimile. Bloomington: Indiana U P, 1962.

_____. *Walt Whitman's Workshop: A Collection of Unpublished Manuscripts.* Ed. Clifton Joseph Furness. Cambridge: Harvard U P, 1928.

Wilson, Edmund. *Patriotic Gore: Studies in the Literature of the American Civil War.* New York: Oxford U P, 1962.

Woodward, C. Vann. *American Counterpoint: Slavery and Racism in the North-South Dialogue.* Boston: Little, Brown, 1971.

_____. *Origins of the New South, 1877–1913.* Baton Rouge: Louisiana State U P, 1971.

_____. "The Price of Freedom" In *What Was Freedom's Price?*, 93–113. Ed. David G. Sansing. Jackson: U of Mississippi P, 1978.

Wyatt-Brown, Bertram. "The Civil Rights Act of 1875." *Western Political Quarterly* 18 (December 1965): 763–75.

Yeazell, Stephen C. "Convention, Fiction, and Law." *New Literary History* 13 (1981): 89–102.

Ziff, Larzer. *Literary Democracy: The Declaration of Cultural Independence in America.* New York: Viking, 1981.

Zweig, Paul. *Walt Whitman: The Making of the Poet.* New York: Basic Books, 1984.

Index